AF700622

Everyday Life in Joseon-Era Korea

Everyday Life in Joseon-Era Korea

Economy and Society

The Organization of Korean Historians, Seoul

Edited and Translated by

Michael D. Shin

Co-translated by

Edward Park

GLOBAL
ORIENTAL

LEIDEN · BOSTON
2014

Cover Illustration: *Banquet in Yeongwangjeong* (Yeongwangjeong yeonhoedo) (detail), late eighteenth century. Part of the series Welcoming Banquet for the Magistrate of Pyongyang (Pyeongyang gamsa hyangyeondo). Thought to have been painted by Gim Hongdo. This part of the painting depicts people near Daedong Gate in Pyongyang. (National Museum of Korea).

Library of Congress Cataloging in Publication Control Number: 2013040417

This publication has been typeset in the multilingual "Brill" typeface. With over 5,100 characters covering Latin, IPA, Greek, and Cyrillic, this typeface is especially suitable for use in the humanities. For more information, please see www.brill.com/brill-typeface.

ISBN 978-90-04-26112-9 (hardback)
ISBN 978-90-04-26115-0 (e-book)

Copyright 2014 by Koninklijke Brill NV, Leiden, The Netherlands.
Koninklijke Brill NV incorporates the imprints Brill, Brill Nijhoff, Global Oriental, Hotei Publishing and IDC Publishers.

All rights reserved. No part of this publication may be reproduced, translated, stored in a retrieval system, or transmitted in any form or by any means, electronic, mechanical, photocopying, recording or otherwise, without prior written permission from the publisher.

Authorization to photocopy items for internal or personal use is granted by Koninklijke Brill NV provided that the appropriate fees are paid directly to The Copyright Clearance Center, 222 Rosewood Drive, Suite 910, Danvers, MA 01923, USA.
Fees are subject to change.

This book is printed on acid-free paper.

CONTENTS

PART ONE

ECONOMY

PART TWO

SOCIETY

LIST OF CONTRIBUTORS

Chung Yeon-sik is a Professor in the Department of History at Seoul Women's University. He is the author of the two-volume work *Tales of Everyday Life in the Joseon Period* (2001).

Han Sang Kwon is Professor of History at Duksung Women's University. He is the author of *Social Problems and the Petition System in the Late Joseon Period* (1996) and other studies of the political and social history of the period.

Hong Soon Min is a Professor in the Department of Cultural Resources in the Graduate School of Records, Archives, and Information at Myongji University in Seoul. He is the author of *The Story of Korea's Royal Palaces* (1999) and *The Scenery of Seoul* (2008).

Jang Dong-Pyo is a Professor in the Department of History Education at Pusan National University. He is the author of numerous studies of local history in the late Joseon period.

Jung Jin Young is Professor of History at Andong National University. He is the author of *The History of Rural Society in the Joseon Period* (1998) and of numerous articles on social history.

Kim Eui-Hwan is Professor in the Faculty of Liberal Education at Chungbuk National University in Cheongju. He is the author of *Salt Production in the Joseon Period* (2006), *The Gwangmu Land Survey and the Socioeconomic Structure of Chungju* (2010), and *Lectures on Korean History and Folklore* (2010).

Kim Kuentae is an Associate Professor in the Department of Korean History at Seoul National University. He is the author of *Agricultural Management of Yangban Families in the Joseon Period* (2004) and numerous studies of the agricultural and social history of the late Joseon period.

Kim Kyung-ran is the Chief Researcher at the Daedong Institute for Korean Studies at Sungkyunkwan University. She has published much research on the local history and social history of the Joseon period.

Kim Sung Woo is a Professor at Daegu Haany University. He is the author of *Sajok and the State in the Mid Joseon Period* (2001) and *The Shift in Local Hegemony in Gyeongsang Province in the Joseon Period* (2012).

Ko Dong-Hwan is Professor of Korean History at the Korean Advanced Institute of Science and Technology. He is the author of *Commercial Development in the Joseon Period* (1998), *The Urban History of Seoul in the Joseon Period* (2008), and *Merchants' Guilds in the Joseon Period* (2013).

Kwon Ki-jung is an Assistant Professor in the Department of History and Culture at Hansung University in Seoul. He is the author of *Hyangni and Local Society in the Joseon Period* (2010), as well as many articles on local society.

Kwon Nae-Hyun is an Associate Professor in the Department of History Education at Korea University. He is the author of *The Finances of Pyeongan Province in the Late Joseon Period* (2004).

Kwon Soon-Hyung is a researcher at the Academy of Korean Studies. A specialist in women's history, she is the author of *Women's Lives and the Institution of Marriage in Goryeo* (2006).

Lee Hae Jun is Professor of History at Kongju National University. He is the author of *The History of Village Society in the Joseon Period* (1996) and *Clan-Based Seowon in the Late Joseon Period* (2008), as well as the co-author of *Traditional Society and Life Culture* (2006).

Lee Hun-Chang is Professor of Korean Economic History in the Department of Economics at Korea University. He is the author of *The Economic History of Korea* (2012) and many articles on economic history in both Korean and English.

Lee Uk is an Associate Professor in the Department of History at Sunchon National University. He is the author of many studies of the economic and political history of local areas.

O Jong-rok is an Associate Professor in the Department of History at Sungshin Women's University. He has written numerous studies of the political history of the early Joseon period.

Oh Soo-chang is Professor of Korean History at Seoul National University. He is the author of *Social Development in Pyeongan Province in the Late Joseon Period* (2002) and *The Framework of Politics in the Joseon Period* (2011).

Edward Park graduated with an A.B. degree in East Asian Studies from Harvard University. He was the main translator of *The Dynamics of Confucianism and Modernization* by Yi Tae-jin (Cornell East Asia Series, 2007). Currently, he is participating in a multi-year project to translate the *Veritable Records* of the Joseon dynasty.

Seo Tae-Won is an Assistant Professor in the College of Liberal Education at Mokwon University in Daejeon. A specialist in military history, he is the author of *The Local Army System in the Late Joseon Period* (1999).

Michael D. Shin is Lecturer in Korean Studies at the University of Cambridge. A specialist on the Japanese colonial period, he is the editor of *Landlords, Peasants, and Intellectuals in Modern Korea* (2005) and the editor and co-author of the forthcoming *Korean History in Maps* (2014).

Sim Jae-woo is an Associate Professor at the Academy of Korean Studies. He is the author of *State Power and Crime in the Late Joseon Period* (2009) and *Confess Your Crime! Understanding Joseon through Crime and Punishment* (2011).

Yeom Jeong Sup is an Associate Professor in the Department of History at Hallym University in Chuncheon. He is the author of *Seo Yugu and the* Imwon Gyeongjeji (2011) as well as many studies of agricultural history.

Yoo Pil Jo teaches at Nangok Middle School in Seoul. He is one of the authors of books by The Association of Korean History Teachers, including *How Should We Teach Our Children About History?* (2002).

LIST OF ILLUSTRATIONS AND MAPS

Hong Soon Min

PREFACE AND ACKNOWLEDGEMENTS

This book originated in a classroom assignment. When I was teaching a Korean text class at Cornell, I assigned students chapters from the original Korean version of this book. Though it was a bestseller in South Korea, I was still surprised to see how much they enjoyed the readings. They said that they enjoyed the book's approach to teaching Korean history, one that differed from the often dry narratives of existing textbooks. By examining history from the perspective of commoners rather than elites, the book defamiliarized aspects of Korea that Koreans often take for granted. For instance, kimchi, often considered to be the national food of Korea today, actually developed very recently in Korean history, with its napa cabbage version becoming widespread only in the late nineteenth and early twentieth centuries. The popular alcoholic drink *soju* likely came from techniques originally developed in Arabia. Because of the students' positive reactions, I continued to use the book and others in the same series in succeeding years. When I began assigning chapters for final translation projects, it quickly became apparent that a translation of the whole book would potentially be very useful in Korean Studies classes. Within a few years, students translated twelve chapters, about half the book, and Edward Park and I then applied for a grant from the Korean Literature Translation Institute. We thank the institute for its support which enabled us to translate the rest of the book and to redo the students' translations. It took several more years to make the book more accessible to students in the English-speaking world. Though the book, first published in 1996, was intended for a general audience in South Korea, it still contained too many technical terms and obscure references for non-Korean readers. In addition to removing such terms, we rewrote many of the introductory sections to the chapters.

We are grateful for the tremendous help that the authors of the book, the Organization of Korean Historians, gave us in revising the manuscript. We held a workshop at Cornell with two of the authors – Prof. Hong Soon Min and Prof. Kwon Ki-jung – and Prof. Baik Seung-Chul of Yonsei University to go over our questions about difficult passages and to review our revisions. Dr. Chung Yong-seo of the Organization of Korean Historians provided important administrative support for publication. We are very grateful to Paul Norbury and Nozomi Goto at Global Oriental for supporting the publication of this book and guiding it to completion; thanks should also go to Manjusha Chandrasekaran for handling the production process. Prof. Oh Young-chan of Ewha Womans University, was very generous in helping us acquiring the rights to images from the National Museum of Korea, where he used to work as a curator. For help in acquiring images, we would also like to thank Ms. Park Sook-Hee, the Head Librarian at the Kyujanggak Archives, Ms. Anja Battefeld of the Museum für Völkerkunde in Hamburg, and Ms. Marine Sangis, Ms. Anne-Catherine Biedermann, and Mr. Christophe Mauberret of the Agence photographique de la Réunion des Musées Nationaux. My wife Shinyoung Kwon provided valuable advice on the translation, and she and our sons, Adam and Luke, provided much support throughout the years it took to complete this book. Edward Park would like to give special thanks to his brother Daniel Park and his father Kyun Park for their assistance and to his wife Christine Park and son Nolan Park for their constant support. Youngchan Justin Choi, a graduate student at SOAS, did the map of the Korean peninsula and compiled the index. Ji-yoon An, a graduate student at Cambridge, compiled the glossary, assisted with proofreading, and provided administrative help. My students Ben Metzler, Dan Anscomb, Kirsten Chaplin, Florence Gracey, and Sam Ruiz proofread the manuscript at various stages and offered helpful comments. For the relevant chapters, the name of the student who did the original translation appears at the end.

This book is dedicated to my students. When they eat kimchi, I hope they reflect upon how much of what is Korean is not ancient but actually a recent development. When they drink a glass of *soju*, I hope they pause for a moment to think about how much rice farmers had to grow to make it. When they travel in the Korean countryside, I hope they are reminded of the lives of the peasants who labored, sang, and danced in the fields and whose often voiceless traces have much to teach us about history.

Michael D. Shin

NOTE ON ROMANIZATION

This book follows the romanization system of South Korea (known as the Revised Romanization system) that was promulgated in the year 2000. One exception is the names of the authors of this volume; they were romanized according to the wishes of the authors. Another exception is for names and places that already have an accepted spelling in the West, such as Pyongyang.

Map 0.1 Map of Joseon

THE INTIMATE PAST: AN INTRODUCTION TO THE JOSEON PERIOD

Michael D. Shin

The kingdom of Joseon (1392–1910) originated in a dramatic coup d'état whose story is known to all schoolchildren in South Korea today. The fall of the Mongol empire in the fourteenth century caused domestic turmoil in the Korean peninsula, just as its rise had done a century earlier. The Ming conquest of the Yuan in China in 1368 had the effect of intensifying internal divisions within Goryeo, the precedessor to Joseon that had been founded in 918. It triggered a debate in the court, with some remaining loyal to Yuan and others advocating support for the new Chinese dynasty. When the Ming threatened to claim part of Goryeo's northern territory, the king supported a plan to invade the Liaodong peninsula in 1388. The pro-Ming Yi Seonggye (1335–1408) was one of the generals assigned to lead the invading force, but upon reaching Yihwa Island in the Amnok River, he turned his army around and returned to the capital, where he seized control of the government. A few years later, he deposed the last Goryeo monarch and founded a new kingdom that he named after the first kingdom on the peninsula, Joseon.

The founding of Joseon proved to be a major turning point in the peninsula's history. It was not ancient enough to be celebrated for the formation of Korean civilization or romanticized as a primordial Golden Age. It could not claim to have unified the peninsula or even to have reunified the country after a period of disunity. Its historical significance lies in the fact that the new state adopted Neo-Confucianism as its ruling ideology, rejecting the Buddhism of the Goryeo kingdom. The transition from Goryeo to Joseon was also a significant moment in agricultural history, as farmers overcame the limitations of fallow-field farming and rice transplanting techniques were introduced. This combination of economic advance and the adoption of a new ideology led to a transformation over the next few centuries in which Confucian institutions, thought, and rituals penetrated the lives of not only the yangban aristocrats but also the peasantry.[1] The monarchy and bureaucracy were reorganized according to Neo-Confucian

[1] Martina Deuchler, *The Confucian Transformation of Korea: A Study of Society and Ideology*, Cambridge: Council on East Asian Studies, 1992.

principles, and institutions such as ancestor worship spread throughout the populace as the Confucian patriarchal family system expanded. These changes resulted in a polity that was one of the longest lasting in East Asian history, outlasting both of its contemporaries – the Ming dynasty in China and the Muromachi shogunate in Japan.

It is a cliché to say that traces of the past are everywhere, but the Joseon period remains as much more than traces and is still a vital part of everyday life in South Korea today. In fact, much of what South Koreans today consider to be 'traditional' Korea actually emerged in the Joseon era. When they think of traditional life, they envisage yangban elites wearing colorful silk clothes and commoners wearing the white garments favored at the time. They picture strongly patriarchal families, whether of royal or commoner lineage, that emphasized filial piety and women's subordination to men. Such images are reinforced by historical dramas set in the era that are among the most popular shows on South Korean television. They are just one example of how the Joseon period continues to be an intimate part of social and political life, imbuing it with the solemnity of tradition and thus giving it stature and prestige.

This book is a translation of a work that was first published in South Korea in 1996. It is the first of a two-volume book that was originally titled *How Did People Live in the Joseon Period?* It was an instant hit, especially as a college textbook, and went through more than ten printings, with a revised edition coming out in 2005. The book represented the culmination of efforts to introduce new paradigms into South Korean historiography. The authors, who are members of the Organization of Korean Historians (Hanguk yeoksa yeonguhoe), were part of a generation that engaged in collective research and attempted to write an alternate history of the Joseon era. Critiquing existing historiography, they shifted the focus of research away from the court and the elites and saw the common people, through their struggles against elite domination, as the true agents of history. This introduction gives a very short overview of the politics, economy, and society of the era in order to give readers the basic information necessary to understand the content of the book. It also discusses some of the major historiographical debates about the period and concludes with a brief examination of the meanings of the Joseon era during the modern period.

Overview of Joseon: Politics, Economy, Society

The Mongols' military campaigns for expansion in the thirteenth century led, directly or indirectly, to the fall of virtually all the major states in the region. They conquered the Jurchen state of Jin and the Han Chinese state of Song, founding the Yuan dynasty. Subjugating Goryeo after three successive invasions, the Mongols did not absorb the country or eliminate the monarchy; instead, they established indirect domination and dethroned kings when dissatisfied with their policies. Though their invasion of Japan failed, the Kamakura shogunate was weakened from having to spend so much of its resources on defense. In Goryeo, the weakening of the monarchy led to social and economic problems with the rise of powerful families who amassed large landholdings because of their ties to the Mongols and connections with Buddhist monasteries. The internal situation became increasingly unstable as the condition of the peasantry worsened because of the devastation of land during the Mongol invasions and because of the severe exactions by the ruling class. The Goryeo state, as well as the Kamakura shogunate, fell not long after being invaded by the Mongols.

Within East Asia, the Korean peninsula was unique in that the end of Mongol dominance coincided with a major ideological shift through the introduction of Neo-Confucianism. Scholars and officials who studied in Yuan China brought back Neo-Confucian ideas and texts that found a receptive audience among those who wanted to establish a new ruling order and undertake a fundamental reform of the country. The founding of Joseon represented, as mentioned above, a reaction against Buddhism, the ruling ideology of Goryeo, which was seen as having become corrupt and unconcerned with the welfare of the people.[2] The promotion of Neo-Confucian institutions undermined the influence of Buddhist monasteries, which controlled much of the land in the country, and led to the replacement of Buddhist customs with Confucian ones. This reaction against Buddhism was part of a transformation of political, economic, and social life set in motion with the beginning of a new kingdom.

In politics, the country continued to be a monarchy with a centralized bureaucracy, but now the system was reorganized according to Neo-Confucian principles. Kings, who all came from the Jeonju Yi clan, were to serve as a moral exemplar, a sage-king. From childhood, he received a thorough education in Neo-Confucianism. The bureaucracy was based on the Tang-dynasty system of three departments and six ministries, altered to suit Joseon's particular circumstances. Rather than the three departments, the highest organ of the bureaucracy was the State Council, and its three top-ranking officials were the Chief State Councillor, Right State

[2] James B. Palais, *Confucian Statecraft and Korean Institutions: Yu Hyongwon and the Late Choson Dynasty* (Seattle and London: University of Washington Press, 1996), pp. 25–26.

Councillor, and the Left State Councillor. Established in the year 1400, it supervised the six ministries and was the successor to a similar organ in the Goryeo state. Following the Tang model, the bureaucracy was organized into six ministries that handled the administration of Personnel, Taxation, Rites, Military Affairs, Punishments, and Public Works. They were not located within the palace grounds but rather in front of Gyeongbok Palace. The head of a ministry was called *panseo*, and the title of the deputy head was *champan*. As in China, there were also offices that had the authority to monitor the king and other officials; they looked for instances of malfeasance and corruption and could remonstrate with the king if his decision was deemed to be improper. The three main offices with this function were the Office of the Inspector General (Saheonbu), the Office of the Censor-General (Saganwon), and the Office of Special Advisors (Hongmungwan). Thus, the Joseon state roughly followed the Chinese model of dividing authority into civil, military, and censorial functions.

As in China, civil officials were selected through an examination that required thorough knowledge of the Confucian classics and skill in composition in classical Chinese. It was based on a curriculum devised by Zhu Xi, one of the founding philosophers of Neo-Confucianism. The civil service examination was formally held once every three years, but there were other occasions when exams would be offered, with those wanting to become a military official taking a separate one. Theoretically, anyone of commoner status could sit the examination; in actuality, the yangban class virtually monopolized the system. The bureaucracy was organized into a complex hierarchy. Similar to China, there were nine ranks of officials, with each rank further divided into senior and junior grades, as they were in the Goryeo period. Thus, the two highest ranks were senior rank one (*jeong il pum*) and junior rank one (*jong il pum*), and the two lowest were senior rank nine (*jeong gu pum*) and junior rank nine (*jong gu pum*). Those of senior ranks one and two and junior rank one were addressed with the title *daegam*; those of senior rank three and junior rank two were addressed with the honorific *yeonggam*. These two groups constituted the *dangsanggwan*, a term meaning that they were the officials who had seats inside when there were discussions at court. Those of lower rank, collectively called *danghagwan*, were addressed as *nari* or *naeuri*. *Dangsanggwan* and *danghagwan* were distinguished by the picture embroidered onto the front of their official robes.

The Joseon government also undertook a reform of the system of provincial administration in its early years. The five provinces of the Goryeo era were reorganized into eight provinces (*do*). The three southern provinces were Gyeongsang, Jeolla, and Chungcheong; the two central provinces were Gyeonggi and Gangwon, and the three northern provinces were Hwanghae, Pyeongan, and Hamgyeong. With the exception of Gyeonggi, the names of the provinces were created by using the first characters of the names of its two most important towns. For instance, Gyeongju and Sangju were the two main towns in Gyeongsang province.[3] Hwanghae province was originally called Punghae, but its name was changed in 1417. The original name of Hamgyeong province was Yeonggil, and it assumed its current name in the year 1509. Provinces, in turn, were further divided into *gun* and *hyeon*, as they were in the Goryeo period.

Agriculture was the main industry of Joseon as peasants constituted the majority of the population. The staple crop was rice with barley, millet, and soybeans as minor crops. As will be discussed below, the founding of Joseon was a turning point in the development of agriculture. By the end of the fourteenth century, continuous cultivation became common; thanks to various advances in agricultural techniques, it was no longer necessary to let fields lie fallow every few years. The technique of rice transplantation was introduced from China at this time, and over the next two centuries, it spread throughout the country. The resulting increase in agricultural production provided the economic foundation for the major changes in the Joseon period. The government placed strong restrictions on commercial activity as Confucian ethics disdained profit-seeking occupations. It granted monopolies over certain products, such as salt and paper, to merchant guilds in the capital. International trade was also restricted at the beginning of the Joseon period. Trade with China had to be conducted over land through the regular tribute missions since maritime commerce was officially forbidden. Most trade with Japan was conducted through the island of Tsushima. In the early Joseon period, there were efforts to introduce both paper and metallic currencies, but these were not widely used until later.

The social status system was another foundation of the Neo-Confucian order in Joseon. The Confucian hierarchy placed scholars at the top, followed by farmers, then artisans, and merchants at the bottom. The social order in Joseon was based on this hierarchy but operated somewhat differently. As explained in this book, the population was classified as either

---

[3] The name of Jeolla province came from the towns of Jeonju and Naju; the others were as follows: Chungcheong (Chungju and Cheongju), Gangwon (Gangneung and Wonju), Hwanghae (Hwangju and Haeju), Pyeongan (Pyongyang and Anju), and Hamgyeong (Hamheung and Gyeongseong).

citizens (*yangin*) or lowborn (*cheonin*). The category of citizen contained a number of classes. The highest social status group in Joseon was the yangban. The term literally meant 'the two orders,' referring to the civil and military officials. Next in the hierarchy was the *jungin* class; the term meant 'middle people' who specialized in technical fields necessary for government such as astronomy, geography, and translation. Commoners without office, such as farmers, artisans, and merchants, constituted perhaps the largest segment of the population. The low born were another large segment of the population, though the extent is still a matter of debate among historians. They were distinguished from other groups by their clothing and their lack of family names. They included unfree people, entertainers, butchers, and others whose professions were considered to be lowly. One of the major objectives of this book is to show how the economy of Joseon was rooted in the social status system. For instance, the fact that only commoners paid taxes, with the exception of the yangban class, had significant implications for the economy. The foundation of Joseon also led to fundamental changes to family structure. As discussed in chapter sixteen by Kwon Soon-Hyung, the spread of Neo-Confucianism led to the strengthening of patriarchy and thus to the increasing subordination of women within the family. During the Goryeo period, there was no distinction between sons and daughters; both were entitled to receive an inheritance from their parents. In the Joseon period, women lost much of their status, increasingly having to follow the so-called 'three obediences' – to their father, to their husband, and to their son.

Historiographical Background

For much of the twentieth century, the dominant paradigm for the study of Joseon history was that of 'stagnation theory.' Originally formulated at the beginning of the century in order to justify Japan's takeover, this theory claimed that Korea had never undergone a feudal period and thus remained at the stage of ancient village economy into the nineteenth century. Unable to generate historical development autonomously, the country required an external stimulus to put it back on the path of history; to Japanese scholars, that modernizing stimulus was of course Japan.[4]

Proponents of stagnation theory have argued that a major factor behind the fall of Joseon was factionalism at court. It is true that many major

[4] For more on stagnation theory, see Owen Miller, "The Idea of Stagnation in Korean Historiography: From Fukuda Tokuzo to the New Right," *Korean Histories* 2.1 (2010).

political incidents involved violent outbursts of factional strife. From the late fifteenth to the mid sixteenth century, for instance, there were four 'literati purges' (*sahwa*) during which up to one hundred members of the losing faction were executed, exiled, or dismissed from office. By the seventeenth century, factionalism became such an integral part of political life that factional affiliation was virtually hereditary. Some Japanese scholars claimed that this was evidence that Koreans were incapable of ruling themselves; thus, factionalism was not simply a dysfunctional state of high politics but also a failure of national character.

One of the main goals of nationalist historiography has been to refute stagnation theory. The first major critiques emerged during the colonial period, but systematic research did not truly begin until after Korea's liberation in 1945. The efforts of nationalist historians culminated in the publication of Lee Ki-Baik's *A New History of Korea* (Hanguksa sillon) in 1967. He showed how each period of Korean history had its own distinctive political, economic, social, and cultural systems, thus establishing that the country did undergo historical development. On the Joseon period, for instance, he noted the development of markets beginning in the seventeenth century; many nationalist historians argued that these markets constituted the beginnings of an indigenous development of capitalism. He also provided a general framework for the emergence and development of a unique Korean civilization from prehistory to the twentieth century. Crucially, its origins began before the emergence of any kingdoms on the Japanese islands. The book became the standard history textbook in colleges for the next two decades, and this conception of Korean history later came to be called 'internal development theory' (*naejaejeok baljeonnon*).

Nationalist history itself began to come under critique by the 1980s, by no coincidence, at the height of the democracy movement.[5] A new generation of historians had emerged who were politicized by two major events: the passage of the Yushin constitution in 1972 and the Gwangju Democratic Uprising in May 1980. The Yushin constitution essentially made Park Chung Hee president for life, and he declared martial law to suppress dissent. After his assassination in October 1979, there was renewed hope for democracy, but General Chun Doo Hwan, in a manner

[5] Yi Seyeong, "1980, 90 nyeondae minjuhwa munje wa yeoksahak" (Historiography and the issue of democratization in the 1980s and 90s) in Gim Yongseop gyosu jeongnyeon ginyeom nonchong ganhaeng wiwonhoe, ed., *Gim Yongseop gyosu jeongnyeon ginyeom Hanguk sahak nonchong*, vol. 1: *Hanguksa insik gwa yeoksa iron* (Seoul: Chisik saneopsa, 1997).

reminiscent of Park's own rise, seized power in a coup d'état. Protests broke out throughout the country in May 1980, and the citizens of Gwangju were able to defeat government forces and take control of the southwestern city for a few days before their uprising was brutally suppressed. Demonstrations opposing the military dictatorships of Park Chung Hee and Chun Doo Hwan were a daily occurrence on college campuses. While some students went on to become activists, others went into academia as opportunities for graduate study expanded in the 1980s. These scholars introduced a new problematic into historiography. Criticizing the elitism of existing scholarship, they turned their attention to the common people and sought to examine the structural roots of their oppression, especially the class system. They also focused on the factors that enabled commoners to engage in resistance against the system. This problematic had obvious parallels with the concerns of democracy activists; the decade was one of the periods when there were direct linkages between historical and political practice. This new historiography, though certainly not without nationalist elements, was often called *minjung* historiography. *Minjung* was a term that generally referred to the oppressed elements of society. Sometimes, it meant people of subaltern status or specifically the proletariat; at others, it signified 'the people' in a very general sense. Though *minjung* historiography emerged through a critique of nationalist historiography, it also made an important contribution to internal development theory. Nationalist historiography in South Korea had not been able to explain the internal factors that led to the creation of the North Korean state; in fact, Lee Ki-Baik's book completely ignores North Korea. *Minjung* historiography enabled an understanding of the division that explained the emergence of both Koreas, claiming that it originated in class conflict in the late Joseon period. This historiographical development reflected the revived interest in reunification within the democracy movement.

After the victory of the democracy movement in 1987, *minjung* historiography struggled to establish itself within the scholarly mainstream. It had originated in informal study groups in universities, and in the mid 1980s, it grew into a disparate group of small historical associations. After 1987, they joined forces and ultimately consolidated into two organizations. The first was the Institute for Korean Historical Studies (Yeoksa munje yeonguso), which was founded in September 1987, and the second was The Organization of Korean Historians, which was founded in September 1988. While the former sought to spread their views on history to the general public, the latter conducted more purely academic historical research. The Organization of Korean Historians started with about

100 members; it was not merely a scholarly association but an active research center. It focused on group research, its members collaborating on research projects that produced books with multiple authors. They published a general history in 1992, *Korean History* (Hanguk yeoksa),[6] which quickly replaced *A New History of Korea* as the standard college history textbook. Its publication marked the beginning of the rise of *minjung* historiography as historical orthodoxy. By the time of its twentieth anniversary in 2008, the Organization of Korean Historians had become one of the major historical associations in South Korea with a membership of about 530 researchers.

Now that internal development theory and *minjung* historiography have become part of the academic mainstream, they have in turn become a target of critique. On a conceptual level, postmodernists have criticized both *minjung* and nationalist historiography for suppressing other viewpoints, calling for the rejection of existing historical orthodoxies. The rise of cultural history has led to a reflection on limitations of the class paradigm for understanding forms of domination. Some scholars, moreover, have criticized *minjung* historiography for exaggerating the level of exploitation in certain periods and the extent of development in others. Much of the criticism has come from economic historians who are just beginning to apply statistical analysis to both premodern and early modern history. They have argued that capitalist development did not begin in the Joseon; rather, it began in the colonial period, a time that has usually been associated with exploitation. As a result of the emergence of new research agendas, debates have flared in recent years about various aspects of the period, but they have achieved little resolution, leading to calls for new paradigms to understand the Joseon period.

The Origins of Joseon

One of the longest running debates on the Joseon period is about the social origins of the kingdom. It is well established that a new class of scholar-officials emerged in the late Goryeo period. Critical of the ruling ideology of Buddhism, they were proponents of Neo-Confucianism that had been introduced to the country in the late thirteenth century. It was at this time that the character *sa* began to be used to designate the literati, as in the term *sadaebu* meaning 'scholar-officials.' These scholar-officials later

[6] Hanguk yeoksa yeonguhoe, *Hanguk yeoksa* (Seoul: Yeoksa bipyeongsa, 1992).

allied with Yi Seonggye to found the new kingdom and became its leading intellectuals as well as the core of the ruling class. The focus of the debate has been about their origins – did they emerge from the same aristocratic families as existing elites, or did they represent the emergence of a new social force? This debate can be seen as an instance of the larger struggle between stagnation theory and internal development theory in Korean historiography.

One of the main historians at the center of this debate is Yi Tae-jin, emeritus professor at Seoul National University. In the 1980s and early 1990s, he wrote a series of articles in which he argued that the new scholar-officials came from a new class of small and medium-sized landlords. Because of advances in agriculture, farmers were increasingly able to abandon the practice of letting fields lay fallow and engage in continuous cultivation. Increased productivity led to the rise of small and medium-sized landlords who were critical of the elites and monasteries that owned large agricultural estates. In Neo-Confucianism, they found an ideology that expressed their worldview and provided a program for fundamental reform that promised to curb the excesses of Buddhism and create a more just and stable society. Yi Tae-jin's work has formed one of the foundations of internal development theory, and many general textbooks in South Korea still follow the general framework of his arguments, including Lee Ki-Baik's influential book.

Some scholars have countered that the new scholar-officials actually came from families belonging to the existing Goryeo ruling class. Criticism of Yi Tae-jin's work has been particularly strong in the United States.[7] The critics have shown that many of the new officials of the early Joseon came from families that had been prominent in the Goryeo era. Many historians feel that the debate will never come to a definite conclusion because of the lack of sources from the period; in fact, the family lineage is known for fewer than half of early-Joseon officials. Another point of contention is the analytic framework that Yi Tae-jin used; it built an argument by establishing connections among various political-economic factors during the Goryeo-Joseon transition. For instance, he noted that there was an increase in the number of officials from the three southern provinces that were the agricultural center of the country. It is also true that Yi Seonggye carried out a comprehensive land reform during the preparations for the new kingdom, and registers for all private and public land were burned. All

[7] See John B. Duncan, *The Origins of the Choson Dynasty* (Seattle: University of Washington Press, 2000) and Deuchler, *op cit.*

these facts suggest that Joseon was trying to establish a new economic foundation for the kingdom; however, there is no 'smoking gun' that can satisfy the requirements of a narrow empiricist.

Periodization

There have also been debates about the periodization of the Joseon era. Until recently, it was common to divide the era into early and late periods, with the Imjin War (1592–1598) and the Manchu invasions of 1627 and 1636 as the dividing point. In recent years, some historians have advocated a tripartite division into early, middle, and late periods. Though there are fundamental differences in historians' interpretations of the Joseon period, the two views on periodization are also rooted in differences in the type of history that is emphasized. The debate is a reminder of how the timing of political, economic, social, and cultural changes can differ greatly and thus how the history of each can provide different understandings of a historical period.

The division of the Joseon era into early and late periods is mainly based on agricultural history. Agriculture developed to the point that farmers no longer had to let fields lay fallow every few years. The increased agricultural production, driven in part by the introduction of rice transplantation from China, was one factor behind the development of Joseon in the fifteenth century, which included the reign of Sejong. Up to that time, fields had been planted according to the method of dry seeding. By contrast, the new technique involved the creation of seedbeds in one portion of the fields with seedlings transplanted to the rest of the irrigated field. By the seventeenth century, rice transplantation had become universal. The combination of labor savings and increased production transformed the economy and laid the foundation for the expansion of markets. Thus, agricultural historians see the Imjin War and the Manchu invasions as a major turning point of the Joseon period. Some historians link political history with agrarian development, seeing the 1623 coup against Gwanghaegun that brought Injo to the throne as inaugurating the late Joseon period. Others note the shift in political discourse that occurred after the two invasions as further evidence of change.

The tripartite periodization is generally based on political history.[8] Initially proposed in the 1950s, it gained strength in the early 1980s with

[8] Go Yeongjin, "Joseon sahoe ui jeongchi-sasangjeok byeonhwa wa sigi gubun" (Periodization and political-intellectual changes in Joseon society), *Yeoksa wa hyeonsil*,

research into the history of calligraphy. This work correlated changing calligraphy style with changes in thought. The fifteenth and sixteenth centuries brought Zhu Xi Neo-Confucianism to its height; in the seventeenth and eighteenth centuries, this foreign ideology became naturalized, leading to the development of a distinctively Korean form of Neo-Confucianism. The nineteenth century saw the emergence of forms of thought that were critical of the Neo-Confucian orthodoxy, such as Northern Learning (Bukhak). The notion of a 'mid Joseon' period developed further through research on political history. Though scholars differ on the exact timing, the Joseon period was divided as follows. The early Joseon period was the time when the newly-rising scholar-officials (*sadaebu*) were the dominant force in politics, ending in the early sixteenth century. The mid Joseon period was defined by the dominance of the so-called *sarim* faction and lasted from the early sixteenth to the late seventeenth century. The *sarim* were scholars in the provinces who began to enter the government when they felt that the dominant *sadaebu* faction was abandoning the true ideals of Neo-Confucianism. The late Joseon period – from the late seventeenth to the nineteenth century – was marked by the strengthening of the monarchy and rule by in-law families (*sedo jeongchi*). Here is one such periodization:

Early Joseon period – Taejo to Yeonsangun	1392–1506
Mid Joseon period – Jungjong to Sukjong	1506–1720
Late Joseon period – Gyeongjong to Gojong	1720–1873

Advocates of this periodization criticized the early-late division for privileging the role of external forces, such as invasions, on Korean history. They also argued that though the two invasions by Japan and the Manchus caused tremendous damage, they did not bring about fundamental changes to Joseon society. There were no changes to the Joseon ruling class, and politics continued to be dominated by factional struggle.[9] A major effort to promote the acceptance of the tripartite periodization was its adoption in a major government effort to write a complete history of Korea. This was the compilation of the fifty-three volume history of Korea published by the National Institute of Korean History (Guksa pyeonchan wiwonhoe) from 1993 to 2003.[10]

---

no. 18 (1995), pp. 84–110. See also "Joseon sahoe reul eoddeoke bol geosinga" (How should we view Joseon society?) in the same issue for a debate on the periodization of the Joseon era.

9 Gim Seongu, *Joseon junggi gukga wa sajok* (Seoul: Yeoksa bipyeongsa, 2001).

10 Guksa pyeonchan wiwonhoe, *Hanguksa* (Gwacheon: Guksa pyeonchan wiwonhoe).

No matter how it is divided, the term 'late Joseon period' does not include the last years of the kingdom since they are seen as properly belonging to the modern period. The late Joseon period generally ends with the beginning of Joseon's confrontation with Western and Japanese imperialism in the mid nineteenth century. Korean scholars often use the term 'Hanmal' to refer to the decades leading up to the beginning of the country's occupation by Japan in 1910. However, the exact meaning of the term is not precise as historians have different notions of when the Hanmal period began. In its narrowest sense, it refers to the years when the country was officially known as the Great Han Empire (DaeHan jeguk), 1896–1910. In some uses, it begins with the country's first contact with modern imperialism, but even on this point, there are varying opinions. For some historians, the period begins with the Treaty of Ganghwa in 1876, the first treaty that the country signed that was based on Western conventions. Others date the period from the time of the foreign intrusions in the 1860s, beginning with the French disturbance of 1866.

The Sarim *and Factionalism*

A major focus of research on the political history of the Joseon era has been the issue of factionalism. Factions were the main actors in Joseon politics from the late sixteenth to the mid eighteenth century. They became connected with both family and scholarly lineages, and membership essentially became permanent. In the struggle for dominance, factions rose and fell; sometimes, one would split into two new factions. During the early modern period, scholars generally viewed factionalism negatively, seeing it as one of the reasons for the country's weakness and Japan's takeover of the country. In recent decades, new interpretations of factionalism have emerged as a result of the efforts of nationalist historians. Some have claimed that the extent of factionalism was exaggerated; others have argued that it was not a dysfunctional form of politics but an integral part of the functioning of a Neo-Confucian polity.[11] Research on factionalism has thus attempted both to refute one of the main claims of stagnation theory and to uncover the workings of the Neo-Confucian state.

Factionalism emerged in Joseon politics together with the rise of the *sarim* faction to political prominence. The term *sarim* is a combination of

[11] Yi Taejin, "Dangjaeng eul eoddeoke bol geosinga" in Yi Taejin, ed., *Joseon sidae jeongchisa ui jaejomyeong*, revised edition (Seoul: Taehaksa, 2003). See also Gim Don, "Joseon sidae jeongchisa yeongu wa guksa gyoyuk," *Yeoksa gyoyuk*, no. 85 (March 2003).

two Chinese characters, one meaning 'forest' and the other meaning 'literati.' The *sarim* were thus scholars located in the provinces who devoted themselves to their studies and did not initially pursue careers in government. They were among the main protagonists in the literati purges that were the main domestic political incidents in the late fifteenth and early sixteenth centuries. Research in the postwar era has made it possible to reinterpret them as part of a transitional stage rather than as evidence of the inherent dysfunctionality of Joseon politics. Until the purges began, the main force in politics had been the *sadaebu* families in the capital region who were descendants of the kingdom's founders, and they were called the *hungu* faction. The *sarim,* who were idealistic Neo-Confucians, were critical of the corruption of the *hungu* faction. They began to move into politics and became a significant force in the late fifteenth century, especially from Seongjong's reign (r. 1469–1494). The main dynamic in politics in the early sixteenth century was the conflict between the two factions, and the literati purges are generally viewed as the *hungu* faction's violent efforts to eradicate the *sarim*. In fact, the *sarim* almost completely disappeared from the government after the third literati purge in 1519 (Gimyo sahwa). According to the current mainstream view, however, the *sarim* ultimately prevailed and took power in the late sixteenth century.[12] By contrast, Lee Ki-Baik saw the literati purges as a conflict not between two different groups but within the new elite that had differing conceptions of Neo-Confucianism. In his view, though the *sarim* lost the political battle, their conception of Neo-Confucian ideology prevailed, becoming dominant by the mid sixteenth century.[13] In short, Lee emphasized the homogeneity of the yangban class while *minjung* historians emphasized the role of class conflict as the underlying dynamic of political change.

Factionalism is thought to have begun in 1575 with the formation of the Easterner and Westerner factions. The split developed out of a dispute over appointment to an important official post that had authority over personnel matters. Supporters of Gim Hyowon (1542–1580) were called the Easterners, and supporters of Sim Uigyeom (1535–1587) were called the Westerners. The names of the factions derived from the location of Gim's and Sim's residences in Seoul. The two factions were also distinguished by their scholarly lineage; the Easterners were the scholarly

[12] Hanguk yeoksa yeonguhoe, *Hanguk yeoksa* (Seoul: Yeoksa bipyeongsa, 1992), p. 135.

[13] Yi Gibaek, *Hanguksa sillon* (Seoul: Ilchogak, 1967). Translated into English as Ki-Baek Lee, *A New History of Korea*, translated by Edward W. Wagner with Edward J. Shultz (Cambridge: Harvard-Yenching Institute, 1984).

followers of Yi Hwang (Toegye, 1501–1570), while the Westerners followed Yi Yi (Yulgok, 1536–1584). The Easterners quickly became the more powerful of the two, but they split into two new factions at the end of the sixteenth century. In the year 1591, the Westerners proposed that Seonjo (r. 1567–1608) designate an heir since he had no legitimate son. Their proposal caused a controversy, and the split emerged over how severely the Westerners were to be punished. The Northerners favored a harsh condemnation while the Southerners took a more moderate stance. Again, the names of the factions were taken from the location of their leaders' residences. The Northerners supported Prince Gwanghae, becoming the dominant faction when he ascended to the throne in 1608, but after he was deposed in 1623, the Westerners came into power.

Within a few decades, another factional split occurred. It began with the debate between the Westerners and the Southerners in 1659 after the death of Hyojong (r. 1649–1659). The king was not the first son of his predecessor, and there was a disagreement on how long Queen Jaui, the second wife of Injo, should wear mourning clothes. Song Siyeol (1607–1689), the head of the Westerner faction, believed that the period should be one year while Yun Hyu (1617–1680), the head of the Southerner faction, argued that it should be for three years, as befitted a first son. The Westerners prevailed in this debate and later succeeded in purging the Southerners from the government; however, they split in the subsequent struggle for power within the faction in 1683.[14] The older members of the Westerners, led by Song Siyeol, formed the Noron faction, and the younger members, led by Han Taedong (1646–1687), formed the Soron faction. The Noron became the dominant faction in the capital and remained so until Yeongjo (r. 1724–1776) established a policy of impartiality (*tangpyeongchaek*), selecting officials equally from all major factions. Nonetheless, yet another factional split occurred in Yeongjo's reign. One of the most famous and chilling episodes from the Joseon period is Yeongjo's ordering the death of his son, the Crown Prince Sado, in 1762. Since a member of the royal family could not be executed, Yeongjo ordered him to be locked in a large rice chest until he died. Officials split into two groups over his decision. The Sipa faction (Party of Expediency) was opposed to it while the Byeokpa faction (Party of Principle) supported the king.

---

[14] A slightly different account of this factional split is given in Patricia Buckley Ebrey, Anne Walthall, and James B. Palais, *East Asia: A Cultural, Social, and Political History* (Boston and New York: Houghton Mifflin Company, 2006), p. 351.

Internal Development Theory

The greatest crisis of the Joseon period was the invasion by the Japanese in 1592 led by Toyotomi Hideyoshi (1536–1598), who had just unified his country. Generally known as the Hideyoshi invasions in the West, it is called the Imjin War (Imjin waeran) in Korea. Landing in the Busan area in spring 1592, three Japanese armies quickly moved northward. They took the capital of Seoul in June, forcing the king to flee. As they approached the northern border, Ming China entered the war, sending a large-scale force at the very end of the year. After suffering repeated losses on land in the early part of the war, Joseon forces fared better at sea. The victories of Admiral Yi Sunsin (1545–1598) in naval battles along the southern coast in autumn 1592 prevented the Japanese navy from providing support to the armies by landing on the western coast. The first invasion ended in mid 1593 as Hideyoshi's forces returned to Japan without achieving their professed goal of conquering Ming China. After years of failed diplomatic talks, Hideyoshi launched a second invasion of Joseon in early 1597 but with less success than the first. The war ended a few months after Hideyoshi's death in September 1598. A few decades later, the country suffered two invasions by the Manchus, the growing power in the region – the first in 1627 and the second in 1636. In the second, Manchu forces captured King Injo after a siege of the Namhan Mountain Fortress; they then forced the king to shift Joseon's allegiance from Ming to the Qing and took two of his sons as hostages, one of whom later became King Hyojong. The successive invasions produced hundreds of thousands of casualties, but its human cost went beyond battlefield deaths. The armies devastated the countryside, leading to a drop in agricultural production as peasants flocked to the cities in search of safety, food, and work. The capital itself suffered much damage as the Japanese burned down three palaces, leaving the government to rebuild itself, restore social order, and revive the economy.

The period of postwar reconstruction is the focus of some of the most heated debates about the period. It is well established that a network of markets developed throughout the country from the seventeenth century. Initially, they were a response to extreme economic conditions. As people flocked to towns and cities to escape the devastation caused by the Imjin War, markets emerged to address the food shortages caused by the sudden population influx. The government allowed them to continue functioning after the wars in order to help revive the economy. One of the most common types of market was the five-day market (*oiljang*). As the term indicates, a town would open a market every five days, and within a region, they were scheduled so that itinerant peddlers could travel around and deliver goods to all its markets. A major debate has focused on the extent and historical significance of the rise of markets in the late Joseon in marking the beginnings of a commercial revolution. Some argue that this development laid the foundation for South Korea's later capitalist development; this is known as the 'sprouts of capitalism' theory (*jabonjuui maengaron*).[15] Critics of internal development theory have disputed the extent of commercialization and asserted that capitalist development did not begin until the late nineteenth or early twentieth centuries.

The work of the historian Kim Yong-sop (Gim Yongseop) shifted the focus of the debate to agricultural history. Kim documented the fact that markets enabled the emergence of a new type of entrepreneurial peasant. They sold much of their harvest in markets and some amassed sufficient wealth to purchase more land and expand their operations. The wealthiest peasants were then able to achieve social mobility by purchasing yangban status. One of the social consequences of the rise of markets was thus the differentiation of the peasant class. While a small number accumulated land and rose into the yangban class, a far greater number became landless and fell to the status of tenant farmers. These developments undermined the economic and social foundations of Joseon's ruling order and thus provide an explanation for the systemic crisis that emerged in the nineteenth century. Furthermore, the differentiation of the peasantry was seen to be the origins of the internal divisions that later became deeper and led to the division of the country in the twentieth century.[16] Kim Yong-sop's work, with its emphasis on the historical agency of the peasantry, had a tremendous influence on the development of *minjung* historiography, as is evident in several chapters in this volume.

In the past two decades, internal development theory has come under critique from a number of quarters. On a conceptual level, postmodernists have criticized its reliance on a linear conception of history and its privileging of concepts such as nation or class.[17] On the Joseon period, the most

[15] For a more detailed discussion of internal development theory, see "Introduction" in Pang Kie-chung and Michael D. Shin, eds., *Landlords, Peasants, and Intellectuals in Modern Korea* (Ithaca: Cornell East Asia Series, 2005). A similar debate occurred in China.

[16] Gim Yongseop (Kim Yong-sop), "Geundaehwa gwajeong esseo ui nongeop gaehyeok ui du banghyang," *Hanguk geun-hyeondae nongeopsa yeongu*, revised edition (Seoul: Iljogak, 1995). An English translation can be found in Shin and Pang, chap. 1.

[17] See the introduction of Yun Haedong, et. al., eds., *Geundae reul dasi ilgi* (Seoul: Yeoksa bipyeongsa, 2006). See also Im Jihyeon and Yi Seongsi, eds., *Guksa ui sinhwa reul neomeoseo* (Seoul: Humanist, 2004).

prominent critics are the scholars associated with the Naksungdae Institute of Economic Research.[18] The institute has done pioneering work in collecting and analyzing statistical data, including agricultural productivity, prices, and wages. Claiming that there was a decrease in agricultural productivity in the late Joseon period, they have argued that the peasant class did not differentiate but underwent a generalized decline.[19] Though statistical research is still in its early stages, they believe that their work constitutes a refutation of the 'sprouts of capitalism' argument.[20] Recently, however, other economic historians have drawn different conclusions with similar data.[21]

The History of Everyday Life

The 1996 publication of this book and its companion volume, with the title *How Did People Live in the Joseon Period?*, marked the emergence of the history of everyday life as a field in South Korean historiography.[22] The Organization of Korean Historians wrote a series of *How Did People Live...* books, including volumes on the Three Kingdoms period, the Goryeo period, and the twentieth century; all have sold well and have had several reprintings. A number of other books on daily life, both academic and popular, have been published since the mid 1990s, and it has been one of the few fields in history to gain a wide readership among the general public.

Though the cultural turn produced tremendous interest in cultural history, studies of everyday life seem to have emerged out of social history. Cultural history remains a minor field within South Korean historiography;[23] most of its practitioners are literary historians, media scholars, or

---

[18] The leading figures in the institute are An Byeongjik, formerly of the Department of Economics at Seoul National University, and his successor Rhee Younghoon (Yi Yeonghun). Yi Yeonghun, *Joseon hugi sahoe gyeongjesa* (Seoul: Hangilsa, 1988).

[19] Gi-Wook Shin attempts to split the difference between the two positions by arguing that the Joseon period was characterized by "involuted social differentiation." Gi-Wook Shin, *Peasant Protest and Social Change in Colonial Korea* (Seattle: University of Washington Press, 1996), p. 34.

[20] Yi Yeonghun, "Hanguksa e isseoseo geundae ro ui ihaeng gwa teukjil," *Gyeongje sahak* 21 (1996).

[21] Jun Seong Ho, James B. Lewis, and Kang Han-Rog, "Korean Expansion and Decline from the Seventeenth to the Nineteenth Century: A View Suggested by Adam Smith," *The Journal of Economic History*, Vol. 68, no. 1 (March 2008).

[22] Jeong Yeonsik, "Hanguk saenghwalsa yeongu ui hyeonhwang gwa gwaje – Joseon sidae saenghwalsa yeongu reul jungsim euro," *Yeoksa wa hyeonsil* 72 (June 2009).

[23] Jeong Yeonsik, p. 299.

scholars in another field of cultural studies. Research on daily life emerged from forms of social history practiced by *minjung* historiography. One of the concerns of *minjung* historiography has been to explore the connections between socioeconomic conditions and political movements. For instance, the differentiation of the peasant class in the late Joseon period has been seen as one of the main factors behind the rise of peasant rebellions in the nineteenth century.[24] After the victory of the democracy movement in 1987, as South Korean society became more conservative and political movements declined, *minjung* historians shifted their attention to examining the daily lives of the *minjung*.

The chapters in this volume illustrate the achievements, promise, and limitations of research on everyday life. Its concrete depictions of how historical forces shaped the lives of the people at the time have been effective in making readers feel a connection to their past. This is especially true for college students taking history classes. They have grown up in a fully industrialized country, mostly in large cities, that appears to have little in common with the agrarian and sinocentric world their ancestors lived in. What is presented in this book is clearly not an idealized past. While filled with stories of the exploitation suffered by the peasantry, it is also careful to note that they were not just victims but also actively engaged in resistance and were as much the agents of history as were the elites. In addition, the book is not meant to celebrate or glorify official nationalism; in fact, it makes it possible to undertake a reexamination of Korean identity. It demonstrates that what people commonly regard as 'traditional Korea' is not timeless but was actually formed in the Joseon period. For instance, we learn that kimchi, the spicy pickled cabbage that is widely regarded as the national food of Korea, did not exist prior to the late Joseon period.

So far, research on everyday life has followed its own separate agenda rather than addressing existing debates on the Joseon period. In fact, the field itself has not generated major debates even among its main researchers. As a result, it is still unclear whether it offers a unique methodology and what its relation is to more established fields such as political or economic history. There has also been little engagement with cultural history as practiced by literary historians and scholars of cultural studies. It seems that the potential of the study of everyday life lies in its ability to transcend existing disciplinary boundaries and encourage dialogue among

---

24 Gim Yongseop (Kim Yong-sop), "Ilje gangjeomgi ui nongeop munje wa geu tagaechaek," *Hanguk geun-hyeondae nongeopsa yeongu*. An abridged translation in English can be found in Pang and Shin, eds., chap. 4.

various fields. On the one hand, social historians have engaged in extensive empirical research in order to write a materialist history of everyday life in the Joseon period. On the other, literary historians have adopted the methods of cultural studies to produce innovative studies of modern literature and popular culture. Dialogue between the two could produce a new understanding of how domination and resistance operated in the Joseon era by examining politics at the micro level. In the coming years, it will be interesting to see whether such dialogues emerge and whether research on everyday life will develop into an indulgence of nostalgia for a romanticized past that never existed or continue to make the past relevant in a way that makes possible productive interventions in the daily lives of people today.

The Meanings of Joseon

The Joseon period has had a complicated and at times uneasy relationship with modernity. Modern identity often defines itself as a break with the past; however, it has not been easy to achieve a clean break with Joseon. One factor is the very length of the period. With its beginnings in the late fourteenth century, it seems to belong to the distant past. The basics of life – food, clothing, and shelter – have all changed greatly since then, especially in the last century with South Korea's rapid industrialization. On the other hand, since it ended in the early twentieth century, it can also feel startlingly recent. Only a generation ago, there were still elderly people who had childhood memories of the Joseon era. Another factor has been the turbulent nature of Korea's modern period during which views on the past have experienced, at times, rapid swings, and, at others, surprising inertia. One example has already been discussed above: the heated debates over the beginning of the modern period. Though some have argued that the end of the Joseon period marks the beginning of modernity, current historical orthodoxy holds that it began centuries earlier in the late Joseon period. The view of Joseon as a transitional period that straddles both the premodern and the modern eras has complicated its place within modern identity. This section gives a brief overview of the changing views of Joseon during the modern period, taking some examples from heritage. For many years, it was rejected for its adherence to Confucianism, and then over the course of the twentieth century, there was a long struggle to reclaim and reconcile it with modernity.

The initial impact of imperialism was to produce a sense of "cultural estrangement" toward Joseon.[25] Encounters with foreign powers in the nineteenth century accelerated the decline of Neo-Confucianism as its ruling ideology. Its status as orthodoxy was already being questioned in the seventeenth and eighteenth centuries as fundamental problems arose in the ruling order, leading to the rise of a scholarly tendency now known as Silhak. The introduction of Western forms of knowledge led to the complete rejection of Confucianism. For instance, *The Independent*, the first vernacular newspaper that was founded in 1896, blamed Confucianism for "bad habits and corrupt practices among the higher classes"[26] and criticized Confucian education:

> [It] destroys all tendency to original force and makes all intellectual production of one monotonous type....Chinese education is mental slavery, and by its jejune routine, its rote and task work paralyzes all mental life. (August 8, 1896)

With the shift to a Eurocentric worldview, China was no longer the 'Middle Kingdom' and was now seen as barbaric, belonging to the bottom tier on the scale of civilization.[27] As a result of the decentering of China, Joseon, which had been confident in its identity as a civilized country, also found itself relegated to barbaric status in the new world order. Many intellectuals saw Confucianism and, in some cases, Joseon's past in general as an obstacle to modernization.

With the beginning of the Japanese occupation in August 1910, Joseon became a source of shame to the Korean people as its weaknesses were blamed for the loss of the country's sovereignty.[28] One term used to refer to Japan's takeover was *gyeongsul gukchi*, which meant 'the country's humiliation in the year 1910.'[29] Colonial ideology reinforced the rejection of the past by declaring Joseon to be backward and stagnant in order to justify Japan's rule. Even under these negative attitudes toward the Joseon period, there were some efforts to recover and reinterpret it as an era whose true history was obscured by Confucianism. It had a few figures

---

[25] Frantz Fanon, *The Wretched of the Earth* (New York: Grove Press, 1968), p. 210.

[26] *The Independent*, June 18, 1896.

[27] Andre Schmid, *Korea Between Empires, 1895–1919* (New York: Columbia University Press, 2002), pp. 56–60.

[28] Yi Tae-jin, "Why Has Yangban Culture Been Denounced?" in *The Dynamics of Confucianism and Modernization in Korean History* (Ithaca, NY: Cornell East Asia Series, 2007), p. 296; see also Gi-Wook Shin, *Ethnic Nationalism in Korea: Genealogy, Politics, and Legacy* (Stanford: Stanford University Press, 2006), p. 46.

[29] The term was used in newspapers published abroad such as the *Dongnip sinmun*, which was published in Shanghai. See "Gaejo (yuk)," *Dongnip sinmun*, September 18, 1919.

who were useful for the construction of national identity. Two of the most celebrated were King Sejong, widely considered to be the greatest monarch of the period, and Admiral Yi Sunsin, its greatest military hero. First, the nationalist movement promoted the native language as part of its effort to protect Korean identity under foreign rule. Though the Korean language has a long history, it had no script until the Joseon period. Sejong invented the script, later called Hangeul, in 1443, promulgating it three years later in 1446. Called *eonmun* or 'vulgar script' for centuries, it now began to be considered the greatest cultural achievement in Korea's history.[30] Modern efforts to celebrate Hangeul's invention began during the colonial period. In 1926, the Joseon Language Research Institute (Joseoneo yeonguhoe) and the publisher Sinminsa organized a ceremony celebrating the 480th anniversary of the promulgation of Hangeul on November 4, as well as a series of commemorative lectures a few days later.[31] This is seen as the beginnings of the later holiday Hangeul Day. Second, in an effort to mobilize resistance against the Japanese, intellectuals looked for historical figures to serve as anti-Japanese role models, but there were virtually none in earlier ages of history.[32] As the only major war with Japan occurred in the Joseon period, Yi Sunsin was lionized as a paragon of anti-Japanese resistance because of his defeat of the Japanese navy during the Imjin Wars. In 1908, the pioneering historian Sin Chaeho wrote a historical novel about him, as did the pioneering novelist Yi Gwangsu in serial form in 1931–1932.[33] In 1931, a movement to preserve the country's heritage began with the campaign to raise funds to purchase the tomb of Yi Sunsin whose land was put up for sale in May of that year.[34] These efforts could not overcome the humiliation of the Japanese takeover; the prevailing view of Joseon contained a mix of shame and pride.

---

30 For example, see Yi Byeonggi, "Sejong Daewang ui Hunmin jeongeum banpo" (Sejong the Great's promulgation of the Korean script), *Byeolgeongon* Vol. 3, no. 2 (May 1928).

31 "'Hangeul' ui saeroun bit oneuli 'Gagyanal" (The new light of Hangeul – today is Hangeul Day), *Donga ilbo*, Nov. 4, 1926; "Gagyanal ginyeom gangyeon" (Memorial lectures on Hangeul Day), Nov. 9, 1926.

32 Jeon Jaeho, "Bak Jeonghui jeonggwon ui 'hoguk yeongung mandeulgi' wa jeontong munhwa yusan jeongchaek" (The making of heroic patriots and the policies toward traditional cultural heritage of the Park Chung Hee administration), *Yeoksa bipyeong* 99 (Spring 2012), p. 119.

33 Yi also wrote other historical novels set in the Joseon period, including *Heo Saengjeon* (1923–1924), *Ilseol Chunhyangjeon* (1925–1926), *Danjong aesa* (1928–1929), and *Sejo daewang* (1940).

34 Yi Jiwon, "1930 nyeondae minjokjuui gyeyeol ui gojeok bojon undong" (The heritage preservation movement of nationalists in the 1930s), *Dongbang hakji* nos. 77, 78, 79 (1993), pp. 760–762.

After the country's liberation from Japanese rule in August 1945, it was expected that historians would reject colonial versions of Korean history and reclaim the estranged parts of its past. However, because the division of the country and the emergence of the Cold War blocked the process of decolonization in the south, there was a significant degree of continuity between the colonial and post-colonial eras in their views of Joseon. People continued to feel a combination of shame and pride toward Joseon; however, it did acquire more layers of meaning. Amidst calls for the 'cleansing' of colonial legacies that undermined 'Korean' identity, Joseon came to be seen more explicitly as a victim of imperialist violence. The most visible sign of victimization was the destruction of the royal palaces. The Japanese colonial government tore down almost all of the buildings of Gyeongbok Palace, the main palace, moved its main gate to another location, and then built the Government-General building in front of the former throne hall. The Japanese also turned Changgyeong Palace into a park and zoo and opened the grounds of many palaces to the public. In the years immediately after liberation, there were some efforts to eliminate the traces of Japanese rule and overcome the sense of estrangement toward the Joseon period. Running south from Gyeongbok Palace to the city hall building, the main boulevard of Seoul, whose name had been changed to Gwanghwamun-tong by the Japanese in 1914, was renamed Sejong Boulevard (Sejongno) in 1946. Hangeul Day was also celebrated in October 1946, the year being the 500th anniversary of its promulgation.[35] In general, however, little was done to restore Joseon-era buildings and heritage sites because of factors such as the cost, the disorder caused by the Korean War and the following years of reconstruction, and the lack of political will among the leadership.

The promotion of heritage began in earnest during the years of Park Chung Hee's dictatorial rule (1961–1979). Initially, Park had a rather negative view of Korean history, seeing little value in the country's past with the exception of a few figures.[36] Even in its early years, however, his administration implemented some measures that set the foundation for its heritage policy. In October 1961, it turned the Office of Former Imperial Property Affairs (Gu Hwangsil jaesan samu chongguk) into the Office of Cultural Heritage Administration (Munhwajae gwalliguk). It formed a

[35] "Hangeul nal ui yurae" (The origins of Hangeul Day), *Gyeonghyang sinmun*, October 9, 1946.

[36] Jeon Jaeho, p. 115; Sheila Miyoshi Jager, *Narratives of Nation Buidling in Korea: A Genealogy of Patriotism* (Armonk, New York: M.E. Sharpe, 2003), p. 83.

Committee on Cultural Heritage in December of that year and announced the promulgation of the Cultural Heritage Protection Law in January 1962.[37] Later that year, it began to change the system of classification of heritage. Up to then, the term 'national treasure' (*gukbo*) was applied to all types of heritage, but now, they were classified into historical sites (*sajeok*), national treasures (*gukbo*), and cultural heritage (*munhwajae*).[38] It was at this time that Sungnye Gate (Namdaemun) was reconfirmed and became more widely known as National Treasure no. 1. The designation of official historical sites began in January 1963 with the announcement of 125 such sites.[39] Though the majority of the sites were in the former Silla capital of Gyeongju and other areas related to ancient history, a number of Joseon-era sites were included such as four of the royal palaces, Sajik Altar, the Royal Shrine (Jongmyo), and places related to Yi Sunsin and Jeong Yagyong.[40] In July 1963, the Committee on Cultural Heritage announced a five-year plan for repairs on heritage sites.[41] The government also devoted a significant amount of funds for cultural heritage in the 1960s. In recent years, the budget for heritage has generally amounted to less than half of the budget for the general administration of culture and arts. By contrast, in the 1960s, it was at least double and, in some years, more than four times the budget for culture and arts.[42]

With a shift in policy in the mid 1960s, Joseon came to play a larger role in the promotion of heritage. When the Ministry of Culture was expanded into the Ministry of Culture and Information in 1968, it adopted a more comprehensive and systematic approach to the promotion of 'traditional' culture.[43] It began to be more active in the restoration of heritage sites, making Joseon a more visible and tangible part of everyday life. Though

---

37 "Munhwajaebeop munhwajae wiwonhoe reul seolchi" (Law on Cultural Heritage – the establishment of the Committee on Cultural Heritage), *Gyeonghyang sinmun*, Dec, 27, 1961; "Munhwajae bohobeop deung gongpo" (The promulgation of the Cultural Heritage Protection Law and other laws), *Donga ilbo*, Jan. 11, 1962.

38 "Gukbo neun 89jong euro" (National treasures [reduced] to 89 in number), *Gyeonghyang sinmun*, Nov. 3, 1962.

39 "Sajeok jijeong" (Designation of historical sites), *Donga ilbo*, Jan. 29, 1963.

40 "Sajeok baekisipo gaeso jijeong" (The designation of 125 historical sites), *Gyeonghyang sinmun*, Jan. 29, 1963. Initially, 121 sites were announced, but four others were quickly added, all related to the Joseon period: Changdeok Palace, Changgyeong Palace, Deoksu Palace, and the Royal Shrine (Jongmyo).

41 "Munhwajae bosu wihan ogaenyeon gyehoek surip" (The establishment of a five-year plan for the repair of cultural hertiage), *Donga ilbo*, July 22, 1963, p. 40.

42 O Yangyeol, "Hanguk ui munhwa jeongchaek chegye 50 nyeon" (50 years of Korea's culture policy system), *Munhwa jeongchaek nonchong* 7 (1995).

43 Jeon Jaeho, p. 118.

Gyeongbok Palace was only partially restored, it had already begun the restoration of its main gate, Gwanghwa Gate, in 1966, albeit with reinforced concrete, completing work in December 1968.[44] Yi Sunsin and King Sejong now played an even more central role in the construction of Korean identity, useful in promoting aspects of South Korea's developmental nationalism. In a country with mandatory military service and living under constant threat of invasion, Yi Sunsin exemplified the military ideal of the modern citizen, especially loyalty to one's country. Park began to celebrate the anniversary of Yi's birthday in 1962; during the eighteen years of his rule, he attended the birthday ceremonies a total of fourteen times.[45] A shrine to Yi, called Hyeonchungsa, was restored and expanded, opening to the public in April 1967.[46] A statue of Yi was unveiled in the center of Sejong Boulevard on May 4, 1968; its location shows Yi's role as the symbolic protector of the nation. Sejong embodied the scholarly qualities expected of its citizens as South Korea's rapid industrialization relied on the promotion of education and science, requiring children to submit to a grueling educational program in order to get into the top colleges. He was given more prominence as his portrait was used on the country's paper currency from 1960. A statue of the king was placed on the grounds of Deoksu Palace in 1968, the same year that the government set a ten-year plan to begin the exclusive use of Hangeul in schools in 1970, the year that Hangeul Day became an official holiday.[47] In 1978, the name of the cultural center on Sejong Boulevard was changed to the Sejong Cultural Center (Sejong munhwa hoegwan). These efforts, however, were not the result of the overcoming of colonialist views of Joseon; in fact, they have been often understood as an effort to obscure the past pro-Japanese collaboration of Park Chung Hee and others in his administration.[48] It seems to be no coincidence that its approach to heritage changed around the time that the Normalization Treaty with Japan was concluded in 1965.

A more general rediscovery of Joseon did not occur until after the end of military dictatorship in 1987 and the end of the Cold War in 1989. One

---

[44] "Gwanghwamun bogwon gaetong" (The opening of the restored Gwanghwa Gate), *Maeil gyeongje*, Dec. 11, 1968.

[45] Jeon Jaeho, p. 120.

[46] "Hyeonchungsa seongyeokhwa jungong" (The completion of the sanctuary of Hyeonchunsa), *Donga ilbo*, April 28, 1967.

[47] "Hangeul jeonyong sebu gyehoek maryeon" (Preparation of detailed plans for the exclusive use of Hangeul), *Donga ilbo*, Oct. 26, 1968; "70 nyeon buteo Hangeul jeonyong" (Exclusive use of Hangeul from 1970), *Gyeonghyang sinmun*, Oct. 7, 1968.

[48] Jeon Jaeho, p. 123.

factor behind the change was South Koreans' growing confidence toward Japan. Though South Koreans continued to feel anger about the takeover, their feelings of inferiority were considerably lessened, if not overcome, with the country's rise as an industrial power.[49] Views of Japan also changed as a result of the refutation of stagnation theory by nationalist and *minjung* historians during the 1970s and 1980s, as discussed above. This scholarship, while acknowledging Joseon's weaknesses, also criticized Japan's claims of modernizing its colony, drawing attention to its expansionist aggressions and the exploitative nature of its policies. The emergence of a new historical orthodoxy helped to lessen the sense of shame at the Japanese takeover. Another factor was the rise of civil society during the democracy movement. Until then, the government had a virtual monopoly over national heritage, but as civil society became more assertive, heritage became more of a negotiation between the two. A third factor was a revival of interest in Confucianism. It was no longer seen as incompatible with modern life as the industrial development of South Korea and other Asian polities (Taiwan, Hong Kong, Singapore) demonstrated that it was not an obstacle to modernization. In fact, they were thought of as a new model of development often called 'Confucian capitalism.' People began to see contemporary problems as the result of the excessive pursuit of Westernization, rather than the lingering effects of Joseon-era Confucianism or Japanese colonialism. For instance, as the historian Yi Tae-jin wrote,

> What then has been the result of blindly following Western civilization for the past one hundred years?
>
> ...Though it could be said that the South has achieved economic development, mutual distrust is high, and social chaos and cultural confusion are prevalent. As a result, people have become desensitized even to immorality and unethical behavior.[50]

---

49 One sign of this change was the publication in 1993 of the bestselling book *There is No Japan* (Ilbon eun eopda) by KBS reporter Jeon Yeook, a dismissive critique of contemporary life in Japan that sold over a million copies. Another bestseller published the same year was Gim Jinmyeong's novel *The Rose of Sharon has Blossomed* (Mugunghwa ggochi pieotseumnida). Selling over six million copies, it told the story of North and South Korea cooperating to produce nuclear missiles that were used to defend against Japanese aggression. "Daeha soseol *Goguryeo* jippil jungin beseuteuselleo jakga Gim Jinmyeong" (Bestselling novelist Gim Jinmyeong: in the middle of writing the roman fleuve *Goguryeo*), *Hanguk ilbo*, Sept. 28, 2012. Another sign of South Korea's growing confidence was the end of the ban on the import of Japanese popular culture in 1998.

50 Yi Tae-jin, op. cit., p. 323.

In a reversal of the thinking prevalent in the late nineteenth century, Joseon culture began to be seen as an antidote to the ills of modern life.[51]

As a result, there was a tremendous increase of interest in the Joseon period in the 1990s. Classical Korean literature became popular as works written in classical Chinese were translated into the vernacular.[52] Lectures and reading groups on the Korean classics at public libraries drew significant numbers of readers. Non-fiction books on the Joseon period also sold well, most notably those written by the historian Yi Deogil (b. 1961). The Joseon era became more prominent in other aspects of everyday life as well. These trends first emerged in the 1980s within the student movement and spread to the general public in the 1990s. Reflecting the interest of the democracy movement, the focus of this interest was not yangban culture but that of the commoners. First, it became more common for people to drink traditional teas at home; in addition to being sold in stores, they became available in vending machines.[53] Traditional teahouses were popular in downtown Seoul and around colleges.[54] Second, a modified version of traditional dress, called *gaeryang Hanbok*, also became popular. Significantly, they were not based on the fancy attire of the elites but on that of the commoner class.[55] Third, there was also a surge of interest in the music of the Joseon era – not so much court music but that of the peasantry. As one of the chapters in this book discusses, drumming and other kinds of music were an integral part of the working day of farmers, as well as of their major seasonal rituals. A revised form of that music, called *samulnori*, became especially popular. The most famous pioneer of *samulnori*, Kim Duk Soo, founded a professional troupe in 1978; by 1994, there were around fifty professional troupes and, according to one newspaper, so many clubs in colleges and companies that they could not be

---

51 In this context, it is not surprising that so many popular dramas set in the Joseon era feature doctors as protagonists, such as *Heo Jun* (1999), *Dae Jang Geum* (2003), and *Maui* (2012).

52 "'Gojeon ilgi undong' pokneolge hwaksan" (The widespread growth of the 'movement to read the classics'), *Gyeonghyang sinmun*, Oct. 7, 1992.

53 "Gajeong eumryosu jeontongcha baram" (The popularity of traditional tea as a family beverage), *Donga ilbo*, Apr 17, 1987; "Japangi deung hwalyong: jeontongcha bogeup hwakdae baramjik" (The use of vending machines and other things: advocating the increased spread of traditional tea), *Gyeonghyang sinmun*, June 7, 1989.

54 Yi Wonjae, "Jeontong chatjip ingi" (The popularity of traditional teahouses), *Donga ilbo*, May 13, 1991.

55 Yi Jinyeong, "Gaeryang Hanbok 'saenghwal uisang' jari jabattda" (Modified *Hanbok* has become established as everyday attire), *Donga ilbo*, Sep 14, 1994; Gwon Yeongsu, "Ssago ibgi pyeonhan gaeryang Hanbok ingi" (The popularity of cheap and easy-to-wear modified *Hanbok*), *Gyeonghyang sinmun*, Feb 13, 1996.

counted.[56] One of the catalysts for the interest in Joseon-era music was the movie *Seopyeonje*, directed by Im Kwon-Taek and released in April 1993. A relatively small-scale film about singers of *pansori*, a form of one-person opera that emerged in the late Joseon period, it became the biggest box office hit in South Korean history as well as the first film to pass the one-million viewer mark. Its popularity led the Ministry to Culture to declare 1994 to be the 'Year of Traditional Music.'[57] At the same time, historical dramas set in the Joseon era became tremendously popular. *Tears of a Dragon* (Yong ui nunmul), about the founding of Joseon, became a big hit in 1996. Drawing ratings of over 30 percent at its height, it ran for 159 episodes for a year and a half. It launched a boom in historical dramas, making them a fixture on South Korean television; in the process, the stories began to be set outside of the palace and focus on the lives of non-elites.[58] These dramas put faces on historical figures from textbooks and taught audiences about titles of officials, names of government offices, and other commonly used terms from the time. The Joseon period has become as tangible, familiar, and commodified a part of material life in South Korea as Hyundai cars or Samsung appliances.

After the end of the military dictatorship, heritage policy placed much emphasis on the elimination of any traces of Japan. In the mid 1990s, civic groups pushed for a reexamination of the national treasure system. They criticized the fact that South Korea still used the names and numbering system for the treasures that had been established by the Japanese colonial government when it created a similar system in 1933.[59] Some groups, in particular, pushed for the Hunmin jeongeum, the original name of the Korean script, to be designated National Treasure no. 1, instead of Sungnye Gate (Namdaemun).[60] After the Office of Cultural Heritage Administration

56 "'Samulnori'ran" (What is samulnori?), *Gyeonghyang sinmun*, Jan. 7, 1994.

57 Sin Bongnye, "Naenyeon eun 'Gugak ui hae'" Munhwa cheyukbu yeonghwa 'Seopyeonje' gyegi seonjeong" (Next year will be the 'Year of Traditional Music' – the Ministry of Culture's decision is influenced by the film 'Seopyeonje'), *Donga ilbo*, Oct. 15, 1993.

58 Gim Hyeonjeong, "Yi Byeonghun peurodyuseo inteobyu" (Interview with the producer Yi Byeonghun), *Ssine 21*, October 27, 2003.

59 Yi Yeonjae, "Munhwa yusando 'baro seugi' munhwajae jaepyeongga-jaejojeong uimi" (Rectifying cultural heritage: the significance of reevaluating and reorganizing cultural heritage), *Gyeonghyang sinmun*, Nov. 29, 1996; Yu Seunghun, "Ilje sigi munhwajae bohobeop ui 'jungjeom boho juui' wa 'pogwaljeok beopje' e gwanhaeyeo" (On the 'priority protectionism' and 'comprehensive legislation' of the Law for the Protection of Cultural Properties during the Japanese colonial period), *Yeoksa minsok hakhoe* 17 (Dec. 2003).

60 Choi Seulgi, "'Hangeul eul gukbo 1ho ro" ([Establishing] Hangeul as National Treasure no. 1), *Gyeonghyang sinmun*, Oct. 7, 1995; Choi Jeonghun, "Namdaemun 'Gukbo 1ho'

formed a small committee to reexamine the existing national treasures, they decided to reevaluate 503 out of a total of 2,197 relics and historic sites.[61] In addition to changing or restoring some names, they supported making no change to the status of Sungnye Gate. They conducted a poll about the gate, and 67 percent of the respondents were in favor of keeping it as National Treasure no. 1.[62]

The most prominent heritage project was, of course, the restoration of Gyeongbok Palace. It began in 1988 with the Roh Tae Woo administration's rebuilding of the Manchunjeon, a building that was actually destroyed during the Korean War.[63] The same year, it decided to continue the restoration by relocating the army units stationed in the palace grounds.[64] In 1991, the government decided to undertake a restoration of a previously unheard of scale by setting the goal of rebuilding all the structures that had been destroyed by the Japanese.[65] When discussions about the restoration began in 1990, there immediately was debate about what to do with the former Government-General building, the "symbol of the remnants of Japanese rule."[66] Most advocated demolition though there were others who proposed preserving or relocating it. According to a Ministry of Culture poll conducted in 1991, 65 percent of the general public and 77 percent of professors and other experts supported demolition or relocation.[67] The Kim Young Sam administration decided to dismantle the building, which had housed the National Museum of Korea since 1986. Work began in 1995 and took two years; only the building's dome and a few other parts were preserved, now on display at Independence Hall in

chan-ban nollan" (The cases for and against Namdaemun as National Treasure no. 1), *Gyeonghyang sinmun*, Oct. 18, 1996. Hunmin jeongeum is Naitonal Treasure no. 70.

61 Choi Jeonghun, "Ilji dangsi jijeonghan gukga munhwajae 503geon 'uri nun' euro jaepyeonggahanda" (Reevaluating with 'our eyes' 503 items of state cultural heritage designated during the Japanese colonial period), *Gyeonghyang sinmun*, Feb. 24, 1996.

62 Yi Gwangpo, "'Namdaemun gukbo 1ho nwaduja' 67%" (67% support keeping Namdaemun as National Treasure no. 1), *Donga ilbo*, Nov. 23, 1996.

63 "Gyeongbukgung Manchunjeon bogwon doenda" (The Manchunjeon in Gyeongbok Palace is being restored), *Donga ilbo*, Mar. 17, 1988.

64 "Gyeongbokgung yet moseub doechanneunda" (Gyeongbok Palace recovers its old appearance), *Hangyeore sinmun*, Sept. 20, 1988.

65 "Minjok jeonggi wa Gyeongbokgung bogwon" (National spirit and the restoration of Gyeongbok Palace), *Donga ilbo*, Jan. 24, 1991.

66 Gim Chasu, "Gu Jungangcheong geonmul cheolgeo geomto" (Considering the dismantling of the former Central Government Building), *Donga ilbo*, Dec. 4, 1990; Gim Chasu, "'Ilje janje ui sangjing' dugoman bwayahana" (Can we do nothing about the "symbol of the remnants of Japanese rule"), *Donga ilbo*, Dec. 6, 1990.

67 "Yet Chongdokbu geonmul 'cheolgeo' apdojeok" (Overwhelming [support] for demolition of the former Government-General building), *Gyeonghyang sinmun*, June 14, 1991.

Cheonan. The desire to recreate the palace exactly as it had been before the Japanese takeover was so great that the government decided to rebuild Gwanghwa Gate once again in 2006.[68] The 1968 restoration not only used inappropriate materials such as concrete but also was not quite in the correct location, out of alignment with the palace's main axis by a few degrees. By 2010, about 25 percent of the buildings that had existed in the late nineteenth century were restored, with plans calling for the restoration to be complete by the year 2030.[69]

The discourse of restoration generally portrayed Joseon as essential to the expression of Korean national identity. For instance, an editorial in the *Donga ilbo* wrote,

> the meaning of the restoration of Gyeongbok Palace cannot simply be reduced to an effort to return to the past by recreating an old palace. First, it has a great significance in reviving the legitimacy of our nation which had been damaged by Japanese aggressions; it is achieving again the true Seoul, the old 600-year capital [of the country]. When a newly restored Gyeongbok Palace stands in front of the former Government-General building, it will enable us to escape from the specter of Japanese rule....The restoration of Gyeongbok Palace...is a restoration of our national spirit (*minjok jeonggi*) and pride. (Jan. 24, 1991)

Joseon was not set apart from other, pre-Neo-Confucian eras of Korean history; it had its place within the line of succession of Korean kingdoms, just as its name suggests. The connection to the very first 'Korean' kingdom was emphasized in the materials used in the palace's reconstruction. The columns were made from pine trees from Mt. Baekdu, imported from China. The mountain has a special meaning for Koreans since, according to myth, it is where Hwanung, the son of Heaven and the father of Dangun, descended to Earth.[70] South Korea also began to promote its heritage internationally by seeking World Heritage status from UNESCO. Though the program had started in 1972, South Korea did not make an application until 1994, leading to three sites being selected in 1995 – Bulguk Temple, Haein Temple, and the Royal Shrine (Jongmyo). This effort was part of "the rapid growth of heritagization in the 1990s" in many parts of the world.[71]

---

[68] Gim Taesik, "Gwanghwamun cheolgeo daejangjeong bongyeok sijak" (The beginning of the dismantling of Gwanghwa Gate), *Hanguk ilbo*, Nov. 19, 2006.

[69] "Gyeongbokgung bogwon jeongbi saeop hyeonhwang" (The state of the restoration project of Gyeongbok Palace). Available on the website of the Cultural Heritage Administration: www.cha.go.kr.

[70] "Baekdusan sonamuro Gyeongbokgung bogwon" (Gyeongbok Palace to be restored with pine trees from Mt. Baekdu), *Donga ilbo*, Dec. 11, 1991.

[71] François Hartog, "Time and Heritage," *Museum International*, no. 227 (2005), p. 10.

There are now a total of ten sites with World Heritage status, five of which are from the Joseon period: Jongmyo, Changdeok Palace (1997), Hwaseong Fortress (1997), royal tombs of the Joseon dynasty (2009), and the villages of Hahoe and Yangdong (2010).[72]

From 1990, Seoul's palaces have experienced a tremendous increase in popularity with both Koreans and tourists. The number of visitors (excluding foreign tourists) in 1992 was 1.27 million, and in ten years, it increased about five times to 6.06 million in 2002, reaching 7.10 million in 2010.[73] The number of foreign tourists also increased tremendously from 297,000 in 1992 to 1.04 million in 2002. Of the main palaces, Gyeongbok Palace has been the most popular. The number of visitors (again, excluding foreign tourists) increased from 3.11 million in 2002 to 3.82 million in 2010; in virtually every year, it had twice as many visitors as any other palace. During these years, there have also been changes in how people interact with the palaces. As they became a more frequent venue for cultural and artistic events, palaces were increasingly visited on family outings.[74] It became so popular for office workers in the area to bring their lunches to the palaces that the Cultural Heritage Administration began to allow them to enter for free in 1996.[75] Couples enjoy strolling along the path outside the walls of Deoksu Palace, despite the saying that those who walk there will break up. Three of the palaces allow wedding photos to be shot on their grounds; during the Lunar New Year and Harvest holidays, people wearing Hanbok are allowed in for free. Not just a destination for school trips, the palaces have become a familiar part of everyday life, just like other aspects of Joseon's culture.

---

72 The other World Heritage sites are Gyeongju (2000) and dolmen sites in Gochang, Hwasun, and Ganghwa; Jeju Island was selected as a World Natural Heritage site in 2007. In North Korea, historic monuments and sites in Gaeseong were selected for World Heritage status in 2013.

73 Gim Geuncheol, "Gyeongbokgung jangnyeon gwallamgaeksu choida ipjang suip eun Changdeokgung 1 wi" (Gyeongbok Palace – first in visitors; Changdeok Palace – first in revenue), *Gyeonghyang sinmun*, Mar. 21, 1993. Statistics on the palaces from 2002 to 2011 are available on the Korean Statistical Information Service website: http://kosis.kr/ (see chart entitled "Gwallam inwon hyeonhwang"). All statistics from 2002–2011 in this paragraph are taken from this website.

74 "Ipjangryo ssago gyotong pyeolli…gajok gogung nadeuri neureo" (Cheap to enter and easy to reach…increase of family outings at the palaces), *Gyeonghyang sinmun*, Feb. 14, 1998; "'Gogung eul saraitneun munhwa gonggan euro' chwijae sucheop" ('Making palaces a dynamic cultural space' – investigative notebook), *Gyeonghyang sinmun*, Apr. 24, 1999.

75 About 220,000 office workers per year visited the palaces at lunchtime. Choi Jeonghun, "'Gogung waseo jeomsim deuseyo' Gyeongbokgung-Changgyeonggung-Deoksugung-Jongmyo jikjangin e gaebang" ('Please come to have lunch at the palace' – Gyeongbok Palace, Changgyeong Palace, Deoksu Palace, Royal Shrine (Jongmyo) opened to office workers), *Gyeonghyang sinmun*, Feb. 27, 1996.

Another element of the changed relation to Joseon was revealed in the aftermath of the burning down of Sungnye Gate by an arsonist on February 10, 2008. As mentioned above, it had maintained its status as National Treasure no. 1 despite some opposition in the mid 1990s. In a 1994 survey of artists by the magazine *Gana Art*, the gate was chosen as the 'symbol of Seoul,' garnering thirty-three of seventy votes.[76] With such a strong connection to the gate, it is not surprising that people regarded its destruction as a tragedy. What was unusual in people's reactions was that, as a psychology professor observed, it became apparent that they thought of the gate as a person or living thing.[77] Citizens, including those living far from Seoul, came to place chrysanthemums near the gate – similar to what is commonly done at funerals in Korea.[78] Naksan Temple in Gangwon province, which itself had lost a national treasure in a fire in 2005, conducted the forty-ninth-day rites for the gate on March 29, a ritual that was not only Buddhist but also usually only done for people. This was the first time that it was done for a national treasure.[79] Sungnye Gate may be seen as an exceptional case; as the same professor commented, it is difficult to imagine that people would react the same way if National Treasure no. 2 were destroyed.[80] However, it can also be seen as representing what all heritage in modern society aspires to be. The gate has become a literal form of 'living heritage' that is a reversal of what the term usually means. UNESCO equates it with 'intangible cultural heritage;' i.e., arts, crafts, rituals, and festivals that have been transmitted from generation to generation to specific individuals or communities. Inanimate and tangible structures from the Joseon era have, in a sense, taken on human qualities. South Koreans feel a deep personal connection to their heritage, akin to that one would have with a friend or even a family member.

---

[76] The Han River came in second, Mt. Bukhan was third, and Mt. Nam was fourth. Yi Yong, "'Seoul ui sangjing' Namdaemun i 1 wi" ('The symbol of Seoul' Sungnye Gate is in first place), *Gyeonghyang sinmun*, Nov. 15, 1994.

[77] Heo Jaehyeon, "Sungnyemun apeseo nunmul eul heullineun iyu?" (What is the reason that people are crying in front of Sungnye Gate?), Feb. 13, 2008.

[78] Choi Suho and Jo Baekgeon, "Bumo sonjapgo…gukhwaggot deulgo…Sungnyemun ap 'chamhoe ui sueop'" (Holding parents' hands…holding a chrysanthemum…in front of Sungnye Gate 'a class in contrition'), *Joseon ilbo*, Feb. 18, 2008.

[79] Yi Hyeokjae, "'Sungnyemun 49jae' Naksansa eseo yeonda" ('A forty-ninth-day rite for Sungnye Gate' held in Naksan Temple), *Joseon ilbo*, Feb. 18, 2008.

[80] It is unlikely that many South Koreans could even name National Treasure no. 2: the ten-story stone pagoda of Wongak Temple, currently located in Tapgol Park in Seoul, which was made in the Joseon period.

These developments since the end of the Cold War all suggest that the Joseon period has become an object of nostalgia. This yearning to return to the era and relive a lost past is one of the main ideological trends of the post-Cold War era in South Korea. This book, however, represents an effort to resist this impulse to nostalgia and, by extension, amnesia. It reminds readers that the richness of life in the period was rooted in the exploitation and suffering of the peasantry. Such narratives defamiliarize the familiar aspects of the past that often go by the name 'tradition,' opening up of the possibility of new dialogues between past and present.

PART ONE

ECONOMY

1. FARMING IN THE JOSEON PERIOD

Kim Kuentae

These days, it would be no exaggeration to say that rice and kimchi are the only dishes on Korean tables that are produced within the country. Most other dishes are made from imported ingredients. The importation of foreign agricultural products has caused serious problems in South Korea including a fall in agricultural prices and the economic decline of farmers. But the government and most of its citizens seem to have little interest in the problems of rural areas. Perhaps this is not surprising since less than ten percent of the South Korean population is engaged in farming, and agriculture generates less than five percent of total GDP. By contrast, farming was the most important economic activity in the Joseon period, with peasants amounting to about eighty percent of the population. The period was a time of major advances in agriculture; in particular, the introduction of the technique of rice transplantation from China led to far-reaching changes in the economy that transformed the lives of the peasantry.

The Expansion of Farmland

One of the major developments in the early Joseon period was a tremendous increase in the amount of land under cultivation. Because of the invasions of the Red Turbans and Japanese pirates at the end of the Goryeo period, many peasants had left their hometowns, and much farmland was left to waste. Rural areas began to recover around the time of the founding of Joseon in 1392 as peasants returned to their homes and reclaimed the land. In the late fourteenth century, farming was mainly restricted to the foot of mountains and other highland areas. It was the movement of cultivation from the highlands to the lowlands that led to the increase in arable land in the country. By the early fifteenth century, the amount of farmland was 2.5 times greater than it had been at the end of the Goryeo period. Much of the new farmland was created through the reclamation of coastal areas, a large-scale project undertaken by powerful families in the central government. In the sixteenth century, there was also much effort to reclaim wasteland in inland regions, increasing the amount of farmland even further.

How farmland was used also changed in the Joseon period. Though the amount of farmland in the northern regions increased significantly through land reclamation, the three southern provinces of Chungcheong, Jeolla, and Gyeongsang still contained the majority of arable land. In the fifteenth century, Gyeonggi province and the three southern provinces contained about sixty percent of the paddy and dry fields in the country. The ratio of paddy to dry fields also differed according to the region. In the early Joseon period, dry fields occupied eighty percent of total farmland, with paddy fields comprising the remaining twenty percent. Eighty percent of paddy fields were located in Gyeonggi and the three southern provinces. Thus, wet-field cultivation was concentrated in those areas, while dry-field cultivation was predominant in Gangwon and the northern provinces. The proportion of paddy fields increased slowly over time. By the end of the nineteenth century, paddy fields occupied thirty percent of total farmland while dry fields amounted to approximately seventy percent. The increase was the result of the conversion of dry fields into paddy fields through the promotion of wet-field cultivation and the expansion of irrigation. Another factor was the continuation of reclamation projects.

Direct Seeding vs. Rice Transplantation

There were several different methods of rice cultivation. Until the beginning of the Joseon era, most farmers cultivated rice using the direct-seeding method, as their ancestors had done. Direct seeding involved planting rice seeds that had been already germinated in fields covered with water. An alternate method was to coat seeds in fertilizer before they were planted in dry fields. In the early spring, farmers would plow their fields a couple of times. In the middle to the late fourth lunar month, they leveled their fields with a harrow and then planted seeds that had already germinated. About a month later, they would begin weeding the fields, a process that would be repeated four or five times up to the harvest.

The technique of rice transplantation involved planting seeds in seedbeds and then moving the seedlings to paddy fields. The Joseon government's policy was to emphasize wet-field cultivation over dry-field farming. This policy became even more pronounced from the seventeenth century when rice could be used to pay the tribute tax. But farming in paddy fields was more complicated and required more labor than farming in dry fields, involving work in all four seasons. As with direct seeding, farmers also plowed their fields once or twice in the early spring. Late in the fourth or early in the fifth lunar month, a seedbed was created in a section of the field about one-tenth of the total area in size. While seedlings were growing in the seedbed, farmers spread fertilizer in their fields that was made with oak leaves and willow branches. From the beginning of the sixth lunar month, about a month after the seedbeds were planted, seedlings would be transplanted to the paddy fields. Clumps of seedlings were planted at sufficient intervals with no more than four or five seedlings in each clump. About twenty days after the transplantation was completed, farmers began to weed the fields, and weeding was done two or three times before the harvest. Fields were plowed again in late autumn and early winter.

The advantage of rice transplantation was that it enabled both an increase in productivity and a decrease in the labor necessary for cultivation. Weeding fields in summer, under a scorching sun, was backbreaking work. Rice transplantation relieved farmers of much of this burden. Farmers now could weed their fields less frequently than those who did direct seeding. In addition, weeding also involved less labor compared to fields cultivated by direct seeding, enabling a reduction of about sixty to seventy percent. Although it reduced the labor needed for weeding, rice transplantation required a large amount of labor for the short period when seedlings were transplanted. As the technique became widespread, a communal labor organization developed called the *dure*. As *dure* assumed a more active role in farming, the work of transplantation became more efficient.

Fig. 1.1. *Rice Transplantation*, Gim Jungeun (aka Gisan), late nineteenth century. (© Musée Guimet, Paris, Dist. RMN-Grand Palais)

Rice transplantation produced higher yields compared to the direct-seeding method because it made the soil more fertile. There were several techniques for improving the fertility of the land. There was *gaekto*, which involved adding new soil to fields in early winter or early spring. *Gibi* was the method of coating seeds with fertilizer before they were sown. *Chubi* was the spreading of additional fertilizer while the rice plants were growing. Rice transplantation increased the effectiveness of *gibi*. While seedlings were growing in the seedbed, farmers cut up oak leaves and young tree branches and spread the mulch in the paddy fields. With the time saved in weeding, they could make compost from the grasses that grew

Fig. 1.2. *Gyeongjikdo* (detail). Late Joseon Period. Painting on a folding screen. The painting shows peasants working on irrigating their fields after finishing transplanting the rice seedlings. (National Museum of Korea)

thick in summer and then spread it over the fields. Rice transplantation also enabled farmland to be used as dry fields from the time the harvest was done in the autumn to early the following summer when the transplantation of seedlings began. After all the rice was harvested, water was drained from the paddies, and barley would be planted and then harvested late in the following spring. The fields were then irrigated again, enabling seedlings to be transplanted from the seedbeds. The double cropping of rice and barley became common in regions south of the Geum River in the mid to late eighteenth century.

Though it had clear benefits, Koreans were somewhat reluctant to adopt the technique of rice transplantation because it also had certain disadvantages. There was a high risk of ruining the entire crop if a drought occurred during the period of transplantation. Because of this risk, the court prohibited rice transplantation during the fifteenth century. Despite this policy, peasants increasingly began to adopt the technique over the years. In the fifteenth century, farmers engaged in rice transplantation only in parts of northern Gyeongsang province and in some areas along the eastern coast of Gangwon province. It became widespread in the northern parts of Gyeongsang province by the late sixteenth century and in all three southern provinces by the late seventeenth century. The spread of this technique was closely connected to the expansion of irrigation facilities. The biggest factor behind its success was the development of a form of irrigation called *bo*. Also known as *cheonbang*, *bo* were reservoirs created by building dams across small rivers or streams.

Yellow Rice and Gray Rice

The spread of rice transplantation also led to the increased production of other grains. With the labor saved by this technique, farmers now had more time to engage in dry-field farming. In the Joseon period, people also consumed other kinds of 'rice' than white rice which was produced by polishing the harvested grain in mills. 'Gray rice' and 'yellow rice' were processed from other kinds of grains cultivated in dry fields. Gray rice was hulled barley, and yellow rice was hulled millet. Many other crops were grown on dry fields, such as beans, but barley was common in the southern regions. When grain stores ran low in the spring, peasants depended on barley for subsistence. The period when peasants went hungry waiting for the barley to be harvested was known as the 'barley hump' (*borit gogae*). It ended around the time of the summer solstice with the barley harvest. Though it was harvested in the early summer, the time for seeding differed according to the variety. There were 'autumn barley' that was planted in the fall and 'spring barley' that was sown in the spring. The practice of simultaneous cultivation of crops became common in the Joseon period. In the fifteenth century, many peasants were already planting beans after the barley harvest. This practice of alternating barley and beans in the same field during a year was called *geuru gari*. Not all beans were cultivated by the method of *geuru gari*; some varieties of beans had to be planted in the spring or early summer to grow properly. Unlike barley and beans, millet was always sown in the spring. Barley, beans, and millet were all grown in the spring, and it was not easy to cultivate these crops on the same fields because of the considerable labor involved in weeding. In the fifteenth century, it was peasants with a small amount of land who began to grow multiple crops. The simultaneous cultivation of barley, beans, and millet became widespread by the early eighteenth century.

In the Joseon period, the method of sowing seeds in dry fields also changed. There were two main methods; seeds could be planted on the ridges created when fields were plowed (*nongjongbeop*) or in the furrows (*gyeonjongbeop*). In the late Joseon period, most dry fields were sown using the method of *gyeonjongbeop*. Since the ridges blocked the wind and kept the furrows moist, crops could withstand drought and the cold better than those planted on ridges. As the plants grew, the soil of the ridges covered up their roots and kept them better nourished. The method of *gyeonjongbeop* became more widespread as the number of cows used for plowing increased. The height of ridges became even more pronounced as plowing methods improved.

Rice transplantation also had a large impact on the lives of the peasantry by making it easier to cultivate labor-intensive cash crops. Cotton was cultivated throughout the country by the sixteenth century after it was introduced at the end of the Goryeo period. Cotton fields had to be weeded about seven times before the harvest. Tobacco was introduced to Joseon at the end of the sixteenth century, with its cultivation becoming widespread throughout the country by the early eighteenth century. It generally required two to three times the labor of other dry-field crops. Since cash crops like tobacco needed much fertilizer, farmers collected grasses in the late summer, when the work of weeding was almost completed, to make compost. Since natural disasters were a constant threat to the lives of the peasantry, farmers throughout the country also grew crops for famine relief. From the early Joseon period, the most important one was buckwheat. From olden times, peasants had planted buckwheat for

Fig. 1.3. *Harvesting Rice*, Sim Sajeong, eighteenth century. (National Museum of Korea)

food when drought conditions made it impossible to grow rice. In the late Joseon period, there was a diversification of the crops used for famine relief. In addition to buckwheat, potatoes were cultivated in the north while sweet potatoes were introduced in the southern regions, improving the ability of the country to withstand drought.

The Sorrows of Landless Peasants

Patterns of land ownership changed over the course of the Joseon period. Not all farmers owned the land that they cultivated. A typical example was the unfree people (*nobi*) who lived on agricultural estates (*nongjang*) that consisted of scattered fields near thatched roof huts surrounding a large tile-roofed house. They tilled the landlord's land, using the seeds and tools provided to them. Some of them received monthly supplies of food from their landlords, but most received only a share of the grain they harvested in the fall. The unfree people's share of the harvest was not determined by convention but differed according to the landlord. Both unfree people and commoners rented land from landlords to cultivate. In these cases, the

Fig. 1.4. *Tadorakchwido*, Gim Hongdo, late eighteenth century. (National Museum of Korea)

tenant shared the harvest equally with the landowner in an arrangement that was called *byeongjak*.

The spread of the *byeonjak* system was a major factor in the decline of the peasantry. Until the early fifteenth century, the government banned the practice of *byeongjak*. The excessive tax burden in this period led to the decline of independent cultivators, and landless peasants farmed the fields of landlords under the *byeongjak* system. Increasing numbers of them were of unfree status. The unfree people working on agricultural estates sometimes deliberately slowed down the pace of their work in order to protest the arbitrary way that landlords apportioned their share of the harvest. As such incidents became frequent, landlords began renting land on the basis of *byeongjak*. By the late sixteenth century, it spread to the point that it became common practice among landlords.

The emergence of the so-called 'landlord system' (*jijuje*) in the seventeenth and eighteenth centuries represented a significant development. In the *byeongjak* system, it had been customary for the landlord to provide seed and to pay the land tax. These gradually became the responsibility of the tenant from the mid-eighteenth century, and by the end of the eighteenth and the beginning of nineteenth century, this practice became common. Though the burdens on farmers increased, it became harder to find land to rent. This was the consequence of land ownership being concentrated in a small number of landlords while the majority of people were landless tenants. In the late seventeenth century, a completely new system emerged – the *doji* system. The land rent was fixed by a contract according to which the tenant had to pay the landlord a set amount every autumn, regardless of the harvest. Tenants preferred the *doji* system to *byeongjak* since the rent averaged less than half of the yearly harvest. Nonetheless, the *doji* system did not always operate to the advantage of the tenant because in years of drought or floods, the amount paid to the landlord constituted a greater share of the harvest.

Another important change in this period was the emergence of a new type of farmer – yet another consequence of the spread of rice transplantation. Mobilizing their households and hiring wage laborers to cultivate their land, they aimed to increase their income by selling their crops at market. Called *gwangjangnong*, these farmers included yangban landlords, commoner landlords, and tenant farmers. Their emergence was a factor that pushed landless peasants to seek their livelihoods outside of agriculture, since it became increasingly difficult for them to find land to rent. In the late Joseon period, it was common for farmers to cultivate small amounts of cash crops such as cotton and tobacco in order to increase their household income. In some regions, there emerged farm households that hired wage laborers and specialized in growing cash crops. But as their profits grew, local officials increased their exploitation of the peasantry, and this led to a gradual intensification of peasant protest.

with Ellen Yuh

2. A TYPICAL DAY AND YEAR IN THE LIFE OF THE PEASANTRY

Yeom Jeong Sup

Genealogies that have survived to the present portray all Korean families as being the descendants of yangban, but the majority of Koreans' ancestors were peasants who were engaged in farming. Landscape paintings depicted farmers working contentedly with vast fields in the background, but such idyllic scenes did not exist in real life. These days, it is commonly thought that peasants in the Joseon period suffered extreme hardship and severe exploitation, performing exhausting work virtually every day of the year. They farmed along the edges of streams and brooks, drenched in sweat and rubbing their aching backs. In the past, they did not have the chemical fertilizers that are readily available today, and very few even had properly made tools. These conditions made it difficult for them to work the land. Today, people speak of the so-called 'barley hump' (*borit gogae*) with a faint nostalgia. But in the Joseon period, it was a perilous time during which people underwent all kinds of hardships in order to survive. As is well known, peasants suffered such grinding poverty that they could barely eke out a living from day to day. Furthermore, the majority of peasants were tenants who had to borrow a few plots of land from large landowners and give them much of the harvest as rent. Even if peasants owned a small piece of land, they would often lose their fields within a few years. Thus, they are usually portrayed as toiling in the fields and performing backbreaking labor only to be painfully exploited by the landlords and the authorities. Is this an accurate picture of the lives of the peasantry?

The Daily Life of the Peasantry

The daily lives of farmers involved long periods of work interspersed with short breaks. They began work at the crack of dawn as the first rays of sunlight appeared in the sky. They ate breakfast only after putting in a few hours of work. In the hot summers, farmers were drenched in sweat, and when a refreshing breeze came, they loosened their clothes and took a short rest. At lunchtime, they had a meal of barley rice with bean leaves as a side dish, sometimes taking a nap afterwards. As the sun set in the mountain ridge to the west, they washed their hands and feet in a stream and headed home where dinner was waiting for them.

Fig. 2.1. *Bringing Food to Farmers Weeding a Field* (Suunyeopchul), Gim Hongdo, late eighteenth century. (National Museum of Korea)

Songs and other kinds of music were a part of the daily routine of farming. They gave voice to the joys and sorrows of the peasantry, providing a glimpse into their lives. Peasants sang while they toiled in the fields to relieve their fatigue and to coordinate their work efficiently. Called *nongyo*, these songs were very diverse, differing according to region, and there was a song for each type of farming work. There was the 'Heukgeoreum Song,' which was sung as farmers carried fertilizer made by mixing soil with things such as compost or lime. The song 'So moneun sori' was for the times when they plowed their fields with a cow. In Jeju Island, farmers sang the song 'Bat ballineun sori' while they used horses in their fields. When they irrigated their fields to cover the rice seedlings, they sang 'Mo jjineun sori.' 'Monegi sori' was the song for transplanting rice seedlings.

When they weeded their fields, they sung 'Gimmaegi sori' while members of the local peasant organization (*dure*) played instruments. The song 'Basim sori' was sung while threshing rice. These songs were sung not alone but in groups, and they have survived to the present through oral transmission.

The Farming Year and the Twenty-Four Solar Terms

The work of farming structured the calendar year for the peasantry. In general, the days for festivals, birthdays, and ancestral memorial rites were set according to the lunar calendar. But it could not be used for farming since seasonal changes corresponded more closely with the movements of the sun. Instead, farmers used the system of twenty-four solar terms that was first developed in China during the Han Dynasty. The yearly movement of the sun was divided into twenty-four points, each of which marked an astronomical event, such as the summer and winter solstices, or a natural phenomenon. By using the solar terms, peasants in the Joseon era were able to compensate for the differences between the lunar calendar and the timing of the seasons.

According to the twenty-four solar terms, the seasons were defined as follows (see Table 1). Spring began with *ipchun* and ended with *gogu*,

Table 1. The Twenty-Four Solar Terms.

Solar Term	Date (solar calendar)	Rice Farming	Other Grains	Food, Clothing, Shelter
ipchun (立春)	February 4	repairing tools (preparation for spring farming)	prepare barley	
usu (雨水)	February 18	burning weeds to make ash	planting seeds of barley	plowing cotton fields, making straw raincoats, making fermented soybeans
gyeongchip (驚蟄)	March 5	spreading ash in the fields (fertilizer)	finish planting barley	planting hemp seed, drying fermented soybeans in the sun

(*Continues*)

Table 1. (*Cont.*)

Solar Term	Date (solar calendar)	Rice Farming	Other Grains	Food, Clothing, Shelter
chunbun (春分)	March 20	plowing paddy fields	planting millet and beans in the barley field, plowing unused fields to prepare to plant millet seeds	planting seeds of the indigo plant (dyes for cloth)
cheongmyeong (淸明)	April 5	planting seeds of *joang* rice (for transplantation) and early rice (direct seeding)	planting seeds of early millet	hatching silkworm eggs
gogu (穀雨)	April 20		planting seeds of adlay (Job's tears)	planting cotton seeds, making a case for silkworms
ipha (立夏)	May 5	planting seeds of *chado* rice (direct seeding) and direct seeding of non-irrigated dry fields	weeding barley fields and planting perilla seeds	feeding silkworms with mulberry leaves
soman (小滿)	May 21	planting seeds of late rice (direct seeding), transplanation of *choang* rice, planting seeds of *manang* rice in non-irrigated fields	weeding of early millet and early beans	weeding of cotton fields
mangjong (亡種)	June 5	transplantation of *chaang* rice	transplanation of tobacco seedlings, repair of flails (for threshing)	cutting down bulrushes to prepare to make rush mats, weeding of cotton fields

Table 1. (*Cont.*)

Solar Term	Date (solar calendar)	Rice Farming	Other Grains	Food, Clothing, Shelter
haji (夏至)	June 21	transplanation of *manang* rice	harvesting of barley; making fertilizer with urine, night soil, and ash made from barley husks; double cropping on barley fields	
soseo (小暑)	July 7	weeding paddy fields	planting beans and millet in barley fields, storing weeds and willow branches in the stable (to make fertilizer)	
daeseo (大暑)	July 23		harvest of early millet, double cropping on millet fields	
ipchu (立秋)	August 7	removal of barnyard millet from paddy fields	planting buckwheat seeds, covering roots of beans and millet with earth	intercropping of radishes in hemp fields (for kimchi), weeding of cotton fields
cheoseo (處暑)	August 23	harvest of early rice	cutting weeds and willow branches into small pieces and storing them in the stable	

(*Continues*)

Table 1. (*Cont.*)

Solar Term	Date (solar calendar)	Rice Farming	Other Grains	Food, Clothing, Shelter
baekno (白露)	September 7	gathering mugwort and tying up in bundles	cutting weeds and oak branches into small pieces and storing them in the stable	planting seeds of napa cabbage (for kimchi)
chubun (秋分)	September 23	harvest of *chado* rice	planting seeds of autumn barley, planting wheat seeds	
hallo (寒露)	October 8	weeding and trimming of oak trees		cut, dry, and store grass
sanggang (霜降)	October 23		harvest of perilla, harvest of late grains	cutting and processing the paper mulberry tree, gathering arrowroot roots to make into rope
ipdong (立冬)	November 7		making earthen huts	gathering reeds and pampas grass to prepare material where silkworms will make cocoons, making fermented soybeans, repairing fences, walls, and windows
soseol (小雪)	November 22	threshing of rice sheaves with a flail	harvest of remaining grains, plowing fields to make furrows	turning over the soil in cotton fields, stacking firewood, cutting pampas grass to make straw thatch

Table 1. (*Cont.*)

Solar Term	Date (solar calendar)	Rice Farming	Other Grains	Food, Clothing, Shelter
daeseol (大雪)	December 7			bartering fish and salt, stacking firewood, gathering cogongrass root, taking care of horses and oxen
dongji (冬至)	December 22		making earthen huts	putting a warm cover on the back of cows, weaving straw mats, making straw thatch
sohan (小寒)	January 5			weaving straw mats, making straw thatch
daehan (大寒)	January 20		preparing barley seeds	collecting horse feces (for use as medicine for heat exhaustion)

Source: Hanguk saenghwalsa bangmulgwan pyeonchan wiwonhoe, *Hanguk saenghwalsa bangmulgwan*, vol. 9 (Seoul: Sagyejeol, 2003), pp. 56–57.

summer was from *ipha* to *daeseo*, autumn was from *ipchu* to *sanggang*, and winter was from *ipdong* to *daehan*. The solar terms indicated the time that farmers had to do tasks such as planting seeds, weeding, and transplanting rice seedlings. Based on information from surviving texts and other seasonal customs from the time, we can discover what work was done in each solar term. *Nongga wollyeong*, a book on agriculture written in the early seventeenth century, discussed the farm work that was done in each of the twenty-four solar terms. In the nineteenth century, Jeong Hagyu (1786–1855) wrote a work of *gasa* poetry, entitled 'Nongga wollyeongga,' that was also about farming during the solar terms.

During the first lunar month, which contained the solar terms of *ipchun* and *usu*, peasants prepared for the upcoming year's farming. This was also the time when the government devoted much effort to promote farming.

In the second lunar month (*gyeongchip* and *chunbun*), farmers did their spring plowing and planted seeds of appropriate crops, as well as raising livestock and digging up medicinal plants. In the third lunar month (*cheongmyeong* and *gogu*), they planted rice seeds in their fields, grafted fruit trees, and prepared foods such as soy sauce, hot pepper paste, and

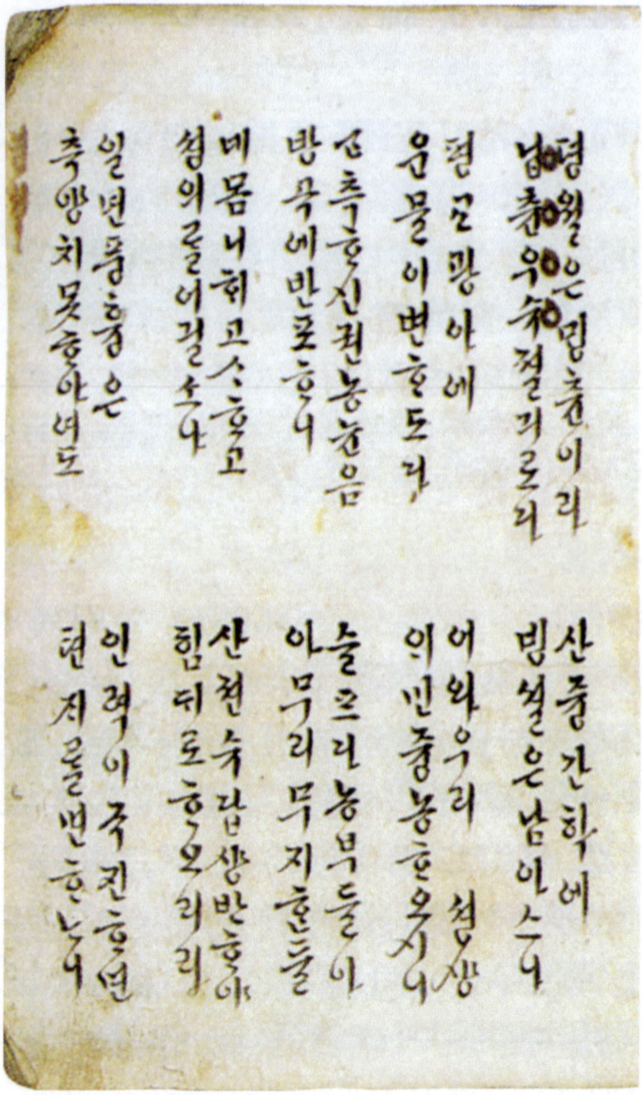

Fig. 2.2. *Nonggawollyeongga*, nineteenth century. A *gasa* poem about farming.

Fig. 2.3. *Plowing a Field in Spring* (Chunilugyeong), Gim Hongdo, late eighteenth century. One panel of a folding screen. (National Museum of Korea)

soybean paste. In the fourth lunar month (*ipha* and *soman*), farming began in earnest with the transplantation of early rice seedlings, intercropping, and the threshing of early barley. In the fifth lunar month (*mangjong* and *haji*), farmers threshed barley, picked silkworm cocoons, and transplanted rice seedlings. In the sixth lunar month (*soseo* and *daeseo*), farmers toiled in their fields in hopes of a bountiful harvest in the fall. They cultivated multiple crops by intercropping, added soil around the growing plants, harvested hemp, did weaving, and weeded the fields through *dure* organizations. In the seventh lunar month (*ipchu* and *cheoseo*), peasants weeded their fields, removed barnyard millet, and planted seeds for radish and napa cabbage to prepare vegetables for winter and for making kimchi. The eighth lunar month (*baekno* and *chubun*) was the time when farmers harvested their crops and felt a sense of fulfillment for a while. In the ninth lunar month (*hallo* and *sanggang*), they focused their energies on harvesting in late autumn. In the tenth lunar month (*ipdong* and *soseol*), peasants harvested radishes and napa cabbage and made preparations for winter. In the eleventh lunar month (*daeseol* and *dongji*), they turned to tasks such as fermenting soybeans, raising livestock, and preparing fertilizer. In the twelfth lunar month (*sohan* and *daehan*), they prepared for the next year's farming, while chilled by the winter winds.

The government tried to eliminate any distractions for the people during the farming season which was defined as beginning in *chunbun* and ending in *chubun*. Hearings for people's complaints would be postponed if they interrupted farming, and even executions were delayed out of fear that they would offend Heaven and bring about a natural disaster.

The Ritual Life of Farmers

The success or failure of a harvest depended on the wisdom and earnest prayers of the peasantry. Their wisdom manifested itself in the way they dealt with various weather conditions such as rain, drought, and strong winds and in the way they chose the appropriate variety of grain for the soil. Veteran farmers, skilled at their work, overcame problems by using the extensive knowledge that they had gained from years of experience dealing with the endless changes of nature. But at a time when technology could not yet mitigate the effects of unfavorable climatic conditions, even skilled farmers turned to the supernatural when there was a natural disaster. To predict the year's harvest, they performed a divination on the first day of the lunar year as well as during each solar term. To determine the proper day to plant seeds and to do weeding, they did numerological readings of the sexagenary cycle based on the principles of yin and yang and the five elements (metal, wood, water, fire, and earth). Farmers used various methods of divination. One simple method was to look at natural phenomena or changes in animals and plants. Another method predicted the year's harvest by relating the various grains to the sexagenary cycle. For example, on the day of *ipchun*, peasants would dig up a root of barley. If the root had three or more branches, then the harvest would be a good

Fig. 2.4. *Plowing a Field*, Gim Hongdo, late eighteenth century. (National Museum of Korea)

one; if there were two, the harvest would be average; and if there were one, the harvest would be bad. This method had a scientific basis as the growth of barley roots was a rough measure of climatic changes in a particular region. Communal games were also a form of prayer for a good harvest, such as a tug-of-war in which the same side was always allowed to win.

The daily life of farmers was punctuated by rituals, ceremonies, and ancestor memorial rites. Most agrarian societies worship agricultural deities, supernatural beings who people believe have the power over agricultural production. The origins of praying to a supernatural being for a successful harvest probably predate recorded history. Historical texts, such as the *Samguk yusa* (Memorabilia of the Three Kingdoms), claim that the origins of these agricultural rituals go as far back as the mythic ages. During the Joseon era, rituals were held at regular intervals in each season and in each solar term. Just as farming was conducted on a yearly cycle, rituals were also conducted on an annual basis. When one ceremony or rite ended, it would be time for the next one to begin. The purpose of these supplications was to satisfy the basic human need for food. The most important ritual was, of course, the ceremony to pray for a bountiful harvest in the upcoming year. It involved a reenactment of the process of cultivating rice. Through a symbolic representation of plenty, it promised a good harvest for the year. The ritual was performed again when farmers sowed seeds. At the state level, the king performed rituals such as the *jeokjeon chingyeong* in which he did some farming and performed ancestor memorial rites at the Seonnongdan. But government rituals were not as diverse nor as filled with earnest prayers as those done by farmers.

Every village in the country had a banner that represented their community. Farmers raised their banner when the *dure* engaged in work, when they performed communal memorial rites, and when they played competitive games with neighboring villages. Banners were made of white fabric with a large image of a dragon or with Chinese-character phrases written in black ink, such as 'The Legacy of Shennong' or 'Farming is the Foundation of the World.'

The Skilled Farmers Forgotten by History

The children of peasants became working members of their households a few years after birth. After they grew up, married, and started a family, they became a full member of the community and had to fulfill their duties to the state. The life of the peasantry was not one of endless suffering, but neither were they living in a world of pastoral simplicity that was free of concern. Over the course of their lives, they gained wisdom, and some truly became expert farmers. There is a famous story about an old farmer's encounter with Hwang Hui (1363–1452), a state councillor, that illustrates how much wisdom peasants had in the Joseon period. One day, Hwang saw a yellow cow and a black cow plowing a field and asked the farmer which one was better. Completely unfazed, he whispered his answer into Hwang Hui's ear so that the cows could not hear. People, both then and now, have shown little interest in this wise farmer whose name is unknown to history. By contrast, Hwang Hui is still today known as an official of unimpeachable integrity.

Today, young people are abandoning rural villages, leaving only old farmers to work the fields. Old and experienced farmers are now treated with disdain, but things were different in the Joseon period when they were respected as experts on farming. When the central government or provincial officials needed advice on agriculture, the first people they turned to were these old farmers. During the compilation of *Nongsa jikseol* (1429, Straight Talk on Farming), King Sejong (r. 1418–1450) ordered the governors of Chungcheong, Gyeongsang, and Jeolla provinces to collect information on farming techniques. The purpose was to gather the knowledge of skilled farmers who had experience with the most advanced agricultural techniques in their regions. In the mid-seventeenth century, when Sin Sok compiled *Nongga jipseong*, he also did research on advanced agricultural techniques that some farmers used in certain regions. These examples show how widely respected veteran farmers were at the time, in stark contrast to today. These experienced farmers were the central force in agriculture, planning, coordinating, and carrying out the daily and yearly work of farming. A family, led by a veteran farmer, was organized according to a division of labor and focused their work – each day and each year – on farming. Farmers thus fulfilled their role as the main historical actors of the Joseon period.

with Yong Suk Cho

3. THE TAX BURDEN OF THE PEASANTRY

Kim Sung Woo

The Tax System of the Joseon Period

Similar to today, people in the Joseon era also paid a portion of their income as taxes and were afforded a variety of rights and benefits such as the ability to hold government office, legal protection, and emergency medical care. In fact, the level of rights given to taxpayers could fool one into thinking that Joseon had already become a modern society. However, if one were to go beyond the codes as written and examine how they actually operated in society, it is clear that this view is superficial.

There were two major differences in how taxes were levied between the Joseon period and the modern era. First, taxes in Joseon period were determined according to social status. In a pre-industrial time, taxes could be levied only on the small proportion of households that were economically self-sufficient. The government classified taxpayers as *gongmin* and non-taxpayers as *samin*. This distinction was reinforced by the social status system which divided the population into commoners and the low-born. In order to encourage the *gongmin* to pay their taxes and provide stability to the tax system, the government guaranteed that the landlord class could own a suitable number of unfree people (*nobi*). The low-born, who were marginalized in the economic system, comprised between thirty to fifty percent of the total population of Joseon; their numbers began to drop rapidly from the first half of the eighteenth century. Second, there were differences in the categories of taxation. In modern society, taxes are levied in every sphere of economic activity while the number of taxes on non-specific economic actors such the household tax or the poll tax are either low or declining. On the other hand, in premodern society, it was necessary to extract as much tax revenue as possible from the commoner class whose numbers were limited. Thus, there were three main categories of taxes in Joseon, the so-called *jo-yong-jo* system: the land tax (*jo*), statute labor (*yong*), and the household tax (*jo*; paid in locally produced goods). In addition to land, the government also targeted households and individual laborers.

Three different kinds of register could be used for tax purposes: the land register, which was compiled every twenty years; the household register, which was updated every three years; and the military register, which was revised every six years. Only household registers were updated regularly. By contrast, land and military registers were not compiled regularly, and strong protests occurred when they were. There was no reason to protest household registers since their purpose was to track changes in the size of the labor force needed by the state as well as trends in the commoner and low-born populations. Because land and military registers were directly used to levy taxes, the amount of taxes assessed could vary greatly depending on how they were recorded. The assessments in land and military registers, once recorded, could remain fixed for decades or even centuries and had a large impact on the lives of taxpayers; it is no wonder that their compilation provoked fierce resistance.

Corruption in handling the tax registers was a serious problem. The process of compilation would begin when an order was transmitted down from the central government to provincial offices and then to local offices. After the register was created, it was sent back up administrative channels to be filed in the appropriate office. There were many opportunities for local elites and officials to abuse their authority. They would lower their tax status or remove their names completely, enabling them to pay little

Fig. 3.1. *Tenants Paying Their Fee to the Landlords* (*Daejiju sojakryo nabip*), Gim Yunbo. (Permission granted by individual collector)

or no taxes. On the other hand, non-elites without connections were assessed a higher tax status than was proper. As a result of the high tax burden, large numbers of the powerless and economically vulnerable peasant class lost all their property. They were also the ones who were most harmed by changes to the taxation system. Taking advantage of their social status to pay little or no taxes, the ruling class and local elites amassed economic power by increasing their landholdings and gaining control over ruined and bankrupt peasants.

The Fiscal System and Social Status

The fiscal system became established by the late fifteenth century. In its first few decades, the government tried various methods to calculate its total revenues and expenditures. During Sejong's reign (1418–1450), the calculation of revenues and expenditures from the land tax was made uniform, enabling land revenues to be determined accurately, and the total amount was fixed precisely during the reigns of Sejo and Seongjong (1455–1468 and 1469–1494, respectively). From that point on, the government estimated tax revenues using the late fifteenth century as the benchmark and adjusted its expenditures accordingly. This system is called the *chong-aekje* in Korean. However, problems began to emerge as the administration of state finances became divorced from economic realities. Since finances were still calculated according to the standards of the fifteenth century, new sources of tax revenue could not be secured even though the economic situation improved. It was necessary for the government to increase its budget in accordance with economic changes, but adjustments could not keep pace with the speed of economic development.

The government revised the tax system in accordance with changes in the country's social structure, but each of the three main types of taxes changed differently. During the Joseon era, the land tax underwent little change since there was little capital for reinvestment and since land required a relatively high amount of labor and material investment. It was also comparatively easy to track changes related to land because it was a fixed asset. On the other hand, the household tax and statute labor, which were greatly affected by population changes and residence patterns, underwent more change. In contrast to the land tax, there were many opportunities to avoid paying the other two taxes. As a result, the government gradually placed more emphasis on the land tax, while the household tax and the statute labor system became supplementary sources of

Fig. 3.2. *Bansangdo*, Gim Deuksin, late Joseon period.

revenue. The household tax and the statute labor system were the taxes that were the most affected by the social status system. The size of a household showed extreme variation depending upon social status and economic situation. The higher a family's social status, the more likely it was to be an extended family. As one went lower in the status hierarchy, the trend was for people to be in small families or to have no family at all. Despite these extreme differences in family structure, the household tax and statute labor were levied generally equally on each household since all families listed on household registers were treated as individual households. As a result, while the two taxes were not burdensome to the extended families of the ruling class, the burden was great for the subject classes that mainly consisted of small families.

During the five centuries of its existence, the Joseon government undertook a few major reforms of state finances and the taxation system. The first was in the late fifteenth century during Yeonsangun's reign (1494–1506). In the late Joseon period, there were two important revisions to the tax system – the Uniform Tax Law (Daedongbeop) in the mid-seventeenth century and the Equal-Service Law (Gyunyeokbeop) in the mid-eighteenth century. They can be seen as efforts to reconcile the fiscal system with social and economic developments, but one constant amidst the changes was the fact that the peasantry bore the heaviest tax burden.

The Suffering of the Peasantry

The taxation system was one of the primary reasons for the suffering of the peasantry, and later reforms provided little relief, even those intended to do so. The first major reform in Yeonsangun's reign increased taxes on the commoners and contributed to the gradual deterioration of the peasant class's economic situation. In contrast to previous kings, he was reckless in his use of state finances and rapidly undermined the fiscal system that had been established in the late fifteenth century. Unable to resolve its budget deficits, the government attempted to raise revenue by revising tribute ledgers which would enable a large-scale expansion of the household tax. It thought that raising the household tax was the best way to minimize the resistance of the ruling class and to increase fiscal revenue quickly.

Corruption in the tax system was of course another factor behind the difficulties of peasant life. Officials embezzled goods at tribute payment offices under the pretext of rejecting them for being of low quality. This embezzlement further increased the tax burden on the peasantry since they had to submit additional tribute goods. Over the course of the sixteenth century, it became established practice to have low-level officials or merchants transport tribute goods to the capital for the commoners (a system called *bangnap*) in an effort to guarantee a supply of tribute goods and to make payment easier. But a significant amount of goods came to be diverted into the wrong hands. The royal family and powerful families took advantage of the *bangnap* system and were able to accumulate wealth steadily. As a result, the peasantry had to pay even more taxes, and state finances continued to suffer from deficits.

The next major tax reform was the Uniform Tax Law that was first implemented in Gyeonggi province in the early seventeenth century. The Imjin War and the Manchu invasions led to renewed calls for reforming the tax system. The most important tasks of postwar reconstruction were to solve the chronic deficits of the government and to regain popular support. To achieve these goals, it was first necessary to reform the *bangnap* system, and the Uniform Tax Law was the attempted solution to these problems. It simplified the system of tax payments for the peasantry; rather than making several different payments, they could now pay all their taxes in rice. Thus, the government had to employ a new method of calculating how much tax revenue it needed. It calculated the total value of tribute goods, local farm products offered to the court, and surplus *bangnap* goods, and then it combined this figure with the revenue from the land tax and the household tax. This total was used to determine how much tax each person had to pay; it was set at twelve *du* of rice per *gyeol* of land, representing a significant reduction of the tax burden on the peasantry. Most of the tribute goods that had been paid by peasants through the household tax now became the responsibility of the landowner, and state finances improved greatly since it was now possible to purchase tribute goods at far lower prices compared to the days of the *bangnap* system.

The Uniform Tax Law dealt a big blow to the ruling class who had been able to amass great wealth under the *bangnap* system. To compensate for such losses, they turned to the military service tax as a new source of revenue. As military service gradually began to function like a quasi-tax, the government attempted to change it into a formal tax. An intense conflict developed between the government which was trying to secure more tax revenue and the peasantry which was trying to escape from the excessive tax burden. The biggest victims were the poor peasants who could not avoid the tax since their names were recorded on the military registers. It was necessary to reduce the military service tax in order to reduce the suffering of the peasantry, but it was also important to avoid worsening the state of government finances. The government's solution was the passage of the Equal Service Law in 1750. The military service tax, which had been levied at two bolts of cotton cloth (or twelve *du* of rice) per able-bodied man, was now reduced to one bolt of cloth per man. This reduction provided significant relief to the peasantry. After collecting the military service tax, the government disbursed funds to each government office, thus enhancing its control over state finances.

However, the overall tax burden was not greatly reduced since a new form of taxation emerged – the grain-loan system. Its original purpose was to provide relief to the peasantry; official granaries lent them grain during the spring famine period, and peasants repaid them after the harvest in the autumn. It was not supposed to be a tax, but from the sixteenth century, the grain-loan system came to be used as an important source of revenue for provincial offices. They began to charge the peasants interest on their loans, and this practice gradually became more exploitative in nature. When the Equal Service Law reduced the revenue these offices received, they made up for the loss through the grain-loan system. By the

Fig. 3.3. *Bubyeokru yeonhoe* (detail), late eighteenth century. Part of the series of paintings entitled *Welcoming Banquet for the Magistrate of Pyongyang* (Pyeongyang gamsa hyangyeondo). Thought to be the work of Gim Hongdo. (National Museum of Korea)

nineteenth century, the three taxes of the *jo-yong-jo* system of taxation came to be replaced by the so-called *samjeong* system. The term *samjeong* refers to the three main taxes paid by the peasantry – the land tax, grain loans, and the military service tax.

How much did the peasantry pay in taxes at the time? Under Joseon's hierarchical social status system, the tax burden was naturally heaviest on the peasant class. Let us examine the average income and expenditure of peasants and see what proportion of their household expenses was devoted to paying taxes. Information can be found in a text from the end of the eighteenth century during the reign of Jeongjo (1776–1800). Appointed as the country magistrate of Myeoncheon in 1799, Bak Jiwon (1737–1805) described the daily lives of peasants in the region in one of his works.[1] He took as an example a tenant farmer whose household had five working people, owned a cow, and cultivated a total of one *gyeol* and two *bu* of both dry and paddy fields. He concluded that the family would not be able to escape from chronic debt because of excessive land rent and taxes. That amount of land would produce 497 *du* of raw grain annually. In a given year, they would pay about 250 *du* for the land rent and seventy-two *du* for the land tax; forty-nine *du*, seven *seung* would be set aside to use as seeds. The household would then have about 126 *du* of grain left to use for the year, which was equal to only about three *seok*, four *du* of rice. Incurring large debts was unavoidable since they also had to pay other taxes such as the military service tax, to repay grain loans, and to purchase daily necessities such as firewood, clothing, and salt. It was not easy for them to reverse their fortunes. Most farm families faced pressure from the authorities to pay their back taxes, and their difficulties sometimes drove them to run off in the middle of the night.

Toward a Modern Tax System

By the beginning of the nineteenth century, the tax system had changed so much that it was hardly recognizable from the one that existed at the founding of the dynasty. In the *jo-yong-jo* system, taxes had been levied on land, households, and individual workers. In return, people were granted rights, thus motivating them to pay their taxes, and the system aimed at the smooth administration of state finances. But the tax system changed radically over time and developed into the *samjeong* system. On the surface, the objects of taxation remained the same – land, households (the grain loan system), and individual workers (the military service tax). But even aspects meant to benefit the welfare of taxpayers, such as the grain-loan system, came to be used as sources of tax revenue. The *samjeong*

[1] The *Hanminmyeongjeonui.*

system thus laid the foundation for the explicit exploitation of taxpayers by the state. Without any protection or benefits from the government, they had no choice but to engage in increasingly radical forms of resistance – from submitting protest letters and refusing to pay taxes to occupying and destroying government offices. These factors were also behind the radicalization of the peasantry over the course of the nineteenth century.

Among the taxes in the *samjeong* system, the household and military service taxes clearly declined in importance. Direct taxes relatively increased in importance, with the land tax being the most important. In the mid-seventeenth century, the Uniform Tax Law had already converted the household tax into a land tax, and in the mid-eighteenth century, the Equal Service Law turned part of the military service tax into a land tax. At the beginning of the nineteenth century, most taxes were levied in the form of *dogyeol*, a system in which the value of all other taxes were calculated according to market prices and then was levied as an addition to the land tax. The integration of various taxes into the land tax was a sign of the diminishing importance of social status in the tax system. It also meant that the ability of the ruling class to engage in arbitrary exploitation was declining. Taxes on the peasantry were steadily on the rise, but the tax system itself was entering a new stage of development. Joseon now stood at a crossroads. On the one hand, the government could create a new tax system that was based on direct taxes and gave taxpayers a balance of rights and obligations. On the other, it could maintain the existing tax system that used premodern forms of violence to suppress their rights and force them to pay their tax obligations. Unfortunately, the ruling class stayed on the latter course until the very end of the Joseon period and ignored the pressing needs of their times.

4. CURRENCY AND THE VALUE OF MONEY

Lee Hun-Chang

As the capital of an advanced industrial economy, Seoul is also the commercial center of South Korea. During the past few decades, a consumer culture has emerged that in many ways is more advanced than that of a Western metropolis. Like other major modern cities, downtown Seoul and other trendy areas are filled with department stores, boutiques, and stores selling the latest goods, many of them imported. These places are crowded with young people whose purchases set the trends for the rest of the country. Both transactions and product life cycles are incredibly rapid; hit products seem to emerge and disappear in the blink of an eye. More recently, e-commerce has undergone tremendous growth; products and services purchased online can be enjoyed immediately or delivered within a day. Amidst all this modern consumption, the city retains traces of an earlier commercial past. Many older types of market remain in Seoul, such as the so-called *jaerae sijang* where many people buy fruits, vegetables, and fish, as well as other daily necessities. Most date back to the early or mid-twentieth century, but some of them, such as Namdaemun Market, have a surprisingly long history going back to the Joseon era.

One of the most important developments of the Joseon period was the rise of markets. From the seventeenth century, a network of markets emerged throughout the country that transformed its economy. The increasing commercialization of economic life led to the widespread use of metal currency. Both markets and metal currency had existed before in the Korean peninsula, but they now penetrated further into the lives of commoners than they had before, becoming permanent parts of the economy. This chapter begins with a brief discussion of the developments in agriculture that led to the rise of markets, and then it examines the types of currency used in the Joseon period. The last section discusses the value of currency – i.e., prices. Research on prices in the Joseon era is still in its early stages, but there is sufficient data on basic commodities to provide another window on life in this period.

How Did Commerce Develop from an Agrarian Society?

One of the preconditions to commercial development was a rise in agricultural production. By the beginning of the Goryeo period, agriculture in the Korean peninsula had reached a relatively advanced state, but it was still necessary for farmers to let fields lay fallow once every two or three years in order to maintain their fertility. Thanks to technological advances, continuous cultivation spread during the eleventh to fourteenth centuries. The practice of fallow farming disappeared by the beginning of the Joseon period. At the same time, a new technique was introduced that brought about a revolution in agricultural cultivation – rice transplantation. Farmers up to that time had engaged in dry sowing, planting seeds directly in unirrigated fields. With the new technique, seeds were first planted in a small seedbed; after the seedlings reached a certain height, they were then transplanted to irrigated fields. As explained more fully in chapter one by Kim Kuentae, rice transplantation enabled a much more efficient use of both labor and land. Peasants could now farm on more land as cultivation moved into lowland areas, and double cropping became possible. After the Imjin War (1592–1598), the technique of rice transplantation became widespread throughout the country, increasing the productivity of land even further.

It is difficult to determine the productivity of land during the Joseon period accurately since statistics from the time are very fragmented and since the system of measurements was different from that of today. Units of measurement were established in the first half of the fifteenth century during Sejong's reign. At that time, land was measured in units of *gyeol* and *bu*, with one *gyeol* equal to 100 *bu*. *Gyeol* and *bu* were not units of area but units of productivity used to determine the amount of tax to be levied from a plot of land. In other words, the units referred to the amount of land necessary to produce a specific amount of grain. For instance, in the fifteenth century, the annual yield for one *gyeol* of paddy field is estimated to have been about 240 *mal*. The size of land in units of *gyeol* thus varied according to its fertility. In the *gyeol-bu* law of 1444, the units were divided into six grades with grade-one land being the most fertile (and having the smallest area) and grade-six being the least. One *gyeol* of grade-one land was equal to an area of 2,986.6 *pyeong*, while grade-six land was four times larger at 11,946.4 *pyeong* (one *pyeong* = approximately 3.3 square meters).

The value of a *mal* was different in the Joseon period than it is today when one *mal* is equal to about eighteen liters. Scholars do not agree on the exact value of a *mal* in Joseon times; estimates range from as little as

Fig. 4.1. *Gyeongjikdo* (detail). Late Joseon Period. Painting on a folding screen. Farmers are threshing grain and making straw sacks after the autumn harvest. (National Museum of Korea)

5.18 liters to as much as 5.976 liters. It was about one-third of its value today. However, the volume of a *mal* differed tremendously according to the region. This was because of a variety of factors – insufficient government regulation, lack of technical expertise, manipulation by merchants and officials, and the underdevelopment of markets at the time. The conversion of *mal* to other units also differed in the Joseon era. Ten *dwoe* has continued to be equal to one *mal*, but unlike today, ten *mal* did not equal one *seom*. Fifteen *mal* was called 'sogokpyeongseok,' and twenty *mal* was called 'daegokjeonseok.'

With this information, it is possible to make a rough comparison with the productivity of land in the twentieth century. From 1918 to 1920, one *danbo* (300 *pyeong*) of farmland had an average annual crop yield of 0.93 *seom* (167 liters). The productivity of land in this period was about twice the level of a grade-four plot in the mid-fifteenth century, if one *mal* is taken to be 5.976 liters. Land productivity continued to increase after the end of the Joseon period. During the Japanese occupation period, the average annual crop yield for one *danbo* increased to more than one *seom*; since the 1960s, productivity has rapidly increased such that the average annual crop yield is now three *seom* per *danbo*. Compared to today, the productivity of land in the Joseon era may seem low. With the spread of continuous cultivation, however, agricultural productivity already reached a high level in the fifteenth century compared to its contemporaries. One consequence of this development was that population density was extremely high. In the year 1500, the population density was twenty-five people per square kilometer for China and eight people for Western Europe (including its overseas colonies); by contrast, it is estimated in Joseon to have approached forty people.

These developments helped to create the conditions that enabled the emergence of markets. In premodern times, the peasantry, who constituted the majority of the population, was largely self-sufficient in terms of consumption. Even in the early twentieth century, when the economy was relatively developed, farm households only sold about twenty to thirty percent of their harvest on the market. Since ancient times, however, farm households have had to engage in trade to acquire some of the goods and products essential to their lives. For example, peasants had to obtain iron farm tools made by artisans, and people in inland regions had to obtain salt from merchants. As agricultural productivity increased, the population grew, and surpluses increased, leading to the expansion of commerce and the growth of markets. As a result, farm households became increasingly dependent upon markets.

When Was Money First Used?

As trade expanded at markets, currency emerged as a means to conduct transactions as well as a measure for value. In premodern society, items used as currency were usually things that could be widely circulated and were easily divisible and storable. It was not until the Joseon period, with the issuance of the *sangpyeong tongbo* in 1678, that metal coins were widely circulated. Compared to countries of a similar level of development, Korea was somewhat late in adopting metal currency.

Even though metal currency was not in wide use, economic transactions were not limited to barter. A variety of materials were used for currency before the Joseon period. According to archaeological research, people were already engaging in trade by the Bronze Age. Through barter, handicrafts were circulated between the coastal regions and inland agricultural areas, and furs, grains, clamshells, and stone coins were used as currency. In Old Joseon, metal currency was minted and distributed, while in the statelet of Jin,[1] it was said that "usually when goods are traded, everyone uses metal as money." From the Three Kingdoms Period, the use of rice or hemp cloth as currency surpassed the use of metal currency, but unlike metal currency, these commodity currencies were only used for internal transactions. During the Goryeo period, rice, hemp, and similar types of commodity currency were already widespread, and roughly woven hemp cloth (*chupo*) was also used as currency. These currencies could easily function as a means for conducting transactions and did not present any major problems as a way to own wealth. Until the early fifteenth century, hemp was the main commodity currency, but cotton replaced hemp as cotton cultivation became more widespread in the first half of the fifteenth century. *Jeongpo* was finely woven cloth officially recognized as currency; coarser *chupo* was mainly used for the smaller daily transactions of poor people in urban areas. In particular, the type of *chupo* called two-*seungpo* was so useless – both for clothing and for sack material – that the government once even prohibited its use as currency. However, it tacitly permitted its circulation since it feared that such a move would harm the livelihood of the poor. This recognition was a sign that commodity currencies had become an essential part of their daily lives.

In both the Goryeo and the Joseon periods, the government made attempts to introduce metal currency. By minting money, it wanted the resulting benefits such as the ability to facilitate tax collection and to store revenues effectively. At the end of the tenth and eleventh centuries, the Goryeo government twice prohibited the use of hemp as currency and put metal currency in circulation. However, since peasants, accustomed to commodity currencies, were reluctant to use metal coins, the circulation of metal currency was limited, far surpassed by that of commodity currencies such as hemp cloth. At the end of the Goryeo period, the government

1 Jin was an Iron Age polity located in the southern part of the Korean peninsula in the third and second centuries BCE before the emergence of the Samhan confederations.

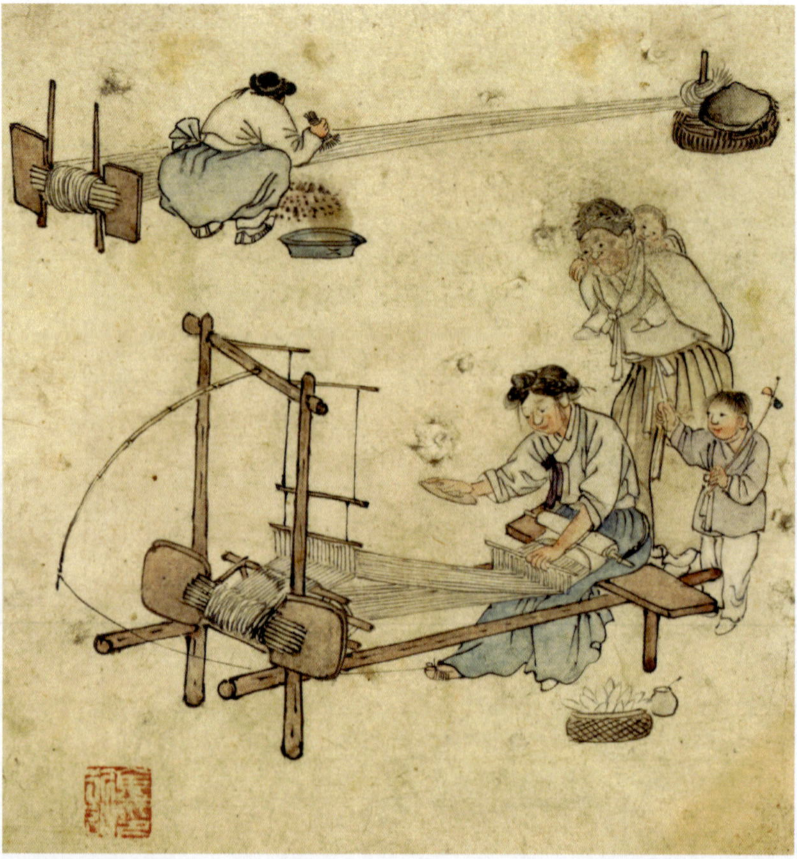

Fig. 4.2. *Weaving*, Gim Hongdo, late eighteenth century. (National Museum of Korea)

tried to introduce a type of paper money called *jeohwa* but quickly abandoned it. In the Joseon period, both King Taejong and King Sejong tried to circulate *jeohwa* and metal coins, but once again, these efforts failed to replace commodity currencies. Efforts at introducing metal coins continued in the seventeenth century.

Why did the attempts to introduce coins or paper money fail? First, commodity currency had many other uses whereas metal or paper currency did not. During the reign of Taejong, the government tried to force the people to use *jeohwa*, but the people thought that unlike rice, hemp, or other forms of commodity currency, "when you are hungry, you cannot eat it; when you are cold, you can't wear it—it is only a piece of a black bag."

The government also could not adequately guarantee the purchasing power of the new currencies, further undermining the people's confidence. Second, the economy had a weak foundation for the circulation of metal currency. In 1473, Sin Sukju (1417–1475) noted that money was not circulating due to a lack of regional markets, emphasizing that they were a necessary condition for currency circulation. Third, another problem was the difficulties in producing a sufficient supply of copper, the base metal for the coins.

Silver was also commonly used in metal currency. In the Goryeo era, the government minted bottle-shaped silver coins, which were used for high-value transactions and for those in remote areas. During the Joseon period, silver currency was mainly used around Seoul by the royal palace, government officials, the ruling class, merchants, and translator officials. Its circulation increased at the end of the sixteenth century since the Chinese army used silver to procure supplies and give rewards to soldiers during the Imjin War. Merchants at the time commented that "other valuables were not saved; one's wealth was determined only by how much silver one owned." Another stimlulus to the circulation of silver currency was the massive influx of silver from Japan in the seventeenth century to pay for imports. In the eighteenth century, however, its use quickly declined. As the influx of silver from Japan stopped, massive amounts of silver flowed out to China to pay for imports and the expenses of tribute missions. The inability of silver currency to establish itself in remote regions also decreased its usefulness.

By the seventeenth century, the economy had developed to the point that it could support a metal currency. It was the result of a combination of factors – the continued development of agricultural productivity, population increase, and the growth of markets. Since silver coins were a high-denomination currency, it became necessary to have low-denomination coins as well. In Gaeseong, a major commercial center, coins were used as the medium for all transactions by the first half of the seventeenth century. From the year 1678, the government implemented a more effective and aggressive currency policy, learning from previous failures, and it led to the widespread circulation of metal currency.

The new currency was a copper-bronze coin called the *sangpyeong tongbo*. One coin was worth one *pun*; ten *pun* was one *jeon*; and ten *jeon* equaled one *nyang*. Coins of higher denomination were introduced later. The *dangbaekjeon*, minted during the regency of the Daewongun, was worth 100 *pun* – i.e., one *nyang*. Minted in 1883, the *dangojeon* had a value of five *pun*. As the minting of coins increased, their usage gradually spread from Gyeonggi and Chungcheong provinces to the whole country by the early eighteenth century. The monetary economy developed to the point that even "old ladies selling vegetables and laborers peddling salt are demanding money instead of grain [as payment]." The government promoted the use of currency through measures such as lending coins at no interest to *sijeon* merchants, using them to pay officials' salaries, and collecting some taxes in money. Convenient for small transactions, metal coins rapidly replaced hemp cloth and gradually became more widely used than silver currency as well. Though metal currency was introduced relatively late, a large amount of money was quickly put into circulation. Between the years 1678 to 1697, the government minted about 4.5 million *nyang* of coins. Taking into account counterfeit coins and damaged coins, the total amount of money in circulation would have exceeded five million *nyang* in the early eighteenth century. With this amount, it would have been possible to purchase 1.3 million *seok* of rice or about ten percent of total rice production – the equivalent of about two to three percent of the gross domestic product (GDP). From 1731 to 1798, the government produced more than five million *nyang* and, from 1809 to 1857, more than six million additional *nyang*. By 1860, the amount of money in circulation was around fourteen million *nyang*. This was equal to 1.8 million *seok* of rice or thirteen percent of total rice production; it is estimated to have been around four percent of GDP.

By stimulating commercial development, the growth of a monetary economy also raised concerns about its effects on economic and social life. At a time when agriculture was the foundation of the economy, one of the greatest concerns of officials was the widespread practice of usury in rural areas. Usurers in villages usually charged fifty percent interest. Originally, loans were made and repaid in grain; for instance, two *mal* of rice lent in the spring would be paid back with three *mal* of rice in the fall. However, with the rise of a monetary economy, everything was conducted in currency instead. Now, a loan of one *nyang* in cash would have to be repaid with 1.5 *nyang* in the fall. The price of rice was high in the spring because supplies were low; it would drop in the autumn after the harvest. If one *nyang* was worth two *mal* of grain in the spring, it could purchase five *mal* in the fall. Because of the use of money, the amount to be repaid was actually more than three times the original amount. Usury created a classic vicious circle in which poor farmers got poorer, bringing many lower-class peasants to ruin.

Because of the prevalence of usury, some officials began to call for the abolition of metal currency. They feared that usury would ruin peasant

Fig. 4.3. Susepae. A form of official identification carried by officials in charge of collecting taxes. (National Museum of Korea)

households and lead to rampant thievery and corruption. After ascending to the throne in 1724, Yeongjo finally agreed to halt the minting of coins. At the time, the supply of coins was insufficient to meet demand. When the government stopped minting coins, the shortage worsened, and the economy, which had become dependent on the use of metal currency, also suffered. Money became so precious that it became difficult for merchants to sell goods to the peasantry. A small number of merchants, who had large stores of money, became more active in moneylending. In the end, the actual consequence of the policy was to worsen the situation of the peasantry, and the government began minting coins again in 1731. Though the country had repeatedly failed at introducing metal currency up to the 1660s, it became such an essential part of the rural economy by the eighteenth century that it could no longer be abolished.

How Did Prices Change?

In the Joseon period, prices were already strongly subject to the laws of supply and demand. Prices are not available for the early Joseon period since coins were not widely used at the time. But it is possible to examine the exchange rates for the main commodities or commodity currencies such as hemp, cotton, and rice in Seoul. According to the official rates set in the mid-fifteenth century, one *pil* of fifth-grade cotton could be exchanged for two *pil* of fifth-grade hemp cloth. In the 1440s, one *pil* of cotton was worth five *mal* of rice, but it declined to three *mal* in the early 1480s and then to two *mal* in the 1490s. In the sixteenth century, it fell to under one *mal* of rice. The main factor behind the rapid decline was that fifth-grade cotton, initially used as a form of currency, was replaced by hemp and that its length gradually became shorter over time. In addition, cotton production grew at a faster rate than rice production during the fifteenth century, and as the population increased, demand for rice also increased which raised its relative price.

How did the price of rice change after the introduction of *sangpyeong tongbo* coins? Since markets at the time were not highly developed, short-term price fluctuations were severe, changing according to the season or the quality of the harvest. When the harvest was bad, it was usual for rice to more than double in price. These price swings constituted such a threat to the livelihood of the peasanstry that it was necessary for the government to devote much effort to stabilize rice prices. Long-term trends in rice prices were closely connected to the currency situation. When the circulation of coinage was widespread, the price of rice increased; prices fell when coins were in short supply or when minting was halted. Commodity prices generally remained stable in the eighteenth century and the first half of the nineteenth century. The average price of rice in Seoul mostly stayed steady at five *nyang* per *seom* in the eighteenth century, with the price being lower in rural areas. For much of the century, there was a shortage of currency. The minting of 1.52 million *nyang* in new coins from 1829 to 1832 resolved the currency shortage, and the large-scale minting of coinage in the 1850s also contributed to price inflation. In the latter half of the nineteenth century, prices of goods began to rise rapidly, driven by increasing rice prices. The minting of the *dangbaekjeon* and *dangojeon* coins in this period caused a sharp jump in prices that destabilized the economy and undermined the livelihood of the common people in the cities.

Other factors such as population and productivity also had an effect on prices. The population of the country rose in the eighteenth century, but in the nineteenth century, it appears to have stagnated or even decreased, along with a decline in the standard of living. Recent studies have shown that agricultural productivity fell in the nineteenth century. These developments decreased the demand for goods which would normally have led to a drop in prices. However, the falling productivity reduced the supply of goods, thus leading to a rise in prices in the second half of the nineteenth century.

What was the purchasing power of one *nyang* in today's currency? As mentioned above, the average price of one *seom* of rice was five *nyang* in the eighteenth century. One *seom* in the Joseon era was approximately equal to sixty percent of today's *seom*, which is equal to 155 kilograms. As of April 2004, the retail price of twenty kilograms of average grade rice is about 55,000 won. Then one *seom* in the eighteenth century would be worth about 250,000 won today, and one *nyang* would be equivalent to 50,000 won (roughly fifty dollars). What were the prices of goods other than rice? The exchange rates for the main taxable commodities were recorded in the *Sokdaejeon*, a revised legal code that was compiled in the mid-eighteenth century. While there were slight regional differences, one *seom* of beans was 2.5 *nyang* or half the price of rice. The price of one *pil* of fifth-grade cotton or hemp cloth was set at two *nyang*, and it was also equal to one *mal* of rice. In the mid-fifteenth century, one *pil* of cotton had been equal to two *pil* of hemp cloth. Between the fifteenth and eighteenth centuries, the spread of cotton cultivation increased the supply of cotton cloth, lowering its value relative to hemp cloth. The price of rice was about 1.0 to 1.8 times the price of barley in the nineteenth century, according to the journals of the Yecheon Bak family in North Gyeongsang province. The relative price of barley was high since it was a valuable source of food at times when other grains were scarce.

5. THE MERCHANTS OF SEOUL

Lee Uk

Seoul, the capital of Joseon, was not just the administrative and political center of the kingdom; it also developed into a major commercial center. The majority of people living in the city were either government officials such as bureaucrats and clerks or poor peasants who had lost their land and worked as laborers. They had to purchase grain and everyday necessities that they could not produce themselves. When King Taejong (r. 1400–1418) ordered the construction of another palace in 1404 and expanded the city, stores and market areas were built. Seoul's location appeared to be favorable for commerce; it was located almost in the middle of the peninsula, just north of the main agricultural regions and at a reasonable distance from its main trading partner, China. Because it was on the northern side of the Han River, it had access to the Yellow Sea and to inland areas further east. Rice and other goods from all over the country were brought to Seoul, mainly as payment for taxes. In the early Joseon period, however, the overall level of commercial activity in the city was relatively low since the government put strict restrictions on commercial activity. In Confucian morality, profit-seeking behavior was disdained, and merchants were at the bottom of the social hierarchy, coming after scholars, farmers, and artisans. Commerce in Seoul underwent development after the Imjin War of 1592–1598. Migration from the countryside increased as people sought to escape the devastation of the war; the increased population created more demand for markets. Merchants came to play a larger role in the economic and social life of the capital. This chapter examines how the merchants of Seoul conducted business and how the nature of commerce changed in the late Joseon period when private merchants overtook government-licensed merchants as the dominant players in markets.

The Sijeon

In Seoul, merchant associations called *sijeon* controlled the sale and distribution of goods. There were only a small number of *sijeon*, and they were mainly located in the area of today's Jongno, one of the main boulevards of central Seoul, where a large number of stores lined the street.

They received exclusive rights over certain goods from the government; for instance, the *ipjeon* merchants had a monopoly over silk, and the *ssajeon* merchants had a monopoly over the sale of rice. By the mid-Joseon period, there emerged a group of *sijeon* that had the responsibility of providing the government's needs for six major products. They were known as the Six Licensed Guilds (Yuguijeon), and they handled silk, cotton cloth, ramie cloth, thread, paper products, and fish products. The positions of *sijeon* merchants were hereditary, passed down from generation to generation, and each merchant had their own shop called a *bang*. For example, merchants belonging to the *ipjeon* would have stores named consecutively the *ilbang* (first store), the *ibang* (second store), and so on. Stores were commonly called *jeonbang*, and the term is a combination of the character *jeon* from the word *sijeon* and the character *bang* meaning store. Originally, the *sijeon* built buildings to conduct their business, but as the number of merchants increased, they would build temporary structures next to the main buildings. These temporary stores were called *gage*, the origin of today's term for 'store.'

There were also merchants who did not belong to a *sijeon*. There were peddlers from the countryside who traveled to Seoul to sell goods, and other peddlers roamed the alleyways of the city, selling goods ranging from fish to brushes. They sold goods to people who could not walk all the way to the *sijeon* just to buy a few days' worth of rice. Markets were active in places such as Ihyeon (Baeogae, near today's Gwangjang Market) and Chilpae (behind today's Seoul Station). However, all of these peddlers and merchants were required to obtain their merchandise from a *sijeon* store.

Fig. 5.1. Rice stores in the Jongno area of Seoul, 1900.

When a commodity was brought to Seoul, it had to be turned over to the *sijeon*, and peddlers could sell only what they had bought from *sijeon* merchants. For instance, if a person needed silk clothes for a special occasion but only had some extra rice, he would first have to sell the rice to the rice store and then use the money to purchase clothes from the clothing store. These steps were necessary for a legal transaction because of the *sijeon*'s monopoly over certain goods.

Wheeling and Dealing for Profit

A sale began with a person called a *yeoriggun*. They were merchants who, since they were too poor to have their own stores, worked for storeowners by bringing in customers from the street. In a normal transaction, merchants tried to sell goods at a profit while customers tried to get them to cut their prices. The amount added to the original price was called the *enuri*. Koreans often say that there is no sale without *enuri*, thinking that the term refers to the haggling over price. But originally, the term referred to the amount that merchants added to the cost of an item. The term *yeori* refers to the amount of profit in excess of the amount taken by

Fig. 5.2. The Chilpae district outside of Great South Gate (Namdaemun), early twentieth century.

the storeowner. In *sijeon* stores, merchants sold goods at a price that included the fee given to the *yeoriggun*.

To illustrate how merchants made a sale, here is a fictionalized episode of an encounter with a customer. Stores had small rooms right inside their main gate, where *sijeon* merchants sat on cushions to receive guests. Mr. Gim is a man who has come to a store to buy silk for his daughter's wedding. Mr. Bak is a *yeoriggun* serving as a middleman, and Mr. Yi is the owner of a *sijeon* store that sells silk. As Mr. Gim strolls into Jongno, Mr. Bak approaches him and asks:

<table>
<tr><td>Mr. Bak:</td><td>What are you looking to buy?</td></tr>
<tr><td>Mr. Gim:</td><td>I need some silk for my daughter's wedding.</td></tr>
<tr><td>Mr. Bak:</td><td>You're in luck. Let me take you to a silk store that
I know well. (Takes Mr. Gim into the silk store. To Mr. Yi)
Will talcha [twenty nyang] be enough?</td></tr>
<tr><td>Mr. Yi:</td><td>Yes.</td></tr>
<tr><td>Mr. Gim:</td><td>How much does a roll of silk cost?</td></tr>
<tr><td>Mr. Bak:</td><td>It costs thirty nyang.</td></tr>
<tr><td>Mr. Gim:</td><td>That's too expensive. Give it to me for ten nyang less.</td></tr>
<tr><td>Mr. Bak:</td><td>If we sell it at that price, we'll lose money.
We cannot sell it at that price.</td></tr>
<tr><td>Mr. Gim:</td><td>Then I have no choice. I'll go to another store then.</td></tr>
<tr><td>Mr. Bak:</td><td>(taking a hold of Mr. Gim)
Hey, you're too impatient!
Wait a minute. We buy a roll of silk for twenty nyang too.
So just pay a little more.</td></tr>
<tr><td>Mr. Gim:</td><td>Then let's make it twenty-one nyang.</td></tr>
<tr><td>Mr. Bak:</td><td>(Eyes Mr. Yi meaningfully, and Mr. Yi signals his approval)
OK, it's a deal. Just pay twenty-one nyang.</td></tr>
</table>

After Mr. Gim leaves with his roll of silk, Mr. Yi gives Mr. Bak one *nyang*.

What just happened? The original cost of the silk was seventeen *nyang*. The storeowner wanted to sell it for twenty *nyang*, adding three *nyang* as the *enuri*. But because of the *yeoriggun*'s bargaining, he was able to sell it for twenty-one *nyang*. The additional one *nyang* in profit is the *yeori*, and it went to the middleman instead of the storeowner. This is why these merchants came to be called *yeoriggun*.

Yeoriggun did not work for a specific store. When they saw a potential customer, they just brought them to a store. If a *yeoriggun* wanted to collect his share of a sale, he had to know the storeowner's intended sale price beforehand, so he could sell it at a higher price. *Yeoriggun* used a secret code to find out the price from the owner without the customer's knowledge. These codes were called *byeoneo*, which were generally based on the principles of *paja* – i.e., separating Chinese characters into their constituent elements to produce words and phrases with different meanings. For instance, the numbers one through nine were represented by the characters *jap* (帀), *sa* (些), *yeo* (汝), *gang* (罡), *o* (悟), *gyo* (交), *jo* (皂), *tae* (兌), and *uk* (旭). Each of these characters contains elements that are the same as the characters for the nine numbers. The word *talcha* mentioned in the above dialogue meant "to take the *cha* element out of the Chinese character *sa*" – thus, leaving strokes that represent the Chinese character for the number two. In other words, *talcha* was a code for the number two, and in the scenario above, it was used to mean a sum of twenty *nyang*. Another example is the term *taljeong*. If the *jeong* element is removed from the Chinese character *gang*, the resultant element forms the character for the number four. Thus, *taljeong* meant 'four' (see Fig. 5.4).

Preventing Illegal Activities in the Market

Merchants in the *sijeon* also had the right to report illegal activities to the authorities and seize the goods of the merchants involved. Targets included people who brought goods to merchants in Seoul not belonging to the *sijeon* and peddlers who sold goods not acquired through a *sijeon* store. Merchants often abused these rights, called the *geumnanjeongwon*, for the sake of profit. One extreme example was the case of a filial man named Gim who had to buy ginseng when his father's illness worsened. The only thing in the house was two *pil* of hemp cloth that his wife had woven. Because the situation was so urgent, he went out to sell the hemp cloth in order to buy ginseng. All of a sudden, a merchant from the *pojeon* (stores with a monopoly over hemp cloth) appeared and deemed his activities to be illegal. The merchant then beat the man and seized his cloth, unmoved by the man's entreaties that his father was seriously ill.

Scenes of abuse were common near Namdaemun (Great South Gate) and Dongdaemun (Great East Gate), two of the main entrances to Seoul. The sounds of wailing were often heard from people who were trying to sell a few bundles of eggs or a jar of pickled fish in order to get food. They loudly bemoaned their fate when their goods were seized by *sijeon* merchants who kept watch near the gates. The *sijeon* merchants would demand that they sell them their goods at less than half the market price, and if they refused, the merchants would forcibly seize their goods, claiming that their activities were illegal.

The *sijeon* merchants even ignored the government's order not to crack down on commoners who were engaging in small-scale transactions in order to make ends meet. The living conditions for poor people were becoming more desperate in the Seoul region, and their resentment against the *sijeon* was gradually growing. The government was concerned about what would occur if they continued to neglect the abuses of the *sijeon*. It abolished the *geumnanjeongwon* of the *sijeon*, except for the largest merchants of the Six Licensed Guilds, and allowed goods to be traded freely. The new policy was promulgated in the year 1791, the fifteenth year of Jeongjo's reign. Since 1791 was the *sinhae* year in the sexagenary cycle, this policy was known as the Sinhae Tonggong. It was a response to the protests of small merchants and poor people in urban areas.

The Rise of Private Merchants

Another factor behind the Sinhae Tonggong was the rise of a new type of merchant who challenged the dominance of the *sijeon* merchants. These new merchants were called the *sasang dogo* – i.e., private merchants. The *sijeon* merchants had acquired the *geumnanjeongwon* because they gave a substantial amount of money to the government. Now another group of merchants emerged who could also provide large sums of revenue to the government. The private merchants generally operated at key locations where goods were brought into Seoul. The most important places included Yongsan, Ddukseom, Mapo, and Dumopo (today's Oksu-dong) along the Han River as well as Songujeom in Pocheon; Songpa, where goods arrived from the three southern provinces; and Darakwon (today's Howon-dong in Uijeongbu), where goods from Hamgyeong and Gangwon provinces were brought into Seoul. With operations based in these places, the private merchants established ties with small-scale merchants in local markets in places such as Ihyeon and Chilpae and with important merchants in provincial areas such as Gaeseong. Their operations became a threat to the *sijeon* merchants in Seoul. With their superior financial resources and networks, private merchants were able to outmaneuver the *sijeon* merchants and gradually gain control over the markets of Seoul.

Out of necessity, the private merchants had to use innovative business methods. Since they did not have special privileges such as the

Fig. 5.3. *Market* (Sijang), Gim Jungeun (aka Gisan), late nineteenth century. (Copyright: Museum fuer Voelkerkunde Hamburg).

geumnanjeongwon, they could not simply wait for customers to come to them, as did the *sijeon* merchants. Instead of waiting for goods to be brought to Seoul, they purchased items directly from the producers. Furthermore, they even used their own funds to pay for entertainment to attract customers. One example was the thriving markets at Songpa where all kinds of goods arrived from throughout the country. To draw people to the market, the merchants at Songpa sponsored entertainments, pooling their funds to hire a performing troupe. This was the Songpa Masked Drama, now designated as an Important Intangible Cultural Treasure (no. 49). Not to be outdone, the merchants of Darakwon in Yangju also organized shows, and these entertainments were the origin of the Yangju Masked Drama, which has also been recognized as an Important Intangible Cultural Treasure (no. 2). Because the private merchants were so aggressively entrepreneurial, they were able to outcompete the *sijeon* merchants, who were dependent on their special privileges, and take control of commerce in Seoul. The Sinhae Tonggong of 1791 represented the government's abandonment of a commercial policy based on the *sijeon* system and a shift to reliance on private merchants.

Rice Riots in Seoul

When the government lifted the restrictions on private trade, the monopolistic behavior of the private merchants caused serious problems. Tensions climaxed with the rice riots in Seoul in 1833. During the third lunar month of that year, the grueling spring famine was at its height – a time when peasants ran out of rice and were subsisting on barley. Meanwhile, Gim Jaesun, the owner of a *yeogaek* (an inn engaging in trade) in Mapo, was extremely worried. He had acquired a tremendous quantity of rice, expecting to make a big profit during the spring famine period, but things did not go as expected. Though he expected rice prices to rise, he had bought too much; the price dropped when the rice hit the market. Gim needed to do something before things got worse. He called for a meeting with Jeong Jonggeun, an owner of a rice store, and other merchants. Gim ordered the merchants to take turns opening their stores so that only one shop would be open each day. As a result, on the sixth day of the third lunar month, the price of rice doubled. Looking to raise prices even further, Gim ordered all rice stores in downtown Seoul to close on the eighth day of the month.

Gim Gwangheon, a royal bodyguard, was very fatigued from being on duty the previous night. He ambled toward the rice stores to buy a little rice for his wife and children who had had nothing to eat for days. On the way, he met his neighbor Go Eokcheol, who had recently moved to Seoul from Jeolla province. Go was panting and seemed very angry. When Gim asked him what was the matter, he replied, "Those bastards! They've now closed down all the rice stores. They weren't content with doubling the price." Enraged at the news, Gim said, "What? They're not selling rice? I'll take care of those bastards." Though he was exhausted from work and hunger, he found himself standing in front of the rice stores.

Gim Gwangheon found a group of seemingly starving people gathering in front of the stores. He became enraged again at the pitiful sight, and to calm himself, he took out his pipe and filled it with tobacco. Noticing some dry firewood lying nearby, Gim suddenly had the thought of burning down the rice stores but restrained himself, thinking of his wife and children. When he spat on the street and turned to go home, he was surprised to find Go Eokcheol standing next to him. Go said, "I can't go back home like this. I'm going to burn down the damned rice stores!" Gim told him, "What are you talking about? Control yourself." "Control myself?" replied Go, "What for? Even if I'm beaten to death, I can't put up with this any longer. I can't tolerate those money-crazed bastards anymore." Trying to calm Go down, Gim momentarily forgot about his own anger.

Pushing Gim aside, Go found a branch on the street and set it on fire. Running toward the closed rice stores, he shouted to the crowd, "Move out of the way! What good is a rice store that doesn't sell rice? Let's burn it down!" He then threw the burning branch onto the roof of the store. With one swift motion, he flung the flaming firewood on the roof. Being made of thatched straw, the roof was quickly engulfed in flames. At the sight of the fire, Gim Gwangheon became caught up in the emotions of the moment. It seemed that people in the crowd felt the same way. As if energized by the crowd, Gim stood in front of them and shouted, "Rice prices are so high because of the damned store owners' schemes. So let's burn down all the rice stores!" Sounds of "That's right!" could be heard from the crowd. Gim and Go led the people to set fire to all the rice stores. A few policemen tried to stop them but could not control the angry crowd.

Gim Gwangheon then ran to the banks of the Han River and also set fire to the storehouses where the merchants kept their rice. He had calmed down somewhat, torn between feeling satisfied and lamenting the waste of the rice. To catch their breath, they rested on some rocks and had a smoke, and as clouds of white dust appeared, they could see policemen rushing towards them. Gim put out his pipe and slowly stood up, feeling as if all his fatigue were suddenly returning. He thought of fighting the police but decided to go quietly, worried that innocent people might get hurt. That very afternoon, Gim was beheaded on the sandy beaches of the Han River. The preceding paragraphs are a slightly fictionalized account of the rice riots of 1833 in which the poor people of Seoul protested against the monopoly of the private merchants. The events of the riots were recorded in historical sources, and it is a historical fact that Gim Gwangheon and Go Eokcheol were its leaders. I made up the fact that Go was from Jeolla province and the details of how he instigated the riot with Gim.

After the Sinhae Tonggong of 1791, the abuses of the *sijeon* merchants decreased significantly. When private merchants gained control over commerce in Seoul, however, they caused similar problems with their efforts to manipulate prices. The entire country felt the negative effects of the private merchants' monopoly over goods. Nevertheless, the government continued to support them, and the people rose up in protest. They risked their lives to fight against the merchants and the government, but their

Example 1: If someone says " *talcha*" (탈차 or 脫此)…
you have to "remove *cha*."

Step 1: Take the character *sa* 些

Step 2: Remove the element *cha* 此

Step 3: The result is the number TWO 二

Example 2: If someone says "*taljeong*" (탈정 or 脫正)…
you have to "remove *jeong*."

Step 1: Take the character *gang* 罡

Step 2: Remove the element *jeong* 正

Step 3: The result is the number FOUR 四

Fig. 5.4. Byeoneo – Breaking the Merchants' Code.

resistance was not strong enough to prevail. The rice riots were perhaps the most dramatic episode in the people's continual resistance to the monopolies of merchants in the late Joseon period. Until the mid-eighteenth century, people had engaged in resistance against the monopoly of the *sijeon* merchants, and afterwards, they fought against the private merchants. The government finally abolished the monopoly of private merchants in the Gabo Reforms of 1894.

with Ellen Yuh

6. THE JOYS AND SORROWS OF THE ITINERANT MERCHANTS

Yoo Pil Jo

In accordance with Confucian principles, the Joseon government emphasized agriculture and regarded commerce and industry with disdain. Confucianism disapproved of profit-seeking activities and put merchants at the bottom of the social hierarchy. However, Joseon's policies were not intended to suppress the development of commerce completely. People needed to buy goods that they could not produce themselves, and merchants sold them products such as salt, fish, and handicraft goods. In addition to government policy, there were other factors that stimulated commercial development, including handicraft production by the peasantry, improvement in their purchasing power, and the development of a market infrastructure. These developments led to the emergence of rural markets called *jangsi*.

There were three main types of merchants who worked at these markets: *gaekju* (brokers), *yeogaek* (commission agents), and *jangdolbaengi* (itinerant peddlers). They were particularly active during the late Joseon period when the country underwent commercial development. *Gaekju* and *yeogaek* owned inns where they also operated businesses that sold goods on consignment, acted as middlemen, and provided financial services. Koreans commonly think that all itinerant merchants in the period were what were called *bobusang*. The *bobusang* were an organization of peddlers that received monopoly rights from local government offices or from the Border Defense Command (Bibyeonsa). Some of them were well connected with high-ranking officials. However, not all itinerant peddlers were *bobusang*, and most of them did not enjoy the same privileges. In fact, most of the people working in markets were merchants and peasants who were exploited by the government or by merchants with monopoly rights. They fought against such exploitation as they worked to make a living. Koreans today are familiar with the exploits of Joseon-era merchants through popular historical novels.[1] These stories portrayed merchants from Gaeseong who travelled to markets all over the country, the itinerant

[1] Such as *Jang Gilsan* by Hwang Seogyeong, *Gaekju* by Gim Juyeong, and *Sangdo* by Choe Inho.

performers who followed them, and the gangs who defended their turf. These characters were not simply products of a writer's imagination; they were based on people who actually existed in the late Joseon period. The rural markets were both places where business was conducted and the site of their joys and sorrows. This chapter examines the emergence of rural markets with a focus on one of the most common types, the so-called 'five-day market.' It also discusses the lives of the itinerant merchants whose livelihoods were dependent on these markets.

The Predecessors of the Itinerant Peddlers

Since the Joseon government allowed merchant associations called *sijeon* to operate stores in Seoul, people living in cities could obtain goods easily. There were also stores in cities such as Gaeseong, Naju, Gyeongju, and Jeonju. By contrast, most rural villages did not have permanent stores; in fact, at the time of Joseon's founding, there were no rural markets that opened at regular intervals in a fixed location – the markets that were the basis for the existence of itinerant merchants.

In the early Joseon era, people in rural areas bought goods from peddlers known as *haengsang*, a term that meant 'traveling merchants selling goods.' They were the forerunners of the merchants called *jangdolbaengi* or *jangdollim*. Since there were no rural markets yet, it would not be accurate to call them *jangdolbaengi*. The *haengsang* existed from the time that people began to trade for goods that they could not produce, going back to at least the Three Kingdoms Period (first to seventh centuries CE). For instance, a Baekje song entitled 'Jeongeupsa' contains a line expressing the wishes of a woman: "O Moon, climb high and cast your light on the road on which my beloved is traveling to sell his goods." They played a greater role in the economy as the amount of surplus goods and the social division of labor increased. In the early Joseon period, traveling peddlers were sometimes considered to be a bad influence on rural society. They travelled to rural villages to sell handicraft goods such as combs, brassware, woodwork, clothing, and farming implements and local products such as salt and fish. The government thought that they were selling unnecessary luxury goods in order to buy up rice and other important staple grains. The wares they handled suggest, however, that they were providing tools for farming and other necessities of daily life.

There were two main types of *haengsang* peddlers. The *yuksang* traveled over land, and the *susang* or *seonsang* traveled by water routes.

Fig. 6.1. *Fish Seller,* Sin Yunbok, late eighteenth century. (National Museum of Korea)

The *seonsang* paid much more in taxes to the government because they carried more goods and transported them more rapidly than overland peddlers, who carried their goods on their backs, in bundles, or by cow or horse. The *haengsang* formed their own organizations, as did the *bobusang* in the nineteenth century, but they were not granted monopolies over certain products. The main motivation behind these organizations was to protect themselves from robbers and from damages caused by the rough condition of roads. The government issued travel authorization papers called *haengjang* to these organizations rather than to individual merchants. Compared to later eras, the *haengsang* had limited opportunities for growth. Similar to all merchants, *haengsang* made profits by buying goods cheaply and selling them at high prices. This was even more true for professional merchants who traveled long distances to sell regional goods. Their pursuit of large profits was risky since markets and commerce were not very developed. The situation changed with the emergence of markets and the development of port trade that, in turn, led to the rise of regional commercial centers in the country.

The Emergence of Markets

Markets had existed in the provinces before the *jangsi* first emerged at the end of the fifteenth century. During the Goryeo period, markets called *juhyeonsi* were opened at irregular intervals. As described in Song dynasty scholar Xu Jing's text *Gaoli tujing*,[2] people of all classes in a region, both high and low, gathered during the day near the local government office to trade goods. The emergence of *jangsi* at the end of the fifteenth century represented the next stage of development of these early markets.

The first rural markets emerged as a response to extreme economic hardship. Toward the end of the fifteenth century, a time of severe famine, people in Muan, Naju, and other areas of Jeolla province held markets in their towns twice a month where they traded for necessities. Known as *jangmun*, they were an effort to overcome the shortages caused by famine. This can be shown through the example of O Huimun, a yangban who took refuge in Imcheon in Chungcheong province during the Imjin War at the end of the sixteenth century. He exchanged rice and barley for dry goods; he also steamed rice cakes and brewed liquor to sell at the marketplace. A similar motivation was behind the opening of the first *jangsi* markets. These developments were possible because a variety of goods were being produced in sufficient quantities and because producers were relatively free to dispose of them as they wished. It is no coincidence that markets first emerged in the region of Naju and Muan in Jeolla province. It was a region abundant in grains and seafood because it was located near the western coast and had vast fields in Naju. In addition, in the second half of the fifteenth century, reclamation was completed of land that had

[2] *An Illustrated Account of Goryeo*; in Korean, *Goryeo dogyeong*.

Fig. 6.2. *Travelling Merchants*, Gim Hongdo, late eighteenth century. (National Museum of Korea)

been devastated by the intrusions of Japanese pirates, and agricultural productivity improved markedly.

Judging by their location, means of exchange, and schedule, it is clear that *jangsi* were fully functioning markets that served the interests of the producers. Most of the people dealing goods at the *jangsi* were farmers or artisans; instead of relying on traveling peddlers, they were able to to buy goods at a low price and re-sell them at a profit. Located within a day's walking distance (twelve to sixteen kilometers roundtrip) from a number of villages, the *jangsi* expanded significantly. The transactions were small in scale, paid for with surplus cloth or grain; later on, coins of small currency were used. The rural markets were held at fixed intervals. They did not become a permanent, full-time market because the main sellers were the producers themselves. They needed time to make the grains, woven goods, and other types of handicrafts that constituted the majority of goods sold at the markets. In addition, they were goods that customers did not need to buy everyday.

The emergence of markets rooted in the rural economy had an impact on the itinerant peddlers. While they continued to visit individual households, they became more dependent on the regularly occurring markets for their livelihood. While they could not enjoy the same huge profits they had in the past, peddlers could do more business because of the larger number of buyers assembled in one location. Over time, there was an increase in both the number of people making a profit and the tax revenues collected by the government as land accumulation by the landlord class forced a growing number of farmers off the land.

The Five-Day Market

First appearing in the latter half of the fifteenth century, *jangsi* gradually spread throughout the three southern provinces and Gyeonggi province. The growth of markets was particularly noticeable from the late seventeenth and early eighteenth centuries when the population of the country surged. Earlier, markets had operated in key military or administrative locations, but now they began to spread to mountain regions where villages underwent development through the efforts of peasants who engaged in slash-and-burn agriculture. The central government's attitude began to shift as well. It lifted its official ban on these markets and even utilized them as a way of gathering people. By the mid-eighteenth century, there were at least 1,000 markets operating regularly. The government remained concerned about the negative effects of markets. During the reign of Myeongjong in the mid-sixteenth century, it was reported that alternating market days among neighboring counties attracted thieves in droves. In Gyeonggi province, where *jangsi* were officially banned after the Hideyoshi invasions in the late sixteenth century, merchants nevertheless set up so many illicit markets that officials complained that goods were not reaching Seoul and the capital region. Because of these disruptions to official distribution networks and the rise in crime, the government became increasingly concerned about the growth of markets and the spread of unregulated markets.

Originally, rural markets were held every ten or fifteen days, but the interval between market days later became fixed at five days. Within a province, neighboring counties coordinated the days on which their markets were held. Each village had a market day every five days, but in the region as a whole, markets were open every day since villages alternated the days of market openings. According to Seo Yugu's *Imwon gyeongjeji*, a scholarly treatise on economic activities in his day, the markets in Chungcheong province, renowned throughout the country for its ramie cloth, were held in the town of Hongsan on the second and seventh days of the month, in Imcheon on the fifth and tenth days, in Hansan on the first and sixth days, in Biin on the third and eighth days, and in Nampo on the fourth and ninth days. For farmers, the five-day market system meant that there was an opportunity everyday to buy and sell at a nearby marketplace, even during the busiest harvest times. The ones who benefited the most were the traveling peddlers. They could spend all day in one market and then travel to the neighboring one the following day. By synchronizing their schedules with those of the markets in a region, peddlers could do business everyday. By the end of the Joseon period, regional markets had become institutionalized with fixed schedules coordinated with neighboring counties.

Though there was not a significant increase in the number of markets in the nineteenth century, commerce in the country became increasingly dominated by a few large markets. Gyeongsang and Jeolla provinces both developed markets relatively early. Even after the end of the eighteenth century, new markets continued to appear in remote areas in small-to-medium sized villages in the two regions. When large markets emerged in major transportation hubs or administrative centers, nearby smaller markets had to shut down or to change their days of operation. The large markets became the main distribution center for smaller markets and offered goods from other regions or countries. Each province had at least one large thriving market,[3] and there were several large markets in Gyeonggi province.[4] The Gyeonggi markets handled rice from the three southern provinces as well as wood products and fish from the east coast.

---

[3] For instance, Pyeongan province had the Jindu market in Bakcheon; the Jeonju county market was a major commercial center in Jeolla province; and Chungcheong province had the Deokpyeon market in Jiksan.

[4] These included Sapyeong market in Gwangju, Songpa market, Anseong county market, and Gongneung market in Gyoha.

Fig. 6.3. Jar Sellers, 1903.

The Joys and Sorrows of the Jangdolbaengi

The development of a countrywide network of markets was the result of improvements in transportation and the efforts of peddlers who travelled around the countryside. The following lyrics from a folk song are an accurate description of their way of life.

Wrap cotton cloth around straw shoes, put on a bamboo hat
Strap on straw shoes on the waist
Running to this and that market
Greeting fellow peddlers
Exchanging all kinds of gossip
Shouting loudly

Through rain or snow
Peddling wares until sundown
Shaking hands and taking leave
Let's meet again tomorrow at the next market

As depicted in the song, the peddlers spent their lives going from market to market – the literal meaning of the terms *jangdolbaengi* or *jangdollim*. They kept an extra pair of straw sandals strapped to their waists as they traveled; after a market closed, they would agree to meet their fellow peddlers at another market the next day.

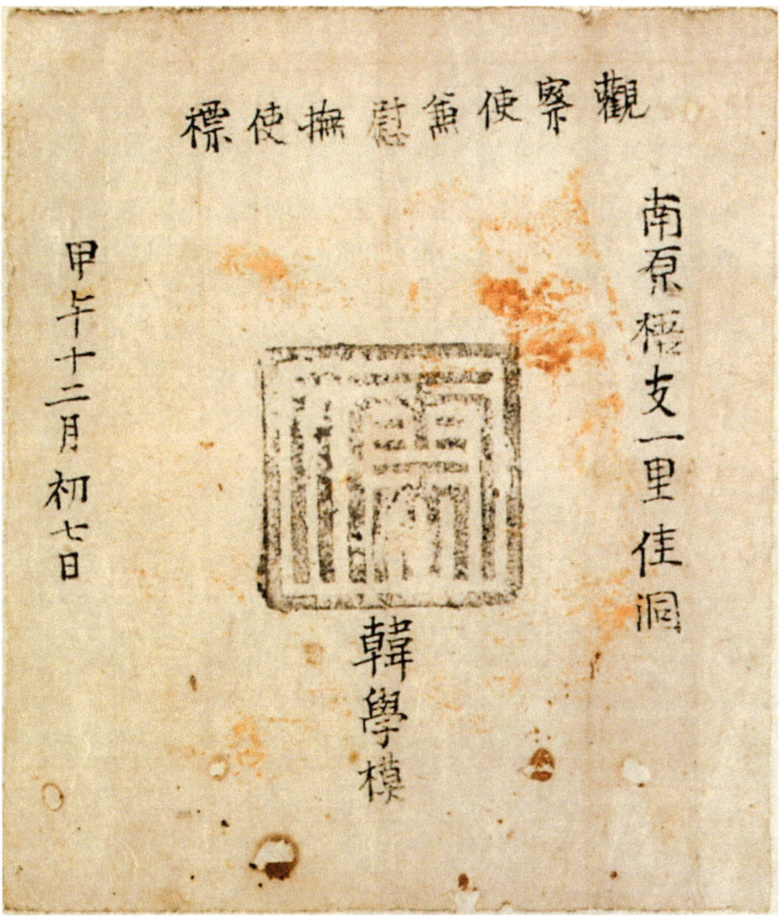

Fig. 6.4. Travel Document, 1894. Issued by the Jeolla provincial magistrate to Han Hakmo of Namwon.

The goods they carried included various grains and high-priced items such as cotton and ramie cloth, paper goods, metalware, and leather goods. They also sold a variety of bulky but inexpensive daily necessities such as salt, dried fish, ironware, plates, and wood or bamboo utensils. After the Treaty of Gangwha (1876) opened the country's markets, peddlers began selling imported foreign goods as well. For transport, some used boats or cattle, and others traveled by foot, using backpacks and A-frames to carry their goods. Regular contact led to a sense of familiarity and closeness among the local populace they served. Peddlers stayed overnight at inns where they could get food, change their straw sandals, and prepare for the next day. The inns were located along major roadways, and eventually whole communities emerged to serve the travelers.

Peddlers spent much of their lives on the road. One example is the merchants of Gaeseong, the former capital of Goryeo, who operated large businesses and had connections with high-ranking officials. While some merchants were able to travel around the nearby villages and return after five days, there were many who left at the start of the year and did not return until the end. This is corroborated by the fact that many babies in the city were born in the same month. During the Joseon period, the number of major roads in the country increased from six to seven and then to ten. Originally used for administrative and military purposes, they now became increasingly commercial in nature. In the Yeongnam region, a new road connected Joryeong and Juknyeong, and mountain passes were built between Cheongju and Sangju and between Gwesan and Mungyeong (Ihwayreong Road). In Hamgyeong province, a new road crossing Cheollyeong Pass to Seoul was built, along with various shortcuts that criss-crossed the province such as Sambang Road and Seolunnyeong Road. Feeder roads connecting the major routes enabled fish such as pollack from Hamgyeong province to be sold in Hwanghae, Pyeongan, Gangwon provinces. Similarly, the growth of commerce also led to the development of water routes. New ports and structures made it much easier to navigate the treacherous waters on the west coast of the country, such as those near the Taean peninsula in South Chungcheong province.

Many of the *jangdolbaenggi* earned very little. Those who sold more expensive products such as cloth or leather goods were relatively better off than those selling cheap goods such as dried fish, salt, and wood products. Some had no permanent home and traveled with their families as they peddled their wares. When males and females had to share the same room, they slept with a screen placed between them. As expressed in the following song, they traveled all around the country without anyone to nurse them if they were sick or bury them if they died.

> As I travel here and there with this heavy pack on my back,
> in the morning toward the East, in the evening toward the West,
> if I get sick, there is no one to care for me.
> People trample over me, and others collect taxes.
> If I hide, I become crow's food,
> How sad – why are our lives so difficult?
>
> (from 'A Prayer for Old Age')

With the exception of the large merchants of Gaeseong or Seoul, most *jangdolbaengi* were very small-scale operators whose profits were taken by the royal family, powerful families, and government officials and by *gaekju* and *yeogak* who controlled the distribution of goods. They later voiced their discontentment during the Gabo Peasants War of 1894. Itinerant peddlers demanded the abolition of taxes collected at the *jangsi* and the prohibition of the corrupt practices of the *bobusang*, freight boat owners, and wholesale merchants.

7. FOREIGN TRADE AND INTERPRETER OFFICIALS

Kim Kyung-ran

The Richest Man in Seoul

> Master Heo lived in Mukjeokgol at the foot of Mount Nam. He was content just to read books, while his wife barely eked out a living by selling embroidery. One day, his wife, crying from pangs of hunger, said to him, "Husband, you've never even taken the civil service examination, so why are you even bothering with such reading?…If you don't like to be a craftsman or a merchant, how about trying to become a thief?" Thus, Master Heo had no choice but to put down his books and go outside, but looking around, he knew no one. He went to Jongno Intersection and asked each vendor he met, "Hello, who is the richest person in Seoul?" In good time, someone mentioned the name of Mr. Byeon. Master Heo finally found Mr. Byeon's home. Upon meeting him, he said, "My family is poor, and I'd like to try something. I've come to borrow a large amount of money." Mr. Byeon said, "Okay" and promptly gave him the money. But Master Heo just left without saying a word of thanks.

This passage is taken from Bak Jiwon's (1737–1805) 'The Tale of Master Heo,' a story about a fallen yangban who seeks the richest man in Seoul to acquire the capital to start a business. Who was this Mr. Byeon, who lent a huge sum of money to a pathetic-looking scholar without giving it a second thought? Though 'The Tale of Master Heo' is a work of fiction, Bak's novels are thought to be a faithful reflection of their time. Since the main characters within the story were portrayed realistically, it is possible that they were based on actual people, especially the character who was the 'richest person in Seoul.' He seems to have been based on Byeon Seungeop, an interpreter official (*yeokgwan*) who lived during the reign of Sukjong (r. 1674–1720).

Byeon Seungeop (1623–1709) was an interpreter of Japanese. He belonged to the *jungin* class whose status was lower than that of the yangban but higher than that of commoners. They were generally lower-level functionaries who specialized in technical fields such as medicine, law, astronomy, and geography, as well as interpreting. Byeon was from a famous interpreter family; his father was Byeon Eungseong, and five of his siblings also were translators. The family seems to have become wealthy during his father's generation, and by the time Byeon Seungeop grew up, they were regarded as one of the richest families in Seoul. When Byeon's wife died in 1696, he caused a stir by lacquering her face – something that was done only for kings. To quell the outcry, he paid hundreds of thousands of gold coins to high-ranking officials at court. Toward the end of his life, when his money lending amounted to 500,000 *nyang* of silver, he began to give money away so that his descendants would not suffer any trouble because of his loans. These facts provide a glimpse into the extent of Byeon Seungeop's wealth.

How was it possible for an interpreter like Byeon Seungeop to become one of the richest people in Seoul with a fortune greater than that of the most successful merchants? The answer can be found in the nature of trade during the Joseon period and the special trading rights enjoyed by interpreters.

Trade in the Joseon Period

International trade in the early Joseon era was mainly conducted through the tributary system. The term 'tributary system' refers to the unique structure of diplomatic relations in pre-modern East Asia. Countries neighboring China regularly sent envoys to China to present tribute goods to the emperor. In return for tribute, China bestowed gifts on them. Through the exchange of tribute and gifts, China's neighbors satisfied their need for trade. Ming China established relations with neighboring countries based on the principles of *sadae* (serving the great) and *gyorin* (neighborly friendship) by granting them investiture. The only exchange it would permit was the officially sanctioned trade conducted by governments through the tribute system. Thus, the level of trade among the East Asian countries, in terms of both frequency and volume, was relatively low.

The nature of trade in the region began to change in the sixteenth century. China adopted a silver-based currency system, and commerce and industry developed, leading to the production of goods such as silk, cotton, and ceramics. Also, earlier European geographic discoveries brought European merchants to China and led to the spread of Chinese goods even to Europe. With the expansion of markets and the growth of non-official trade, China could no longer cling to the tribute-based trade system. Another turning point in East Asian trade was the outbreak of the Imjin War in 1592. From the year 1593, in the midst of the war with Japan, Joseon conducted trade with China at Junggang (Nanja Island in the Amnok River) to obtain warhorses and supplies for famine relief. Due to severe food shortages, there were many regions where it was difficult to exchange one *pil* of cotton for one *mal* of unhulled grain, but in Junggang, it could purchase around twenty *mal* of rice. Traders dealing in silver, copper, and cast iron are estimated to have made a profit of ten times over the original price. Junggang developed into the first international market (*gaesi*), and from the seventeenth century, international markets were opened in places such as Hoeryeong, Gyeongwon, and Zhamen (K. Chaengmun) as the government sanctioned trade at these locations. The emergence of these markets was not the only sign of the growth of trade. Private trade

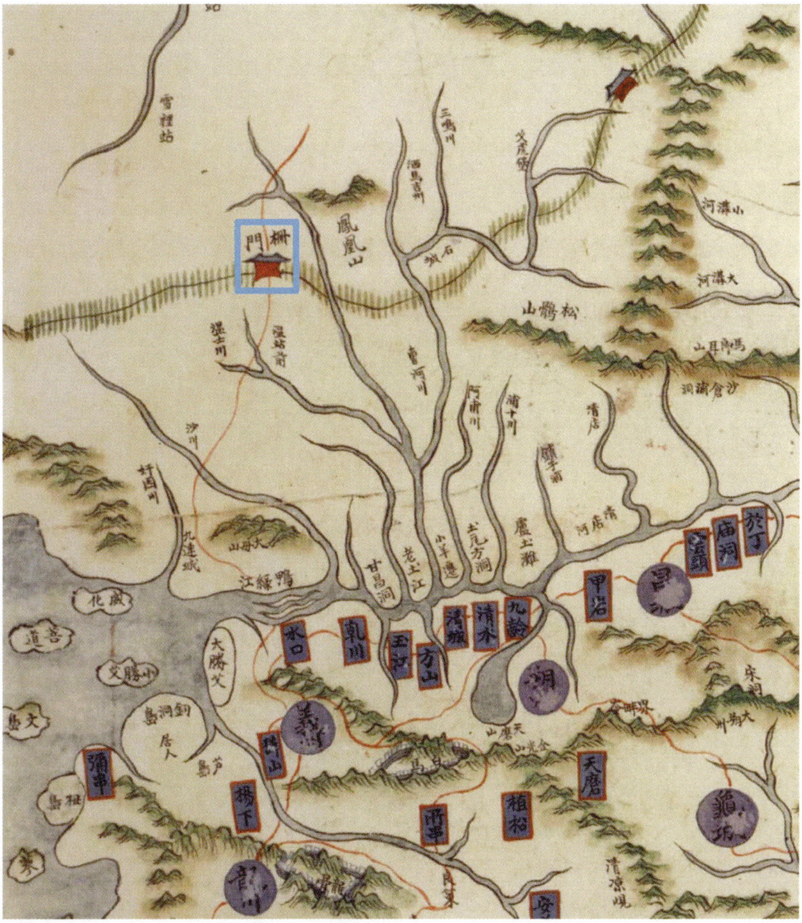

Map 7.1. *Haedong jido* (Map of Joseon), mid eighteenth century. The blue rectangle indicates the location of the Zhamen international market. (Kyujanggak Institute for Korean Studies)

was also conducted on a large scale in markets called *husi.* Merchants from both countries actively engaged in trade since the markup on goods ranged from ten to twenty times the original cost. The official trade in tribute goods gradually lost ground to the vibrant private trade.

Fig. 7.1. *Japan House* (Waegwando), Byeon Bak, eighteenth century. (National Museum of Korea)

Trade also began to increase with Japan, its other main trading partner. Joseon had broken off relations with Japan because of the Imjin War, but after Japan returned its prisoners of war, relations between the two countries were restored in 1609. Trade also resumed through Japan House (Waegwan), gradually increasing in volume. Joseon played the role of a middleman, exporting silk and thread imported from China and receiving silver from Japan as payment. This intermediary trade provided Joseon a profit of at least three times the original purchase price. Some people were able to take advantage of the increase in trade and amass tremendous amounts of wealth. There were private merchants who were involved in the *husi* trade, but the central figures were interpreters, such as the character of Byeon Seungeop in 'The Tale of Master Heo.'

The Rise of Merchant Interpreters

Interpreters were important officials who were indispensable to the conduct of Joseon's diplomacy. They accompanied envoys to China and other countries, and when foreign envoys arrived in Joseon, they interpreted for the king and his ministers. Taking advantage of their position, they openly engaged in trade and were called *sangyeok* (merchant interpreters). *Sangyeok* became the official term used by government officials who looked down on the trading activities of interpreters, particularly their smuggling. To become an official interpreter, it was necessary to pass the *yeokgwa* civil service examination. From the beginning of the Joseon period, it was offered every three years, as were the examinations for civil and military officials. There were additional opportunities to take the *yeokgwa* when the government held special examinations to celebrate an auspicious event. In the late Joseon period, additional civil service examinations were held often in addition to the regularly scheduled ones. The number of interpreters in the Sayeogwon (Training Center for Interpreters) increased to around 600 in Sukjong's reign (1674–1720). But the government actually only needed fifty or sixty of them.

Interpreters became involved in trade because the government was unable to pay all of them a salary. There was not enough work for all passers of the *yeokgwa* examination, but the government feared that the conduct of diplomacy would suffer if they abandoned their profession. As a temporary solution, the government created a rotation system for interpreters. A number of people would take turns performing the duties of a single post and share the salary. This system was an attempt to utilize all

Fig. 7.2. *Procession of Envoys* (Tongsinsa haengnyeoldo), probably seventeenth century. The official on the second horse behind the litter is an interpreter (*yeokgwan*). Painting of a diplomatic mission to Japan in 1636. (National Museum of Korea)

passers of the examination and prevent them from turning to other occupations. However, because the amount that they received was insufficient to make a living, they had to find their own way to supplement their income. From the early Joseon period, it was common for interpreters to trade goods secretly on their trips abroad. Having failed to solve all problems with the rotation system, the Joseon government allowed interpreters to bring a certain amount of goods with them and officially permitted them to engage in private trade within certain limits. It was a kind of compensation for the flaws of the rotation system.

Intermediary Trade with Qing China and Japan

How much trade was conducted by the interpreters, and what kinds of goods did they take with them? Let's examine the case of the interpreters of Manchurian who traveled frequently to the Qing capital of Beijing. The main product that they handled was ginseng. It was valuable since it was popular in China for its medicinal uses and could be sold at a high price.

This trade was commonly known as *palpo* trade. Ginseng roots would be grouped into bundles of ten called *po*, and the term *palpo* referred to a set of eight of these bundles. In other words, they could trade up to eighty roots of ginseng. The *palpo* quota did not limit interpreters to selling ginseng. Supplies were insufficient to satisfy even domestic demand since wild ginseng had to be gathered, and its cultivation was not possible until the early eighteenth century. From the mid-seventeenth century, one root of ginseng was valued at twenty-five *nyang*; the quota was set at the equivalent of eighty roots of ginseng or 2,000 *nyang*. This amount was equal to several thousand *seok* of rice – an indication of the high volume of private trade that translators engaged in. The amount of their trade would sometimes exceed the *palpo* quota. Each government office in Seoul was also allowed to trade goods up to the *palpo* limit, and interpreters handled this trade for them. This was the so-called *byeolpo* trade. With the profits from the *byeolpo* trade, they were able to earn more than they were officially allowed through private trade.

In addition to interpreters, there were some wealthy merchants who participated in private trade, both legally and illegally. They paid money to government offices to become their trade official. As private trade became more active, the potential for corruption increased, and Qing officials began to demand bribes. The government provided the silk presented to the Qing court, but the merchants and interpreters had to provide the funds for bribes. As the amount of the bribes increased, the government helped them to acquire funds in order to maintain friendly relations with China. The government directed government offices to lend its silver to interpreters for this purpose; this was called 'public-use silver.' It provided a legal channel for interpreters to borrow funds from government offices for their trading activities.

With these privileges, interpreters were able to accumulate enormous wealth during the seventeenth century. One of the most profitable businesses seems to have been the intermediary trade between China and Japan. Since Japan did not have diplomatic relations with Qing, no envoys travelled between the two countries, and because of Qing's prohibition of maritime commerce, no trading vessels did as well. Japan could import Qing goods only through Japan House, which was located in Joseon territory in Dongnae. In Japan, demand for Qing silk and silk thread was growing rapidly at the time. The interpreters and merchants engaged in unofficial foreign trade imported silk and thread from China and exported them to Japan. Interpreters specializing in Japanese sent by the Sayeogwon

Fig. 7.3. *Songchao tianke guiguo shizhang* (detail), Chinese painting depicting Ming officials sending off Joseon envoys on their journey back to their country. (National Museum of Korea)

were the leading figures in the trade at Japan House. By working through these colleagues, interpreters were easily able to sell goods imported from Qing. Exports to Japan amounted to tens of thousands of *nyang*; at its height, its value reached around one million *nyang*. Trade was so profitable that exported goods were sold at two to three times the import cost. In fact, Byeon Seungeop, the model for the character from the Bak Jiwon story mentioned at the beginning of this chapter, was an interpreter of Japanese. The fact that he was thought to be the richest man in Seoul is an indication of how much money could be made through the intermediary trade conducted at Japan House.

The Decline of Trade by Interpreters

During the seventeenth century, interpreters were able to accumulate tremendous wealth, and their trade acted as a stimulus to the domestic economy. One consequence of the intermediary trade was a large influx of silver into Joseon. The circulation of silver currency increased, and coins came to be used as a supplemental form of currency. Foreign trade also stimulated the development of domestic agriculture, handicraft industries, and commerce and thus played an important role in promoting the growth of markets within the country.

The interpreters who engaged in intermediary trade suffered a heavy blow to their business in the early eighteenth century. When Qing China and Japan restored diplomatic relations, direct trade also resumed between them. China set up a trading house in Nagasaki, and the silk and thread that had been obtained through Japan House were now brought to Japan on Chinese and Dutch ships. The intermediary trade that had generated such large profits for Joseon interpreters now began to decline. In addition, the Joseon government banned the import of silk and thread, the major products of the intermediary trade; it even forbade government offices from lending silver for use in trade. Because of these changes, interpreters were no longer as actively engaged in trade as before. However, this did not mean that Joseon's foreign trade became stagnant. As the role of interpreters decreased, smuggling by domestic merchants from Gaeseong, Uiju, and other places became prevalent, and trade even increased compared to earlier periods. Private merchants gradually increased the volume of their trade through the *husi* markets that emerged after the closure of the *gaesi* international markets in Junggang and Zhamen where official trade had been conducted. Imported through the smuggling of private merchants, goods reached not just cities but also households in remote villages through their merchant associations. With the loss of the domestic market, interpreters came into conflict with private merchants, and they gradually lost their dominant position in trade.

8. SALT: WHITE GOLD

Kim Eui-Hwan

Korean food is known for being spicy, but it also contains a lot of salt. South Koreans ingest fifteen to twenty grams of it a day, more than two to three times the World Health Organization's recommended amount of six grams per day. Seasoned foods such as kimchi, soy sauce, hot pepper paste, and salted fish all have a high salt content as do the instant foods that are so popular today. Not surprisingly, the incidence of related diseases is high in Korea, including heart attacks, osteoporosis, stomach cancer, and 'silent killers' such as high blood pressure and strokes. Koreans now are very interested in healthy foods and are trying to reduce their salt intake.

Today, salt is so commonplace that it can be bought in supermarkets and found in homes all over the world. In the past, however, salt was a precious commodity that was difficult to produce. In ancient Rome, the price of salt was so high that soldiers were paid in salt rather than grain or money; in fact, the word 'salary' comes from the Latin word *salarium* whose origin is the word 'salt.' The Chinese characters for the word salt (素金, *sogeum*) include the character for gold (*geum*). In other words, salt was regarded as 'white gold.' In the Joseon era, salt was also a valuable commodity and a major concern in the lives of the people. It had long been known that salt intake was essential to human health; for instance, King Sejong would drink salt broth when he was ill. The government also regarded salt as a key resource in the administration of the country. This chapter discusses the production and distribution of salt in the period, as well as its economic and political importance.

The Importance of Salt

During prehistoric times, people ingested salt by eating clams, oysters, shrimps, fishes, and animals that they hunted. As agriculture developed and grains and vegetables became staple foods in the Neolithic Era, salt deficiency gradually became a problem, and it became increasingly necessary to ingest salt by other means. As a result, from olden times, there was a custom in inland regions of drinking the blood of animals and livestock that were killed since blood was regarded as important as meat as a source of salt. From the ancient period, human settlements expanded from coastal regions and riverbanks into inland regions, and agricultural production increased. In the process, demand for salt increased, and salt production began in earnest. Up to the Joseon period, salt was always valuable in inland regions far from the coast. The Jurchen people were originally from Ninguta (today's Ning'an) in Manchuria, a region that did not produce salt. They would cross the border and capture Joseon officers and soldiers, demanding salt in exchange for their return. Such incidents occurred repeatedly since acquiring salt was a matter of life or death to the Jurchens. In the late Joseon period, soldiers stationed in Samsu and Gapsan in Hamgyeong province took salt, rather than grain, to exchange for money to cover the cost of their military service.

Salt was used in Korea for pickling radishes and other vegetables to make kimchi. The use of red pepper powder in making kimchi started only in the late Joseon period. At the time, frequent rainfall decreased salt production, causing prices to rise dramatically. People began to use red pepper to reduce the amount of salt used and to preserve the kimchi for a long time. Salt was also used in making sauces and pastes and in storing and processing fish, and it was used in relief efforts in times of severe famine after a bad harvest. People suffered from swelling because they ate pine needles, pine bark, and plant roots instead of grain. Salt was useful because it counteracted the toxins in them. When palaces and temples were built, floors of buildings would be covered in salt in order to reduce moisture and repel harmful insects.

How Was Salt Made?

Koreans are sometimes surprised to learn that salt is mined like coal in places near the Himalaya Mountains, such as Nepal, or in the middle of a desert in Africa. That is because we think of salt as only being produced in the ocean. Salt mining in Poland began in the thirteenth century, and today, a famous tourist attraction is a cathedral near Krakow, complete with decorative details, carved within a former salt mine. The formation of rock salt began when salt settled on ocean floors; many years later, land or mountains would be created through changes in the earth's crust. In the process, salt would be formed into rocks. In China, salt was made from wells in Sichuan province and from saltwater lakes in Shanxi province. In Korea, salt was produced by evaporating seawater in salt kettles.

Koreans started producing salt from seawater long ago when agricultural cultivation began and human settlements moved to inland regions.

The method of production at the time is still not fully known today. It is thought that people collected salt that formed naturally along the seashore or made salt by placing seawater in pots and boiling off the water. At the end of the Unified Silla period, there was a technological advance in salt production. The first step was to create a salt field and evaporate seawater; the result was concentrated saltwater that would then be boiled to produce salt. If seawater, which has three percent salt content, were boiled directly, the process would consume much fuel, and the yield would be very low. Creating salt fields and evaporating seawater increased the salt concentration before the water was boiled down. However, even in the Goryeo period, the use of salt fields was limited to a few regions in the south and west coasts of the country.

In the Joseon era, the method of salt production differed according to the region. Making salt fields was easy along the southern and western coasts where tidal flats were developed and where there was a large difference in water level between high and low tide. Salt fields without embankments were made in the shape of a truncated cone, and salt wells were built to collect the concentrated saltwater. This was the primary method used on the west coast of Korea. Another method was common on the south coast, as well as parts of the west coast. Cows with harrows were used to upturn the ground of salt fields two or three times a day after the seawater receded during the waxing and waning phases of the moon. The soil of the tidal flat was exposed to sunlight, creating salty earth containing grains of sand covered in salt crystals. After seawater covered the salt fields and receded, they would be plowed again, increasing the salt content of the soil. A device called a *deongipan* was used to break up the soil into fine pieces so that salt would stick better to it. After repeating the process several times, the salty soil was then packed with a soil leveler (*narae*) around a salt well (*ungdeongi*) 1.5 meters deep located in the middle of the salt field. Seawater was brought in again; when the soil filled with salt crystals was covered, concentrated salt water gathered in containers. People used yokes to move the saline water, which would have a salt concentration of fifteen to eighteen percent, to salt huts to protect it from wind and rain. The saline water was then put in salt pots made of iron or seashells and boiled to make salt. These salt wells were also called *tongjarak* in Chungcheong province and *seotdeung* in Jeolla province.

Along the east coast of Korea, it was difficult to make salt fields since there were no tidal flats. People put seawater in kettles and boiled it to produce salt. Some regions in the east used another type of salt field that was artificially created using clay soil and was shaped into a grid. After clay soil was spread on the floor of the salt field, people used gourds to pour seawater onto it several times to infuse the soil with salt. Saltwater was poured on once again, and then the saline water was collected and boiled to make salt. This method was also used in Japan and Indonesia.

Salt was produced mainly during the spring and autumn when rain was infrequent. Even then, it was only possible during the twelve days each month when the moon was in its waxing and waning phases. The amount of salt that could be produced was limited, and its price was very high, more than half the price of rice. Since salt production was very dependent on the weather, people felt that it was "in the hands of Heaven." People had to do arduous work all day under a hot sun to make salt; it was so difficult that serious criminals were sentenced to roast salt as punishment. To make the work more bearable, there were folk songs and games related to salt.

The tools used to make salt in the south and west coasts differed from those used in the east coast. When salt was made by boiling seawater, the heat had to be at a very high temperature. Iron pots were used since earthenware pots made with oyster and clam shells could crack easily. People in the south and west did occasionally use earthenware pots since concentrated saline water could be boiled at lower temperatures, but iron pots were generally used since they were more durable. For firewood, tree

Fig. 8.1. Farmers using a harrow in a salt field. (Photograph by the author)

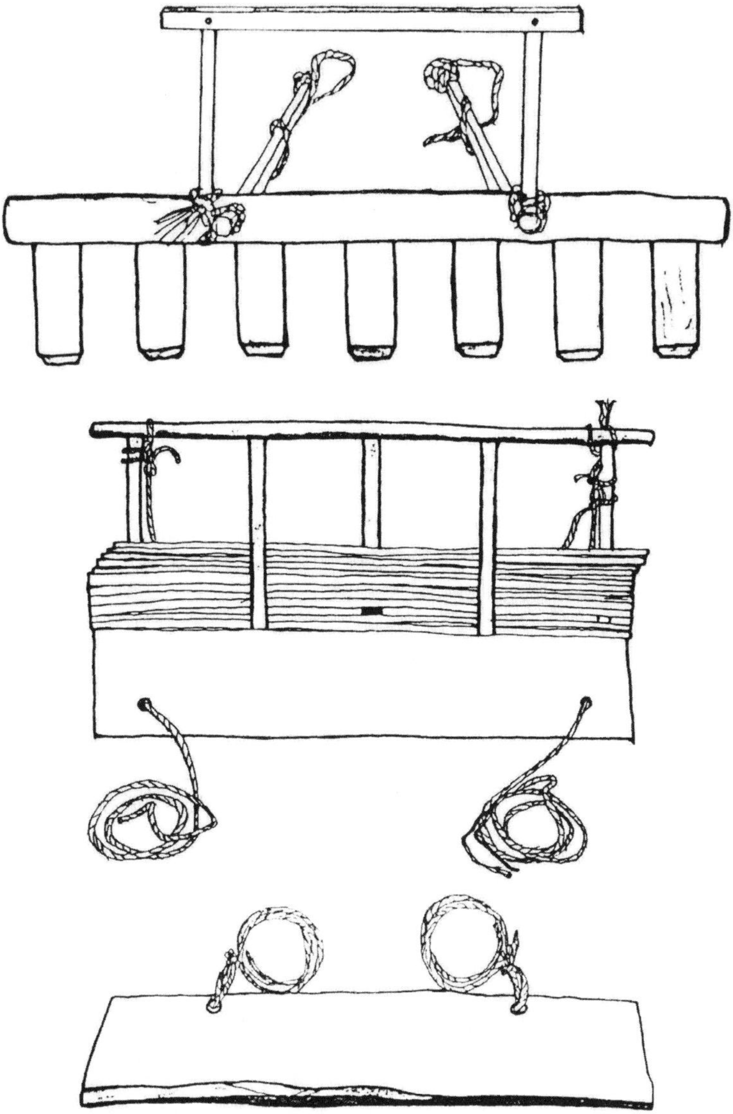

Fig. 8.1. (*Cont.*) Harrow (*sseore*) (top); Soil Leveler (*narae*) (middle); *Deongipan* (bottom).

branches and plants were used with earthenware pots, and pine, which burned at a higher temperature, was used with iron pots.

The methods of salt making remained largely unchanged until the late Joseon era. From the seventeenth century, productivity increased significantly with the development of salt fields that used embankments.

Fig. 8.2. *Tongjarak* (photo, left); *Hamsutong* (right). (Photograph by the author)

This new method first appeared in places such as Yeongheung and Muncheon in Hamgyeong province and in Myeongji Island in the Gimhae region. An embankment enabled people to make salt when the moon was not in its waxing and waning phases, even without a large difference between high and low tide. But this method produced, at most, only five *seom* per salt pot per day, and at least five people were needed to handle each pot. The cost of labor and fuel was so high that it amounted to over two-thirds the total cost of production. In the nineteenth century, salt remained an expensive commodity comparable in value to gold. Salt production began to modernize its methods in the year 1907. It underwent a major transformation with the shift to producing sun-dried salt that had twenty-percent mineral content. There is even a monument commemorating the new process in the city of Incheon.[1] Sun-dried salt is now on the verge of disappearing because of excessive land reclamation and the import of cheap foreign salt. Salt is now made by electrolysis; seawater is passed through an ion exchange membrane to produce salt that is ninety-eight percent pure.

How Was Salt Distributed?

Salt produced on the coasts was transported over land and water routes, reaching even remote inland regions. The path from producer to consumer was a long journey sometimes hundreds of miles long. Merchants traveled from seas, rivers, and major inland areas to markets and even remote mountain regions to sell salt, carrying their goods by boat, A-frame, and on their backs. One example was King Micheon (?–331) of Goguryeo, who worked as a salt peddler before becoming king. Throughout the country, there are many places with names related to salt, such as Yeompo, Yeomchang, and Yeomti – all containing the Chinese character for salt, *yeom*.

While coastal regions were the centers of salt production, the center of salt distribution was the capital. From the seventeenth century, Seoul developed into a major commercial city with the development of maritime trade. Places such as Mapo and Yongsan became more than a shipping hub and developed into a distribution center for the entire country. Salt, grains, fish, and other products from all over the country were brought by boat to the Gyeong River near Seoul and then sent out again. Provincial ports, linked to nearby markets, became local distribution centers that handled salt, grain, and other products. In the second half of the eighteenth century, *yeogaek* owners in port areas acted as middlemen in salt distribution. For their services, they charged a portion of the price of the commodity or collected five *pun* or one *jeon* per *seom* of salt. They had the right to handle the distribution of commodities such as salt. This right could be sold, inherited, and transferred, and its price could exceed 400 *nyang*.

---

1 The monument is located in Simjeong-dong, Bupyeong-gu.

Fig. 8.3. *Salt Seller* (Sogeum jangsa), Gim Jungeun (aka Gisan), late nineteenth century. (© Musée Guimet, Paris, Dist. RMN-Grand Palais)

During the Joseon period, the merchant houses called *sijeon* dominated commerce in Seoul. The government gave them monopoly rights over specific products in return for handling certain duties. The merchant houses that had a monopoly over the sale of salt were called *yeomjeon*. Some of the major salt merchants in Seoul were the Gyeongyeomjeon, Mapo Yeomjeon, and Yongsan Yeomjeon. They came from diverse social backgrounds, including many unfree people (*nobi*) of powerful families and palace estates as well as many commoners. There were also yangban and other wealthy families that used the profits from making and selling salt to buy up land, becoming large landlords. Prominent examples include the Bak family of Namyang, the Yi family of Seosan, and the Mun family and the Cheon family of Amtae Island. When the salt business generated large profits, armies such as the Hullyeon Dogam sold salt through unlicensed private merchants, and merchants houses competed with each other for the rights to handle and sell salt. The *yeomjeon* in Seoul purchased large amounts of salt from Hwanghae province and other salt-producing regions and had it transported to Seoul by boat. *Yeogaek* owners then delivered it to the *yeomjeon*. The merchant houses handled the sale of salt to consumers. They could set the price however they wished; they generally sold salt at a price of one to two *jeon* for one *seom* of salt and sometimes charged even higher prices. Utilizing their monopoly position, the merchant house sometimes set the price of salt at less than half the market price. If merchants did not follow suit, the merchant house would prevent them from selling salt. To avoid the interference of the merchant house, merchants gave government offices such as the Royal Treasury a share of their profits in return for protection. To resolve this situation, the government allowed merchants to sell salt freely if they paid a fixed tax to the salt merchant house. The monopoly of the salt merchant houses lasted until the Sinhae Tonggong reform of 1791 during Jeongjo's reign.

In the late Joseon period, one *seom* of salt generally cost around two to three *nyang* which was half the price of rice. In years when heavy rainfall decreased salt production, the price rose to over four or five *nyang*. Salt was most expensive during the spring, when it was needed for famine relief efforts, and during the rainy season in the months of July and August. Salt merchants made their profits not only by transporting salt over long distances but also through seasonal price fluctuations. Along the Nakdong River, the local military office (*tongyeong*) forbade merchants from selling salt and monopolized the business for itself. This caused many problems, including an increase in the price to over ten *nyang*. When salt was transported from downstream to upstream areas to be sold, merchants made a profit of as much as five to six times its price.

The distribution of salt also had important cultural effects. Salt sellers communicated news from other regions and played a role in spreading culture; occasionally, they also became involved in romances, as depicted in literary works. In addition, Andong salted mackerel, a dish popular today, was created when people began salting fish being transported from the southern coast to prevent it from spoiling.

Salt and State Finances

The Chinese character for salt, pronounced *yeom* in Korean, is a compound made up of the characters for 'subject,' 'saltwater,' and 'dish.' The elements of the character suggest that salt was subject to control by the state. From the beginning of salt production, governments in both the East and the West have tried to establish control over it because of the tremendous profits it could generate in a relatively short period of time. In the past, it was said that the best way to make a country prosperous and to provide relief to the people was to make salt. For ancient states, salt was an important item of trade, along with iron, for the expansion of its military and economic influence. Those who controlled salt would become the main power group in the government.

Kingdoms in the Korean peninsula also devoted much effort to securing a supply of salt. Goguryeo subjugated the state of Okjeo on the eastern

Fig. 8.4. *Old Woman Selling Salt* (Maeyeompahaeng), Gim Hongdo, late eighteenth century. (National Museum of Korea)

coast of Korea to obtain salt and sea products. The fact that Okjeo people transported salt a distance of 1,000 *ri* to the Goguryeo capital shows how concerned Goguryeo was about acquiring salt. King Gwanggaeto (r. 391–413) also conquered Yanshuei, a salt-producing region in Manchuria, to increase the country's sources of salt. The Goryeo kingdom also placed much importance on salt. At the end of the Goryeo period, it considered collecting a tax on salt in order to replenish the state treasury. State finances had become depleted because of the tribute demands of Yuan China, and powerful aristocratic families and Buddhist temples owned the majority of farmland and salt fields in the country, monopolizing its profits. King Chungseon (r. 1298, 1308–1313) established a government monopoly over salt in order to improve state finances and to contain the influence of the powerful families.

During the Joseon era, the government's policy on salt underwent a number of changes. In the early Joseon period, individuals were generally allowed to own salt fields and to produce and sell salt. In return, the government collected a fixed amount of tax from the producers. Towards the end of Sejong's reign, Joseon implemented a monopoly system to use salt revenues to purchase grain for famine relief. However, it was soon abolished because it actually caused severe shortages. The government's policy at the time entrusted the production of salt to expert salt makers and its distribution to merchants, regulating the system by levying taxes. The Ministry of Taxation used salt tax revenues to acquire grain and weapons for the military.

Salt policy changed in the early sixteenth century after the de facto abolition of the Office Land System (*jikjeonbeop*) in 1556 and its complete abolition during the Imjin War (1592–1598). The government adopted a new land policy, called the *jeolsu* system, in an effort to help the economy recover from the destruction of the war. Much land had been abandoned, and the government granted people and institutions the right to reclaim a parcel of uncultivated land. Since the *jeolsu* system granted prebendal rights to salt fields to royal relatives and central government offices, little of the tax revenue from salt went into the state treasury. As the system expanded and the government's financial situation worsened, some called for its abolition and the return of prebendal rights to the state, but these efforts were not successful because of the power of entrenched interests. Prebendal rights had been given to people close to the king, and they received tremendous benefits from them. In the second half of the seventeenth century, the government prohibited existing palace estates from accumulating more land under the *jeolsu* system and limited new palace estates to three parcels of land. The system was completely abolished when the Equal-Service Law (Gyunyeokbeop) was put into effect in 1750, and prebendal rights were returned to the Office of Equal Service.

In the late Joseon period, the government regulated salt production not through granting monopolies but by levying taxes. It would have been difficult for them to operate and maintain the facilities needed to make and sell salt directly. There was also the danger of saturating the market for salt. During the Joseon period, there were only a few years when the government established a state monopoly over salt; for most of the period, high-level government offices and the palace estates of royal relatives and in-laws had the rights to collect taxes on salt.

The government turned to salt production when state revenues were insufficient, as happened at the end of the Goryeo period. When funds were urgently needed in the Joseon period, it established its own production facilities and used the profits to replenish the treasury. For example, during the Imjin War, it adopted the proposal of Yu Seongnyong (1542–1607) to establish salt fields, making and selling salt directly. The government also began salt production after the Manchu invasions to prepare tribute goods for Qing China. It established facilities to make salt from saltwater in places such as Seosan and Taean. It was so successful that salt revenues amounted to seven to eight percent of the Ministry of Taxation's budget. Salt was also utilized in times of famine. The country suffered many years of poor harvests when the government faced financial difficulties. It was necessary to find other ways to secure enough grain and salt to provide relief for the starving people. During Yeongjo's reign (1724–1776), the government established salt fields in Myeongji Island in the Gimhae region. They used seawater to make salt, and the revenues were used to purchase relief grain and to provide for other needs.

with Ellen Yuh

9. SEEKING WORK AT MINES

Oh Soo-chang

The Korean peninsula has been known for its mines since at least the Three Kingdoms period, but the exact origins of mining are unclear. As a very mountainous region, minerals can be found all over the country, but the best mines are concentrated in the north. Geography and climate dictated that the southern regions would be the center of agriculture with its fertile land and plentiful rainfall. The mountainous northern regions did not have much arable land, and rainfall was not sufficient to enable proper irrigation of paddy fields. However, the north was active in commerce and mining with mountains rich in copper, gold, and iron. In the late nineteenth century, foreign powers sought to extract mining concessions from the government. The Unsan mine in North Pyeongan province was granted to an American concern in 1895, later developing into one of the world's leading producers of gold. Mining continues to be a major industry in North Korea today, producing important minerals such as magnesite, tungsten, and zinc. This chapter provides a brief overview of the development of mining in the Joseon period and also examines the lives of the various people who worked in the mines. Initially tightly regulated by the government, the mining industry gradually became dominated by investors who provided capital and hired workers who received wages for their labor. During the end of the eighteenth and the first half of the nineteenth century, it transformed into an industry based on capitalist principles.

A Brief History of Mining

In the early Joseon period, the government's policy was to discourage gold and silver mining. The peasantry was also opposed to mining since they would be forced to do difficult labor without receiving any benefits. They bribed government officials and technical experts to submit false reports that their regions had no gold. Magistrates and local officials were also reluctant to develop mines because of the added obligations they would entail and the stiff resistance of the peasantry. The Great Code of 1469 (Gyeongguk daejeon) prohibited digging for gold and established regulations for its mining. In the fifteenth century, mining focused on iron ore rather than gold and silver; iron was used to produce daily necessities, weapons, and other metal goods. Mine workers did not work there by choice; the peasants residing near the mine were conscripted for compulsory labor. They had to extract ore, transport it, prepare firewood, and smelt the iron. Private mining production did exist, but it was strictly controlled and taxed.

Mining underwent gradual development over the succeeding centuries as the government loosened restrictions on it. When trade with China expanded in the sixteenth century, silver was needed to pay for the increased imports of silk. In addition to the official government mines, people engaged in illegal private mining of silver. In silver mining regions such as Dancheon in Hamgyeong province and nearby areas, independent miners emerged, having learned techniques when they worked as forced or paid labor in government mines. However, silver mining was still not a lucrative profession. Even in the reign of Jungjong in the sixteenth century, the residents of Dancheon did not have any fixed assets and were much poorer than other people in the province. In the seventeenth century, the government stopped direct management of mining operations, shifting to a system of indirect regulation through the collection of taxes. After the Manchu invasions in the seventeenth century, King Hyojong

Fig. 9.1. Unsan gold mine, early twentieth century.

advocated an invasion of Qing China, and the production of iron, sulfur, and wrought iron – all used to make military goods – increased. The most sought-after mineral in this period was still silver. In the middle of the century, the government opened silver mines in places such as Paju, Gyoha, Goksan, Chuncheon, and Gongju and levied taxes on them. By 1687, about seventy silver mines had been built across the country, and the largest one was the mine in Dancheon. Government authorities forced peasants in the surrounding area to work in the mines, and they did most of the work except for tasks such as digging or refining which, at the time, required specialists known as *jangin*.

The next stage of development came at the end of the seventeenth and the beginning of the eighteenth centuries, when the Ministry of Taxation took control of mining; particularly, lead and silver mines. The ministry had the authority to appoint merchants in Seoul as officials called *byeoljang*, allowing them to open mines and collect taxes on them. The people in charge of the actual mining were called *jeomjang*, whose skills were more advanced than those of earlier mine workers. If they discovered a deposit of silver ore, they would notify the office in the capital. After a *byeoljang* was appointed to open the mine officially, workers called *yeongun* (lead miners) or *eungun* (silver miners) would gather in the area. Forced off their land, they were so unable to make a living that their names were not even recorded in household registers. They were more like wage laborers, receiving fixed wages either once a month or once a year. In the first half of the eighteenth century, it was said that hundreds or even thousands of workers gathered at the mines, depending on the size of the deposit.

At the end of the eighteenth century and the early nineteenth century, private mining began to emerge. Under the government's inefficient system of regulation, silver mining actually declined, but the development of gold mining, which was highly profitable, was very active. It became increasingly common for miners to be paid wages and to work together with their families.

Selling One's Labor to Survive

Who were the people who came to work in the mines? A good amount of information can be found in the texts produced in the aftermath of the Hong Gyeongnae rebellion of 1811–1812. Mine workers were generally poor peasants who had lost their farmland or were overwhelmed by famine.

Marginalized both socially and economically, they came from all over the country and worked as day laborers or peddlers. For example, Choe Dongi was a poor twenty-two year old merchant, who travelled throughout the region. Originally from Gaecheon, he came to a village in Unsan and worked for someone selling earthenware. During an average market day, he would sell four *jeon*, five *pun* worth of goods, netting him about one *jeon*. Lacking a household register or identification tag, he wandered around begging for food; he once went to Pyongyang and sold herring. One day, he took five *jeon* and went to a wealthy family's home to buy some grain, but the owner refused to sell to him. Out of spite, he robbed the house with his brothers and comrades after the outbreak of the Hong Gyeongnae Rebellion. He then reported the father and sons of the household to the government army, claiming that they were on the side of the rebels. Choe Intaek was forty-three years old and lived in Jindu, making his living ferrying people across the Daeryeong River. Gim Durisan was fifty years old and supported himself by carrying people's goods around the marketplace. Forty-three year old Yun Ibok was a poor commoner renting a room in someone else's house, while fifty-eight year old Sin Bongdeok was so poor that he volunteered to go mining. These people lacked the specialized skills and tools needed for mining; the only thing they possessed was the sheer labor of their bodies.

The people were paid one *nyang* in advance as wages. The people hiring laborers at the time convinced people that this amount would be enough for a family to survive for a month while the head of the family was away working in the mines. There were some like Yun Ibok who received as much as three *nyang* in advance. Yun later stated that in a time of famine, he could not pass up the opportunity to receive such a large sum. These laborers did not actually end up working in the mines. The ringleaders of the Hong Gyeongnae rebellion had spread false rumors that gold mines were opening in Unsan in an attempt to recruit troops for the insurrection. The people were taken to their base in Dabokdong and were used to support the troops undertaking a siege of Gasan and Bakcheon. Despite this deception, the fact that people flocked to the mines clearly shows how the poor people of Pyeongan province, unable to make a living on their farms, sold their labor in order to survive in the early nineteenth century.

The Lure of Mining

Gold collectors were in slightly better circumstances, as Bak Jiwon described in *Jehol Diary*. In 1780, when he went to China as part of an official mission, he traveled to Bakcheon in Pyeongan province. Along the road, he met many men and women carrying goods and bundles who were heading to the Seongcheon gold mine with their families. They carried the implements needed to harvest gold – chisels to dig through the ground, sacks to hold the dirt and stones mixed with gold, and baskets to sift out the dirt and pebbles. Even though the tools were rudimentary, they allowed families to work on their own and reap the rewards for themselves. Those who were unlucky would find only three or four grain-sized pieces of gold, but a lucky person could find more than ten. It was not very hard work to go through one sack of earth a day, but it could provide enough to eat; if one were extremely fortunate, a person could become rich instantly.

This kind of mining was more profitable than farming. Each day, a person could find at least six or seven *pun* worth of gold, which could be exchanged for two or three *nyang* of money. This amount could purchase a half *seok* of rice. By comparison, Choe Dongi, mentioned above, made one *jeon* selling goods all day at the marketplace (with one *nyang* equal to ten *jeon*). The prospect of such earnings drew not only large numbers of peasants who abandoned their farms but also all kinds of 'undesirables.' Another example is the gold mine in Seongcheon in Pyeongan province. It was said, with some exaggeration, that the mountain area was overflowing with rice and various goods and was crowded with more than 100,000 people as well as vendors selling everything from liquor to food, rice cakes to

Fig. 9.2. *Looking for Gold* (Geumjeom moyang), Gim Jungeun (Gisan), late nineteenth century. (© Musée Guimet, Paris, Dist. RMN-Grand Palais)

toffee. According to a 1780 report by Yu Uiyang, even at the time he was just a magistrate (*busa*), the Seongcheon mine produced about 20,000 *nyang* of gold in weight. This was equivalent to about 800,000 *nyang* in money.

The sudden growth of mining became a major concern for the government. In the second half of the eighteenth century, gold panning emerged in the Daedong and Cheongcheon river basins, drawing large numbers of peasants. Both silver and copper mining also underwent rapid development. Peasants were not only abandoning farming but also damaging the land, leading to a decline in agricultural production. Even a relatively progressive king such as Jeongjo implemented strict measures to force people to return to their villages. He was worried that the people at the mines were abandoning farming to seek an easier life and that mines were becoming hotbeds of crime. Another concern was that gold was flowing out to China. For the peasantry, however, the lure of mining went beyond the prospect of a high income; it was a type of economic activity where a person's earnings would be commensurate with one's effort and technical skill. At the end of the eighteenth century, King Jeongjo promulgated a series of measures to forbid gold mining but all ended in failure. The mining industry continued to grow, and the number of mining workers increased once again. In the first half of the nineteenth century, a government official noted, "People following profit is like water flowing downward. As long as such enormous profits exist, we cannot control the situation even if we forbid [mining] and beat them every day."

The Emergence of Private Mine Operators

Poor farmers and peddlers were not the only people at the mines. The types of people varied according to the time period. In the sixteenth century, the people who managed silver mines were officials sent by the central government. They commandeered peasants to work in the silver mines or worked through wealthy merchants to recruit laborers. In the seventeenth century, there were many mines that were operated by army bases; officials appointed by the government continued to manage the mines, but they were very different in nature. Familiar with the geological conditions of their regions, they were generally appointed to their posts in return for finding a deposit of ore, living in the mines that they operated. Though some had passed the military service examination or were officials in sinecure posts, most of them were ordinary commoners. Their goal was to rise in social status rather than simply to seek financial gain. From the end of the seventeenth century, the Ministry of Taxation was put in charge of lead and silver mines, acquiring the authority to appoint the mine operators. The nature of these managers began to change significantly. Wealthy merchants, seeking large profits, started to become involved in lead and silver mining. Using their connections with high-ranking officials, they got themselves appointed as officials by the Ministry of Taxation and became mine operators. In return for building a mine and collecting taxes, they received as much as two-thirds of its total production. Because of this potential for wealth, there was fierce competition to gain control over mines. Conflicts between officials sent by the Ministry of Taxation and the managers who lived in mining areas sometimes even led to murder.

In the second half of the eighteenth century, there were mine operators who accumulated tremendous amounts of capital. It was no longer possible to maintain the existing practice of appointing operators as officials of the Ministry of Taxation. A new system was officially established in which the local magistrate was put in charge of supervising the development of mines and of collecting taxes. One consequence was that it gave more freedom to those with capital. There was an increase in illegal mining without a government permit, a practice known as *jamchae*. It was the result of the fact that increasing numbers of landed elites and large merchants served as financial backers for silver mines. They had the capital necessary to hire workers, had both status and ability, and had connections with officials higher in rank than the local magistrate. Merchants and moneylenders gradually became the leading figures in gold mining rather than mining specialists. Sometimes, they were even directly involved in finding workers for their mines. Some of them became organizers of the Hong Gyeongnae rebellion; they were the ones who advertised the opening of mines in order to bring workers to the region. For example, Gang Deukhwang operated a sizable business with his father in Jindu, also serving as a local military officer; he brought many people to the rebel base with the promise of an advance for working in a mine. Gim Yeojeong, who also recruited many people to the cause, had a large business in Jindu with his father, and their boats brought their goods to customers as far away as Jeolla province. Although they lied about their involvement in mining, their backgrounds do reveal some aspects of gold mining at the time.

At the end of the eighteenth century and first half of the nineteenth century, a new kind of mine operator emerged called *hyeolju* or *deokdae*.

As gold mining rose in importance, people were needed to locate new veins and take charge of operations once the ore extractable by panning was exhausted. The main qualifications for a mine operator were experience in mining extraction, familiarity with the region, and close ties with government officials or merchants. Funds for facilities and operating expenses came from financial backers who directly operated the mines themselves. Some *hyeolju* and *deokdae* did become mine owners, but some were involved in scandals resulting from mismanagement. One example is a murder that occurred in 1799. After failing at silver mining, Bak Jongjeong and Bak Changbaek, both from Hamgyeong province, made plans to develop a gold mine in secret during a stay at an inn. Fearing that they would be reported to the authorities, they went to see the *pungheon*, an officer of the *yuhyangso*, to ask the village not to report them to the authorities. They found out that the head of the village was indeed going to report them, and after the head refused their requests, they waited by the road and murdered him.

10. WHEN DID JOSEON'S POPULATION REACH TEN MILLION?

Ko Dong-Hwan

Korea underwent tremendous population growth during the twentieth century. Despite all the turbulence of the modern period, the population of the peninsula quadrupled. The country began the century with around seventeen million people. In the year 2009, the population of South Korea was about forty-eight million, ranking twenty-fourth in the world – similar in size to Spain and South Africa. North Korea had an estimated population of about twenty-four million in 2009, which ranked fifty-first in the world. Countries of comparable numbers include Yemen and Mozambique. If the two Koreas reunified, the total population of seventy-two million would rank eighteenth in the world. It would have more people than France, Congo, and Turkey, but fewer than Germany, Egypt, and Iran. The city of Seoul has undergone perhaps even more remarkable population growth. Its population was almost 10.5 million in 2009, which made it the eighth largest city in the world. In terms of the entire metropolitan area, it would be the second largest, behind only Tokyo.

Joseon also experienced significant demographic change during the 518 years of its existence. At its founding in 1392, the population was about 5.5 million people, and it was around seventeen million at its end in 1910. As the title indicates, this chapter begins by trying to answer the question of when the population of the country reached ten million. Though this is an arbitrary number, it can serve as a rough indicator of the achievement of a certain level of economic and social development. European countries generally did not exceed the ten million mark until they were well into the modern period, with the exception of large polities such as France and the Holy Roman Empire. The population of Spain reached ten million in the late eighteenth century, and England did not do so until the early nineteenth century. In the case of the United States, it surpassed ten million some time in the 1820s. By contrast, the population of Japan increased to ten million by the year 1500 at the latest. Joseon's population reached ten million probably a little later than Japan but earlier than many European polities. Since population change is one of the main determinants of human life, examining its underlying factors can reveal much about a historical era. This chapter discusses the Joseon government's method of collecting population data, its relation to the social status system, and the urbanization of Seoul in the late Joseon period.

Population Statistics and Household Data

Though the Joseon government did collect data on its population, its census counted households rather than individuals. A census was supposed to be conducted every three years to update the household registers (*hojeok*). Each household submitted a household report to their local government office, which compiled the information and sent it to the central government. The census was not based on data directly collected by the government but on voluntary reports from households. The government compared the new data with that of the previous census and updated their household statistics. For several reasons, household registers were of limited accuracy in measuring the actual changes in population. First, during the Joseon period, people were divided into four main age groups – old (老, *no*), able-bodied (壯, *jang*), weak (弱, *yak*), and child (兒, *a*), but it was customary not to record children less than ten years of age because of the high infant mortality rate. Second, census data was not seen as essential to formulating government policy as is the case today. Instead, the government saw the size of households and the population as a measure of the virtuous rule of the king. Since the number of households increased in times of peace and prosperity, an increase in households was viewed as a manifestation of kingly virtue. The number of households under his rule was presented to the king in a ceremony called the *heonminsu*. The Joseon government had much less interest in measuring the population accurately than modern-day governments do.

Of course, the government used household statistics for more practical purposes as well. First, they were used to calculate the number of taxpayers. The census counted the number of households and of able-bodied men who could fulfill their military obligation or provide statute labor rather than measuring population change. The data were not directly used to set economic policy or to address the problems of its citizens. Second, when local magistrates were evaluated on their performance, one of the criteria was the change in the number of households. The government's goal was more to firm up state finances than to demonstrate the king's virtuous rule. Even if the population had decreased because of an epidemic or severe famine, they reported the same number of households to the government in order to receive high marks on their evaluation. On the

Fig. 10.1. *Banquet in Yeongwangjeong* (Yeongwangjeong yeonhoedo) (detail), Thought to be the work of Gim Hongdo, late eighteenth century. This part of the painting depicts people near Daedong Gate in Pyongyang. (National Museum of Korea)

other hand, when the population rose rapidly during an upturn in the economy, local magistrates reported just a very small increase in population. If they reported the actual figure, the amount of taxes levied on the village would have increased, and they wanted to avoid submitting more tax revenues to the government.

Thus, household data were not a reliable measure of Joseon's actual population. A recent study has even argued that household statistics underestimated the population by about sixty percent. Nonetheless, they

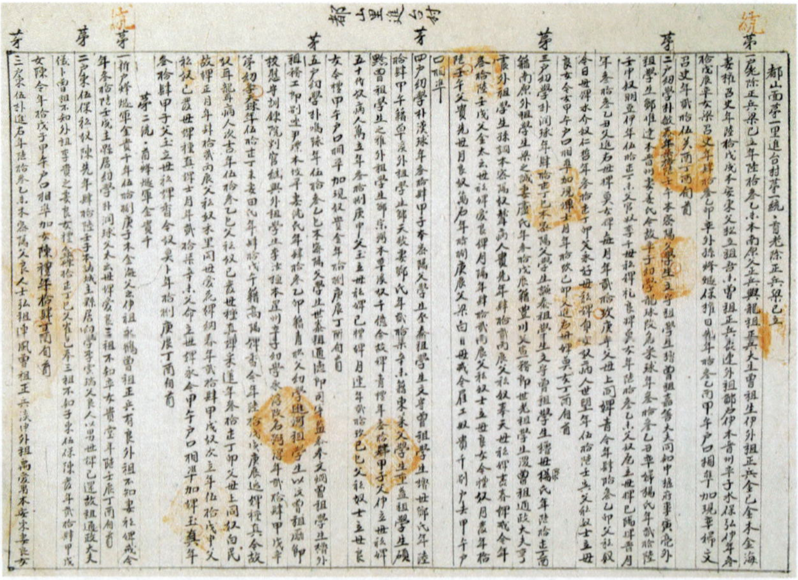

Fig. 10.2. Household Register from Danseong, 1717.

are still valuable sources for researching population change. Since data were collected every three years for hundreds of years, trends in the statistics can be used to confirm changes in the size of the population. There are very few other countries or polities where household records were compiled in a consistent manner for such a long period of time.

Overview of Population Change

Population is a complex social phenomenon that is determined, in the first instance, by natural and biological processes. Joseon had the high birth and high morality rates that were characteristic of premodern times. The rate of population increase is estimated to have been less than one percent per decade. In general, population growth was determined more by the mortality rate than by the birth rate. Famine, epidemics, and war had a large impact on mortality rates. Most of the deaths from disease were of young children and the destitute, those likely to have been underrepresented in official government data. Thus, the impact of disease on the overall population in pre-modern societies is generally less apparent in the official data than that of other factors, such as drought, flood, and other natural disasters.

Table 1. Population Change in the Joseon Period.

Year	Population according to household statistics	Estimated actual population
1393	301,300	5,572,000
1440	692,475	6,724,000
1511		10,010,000
1543	4,162,021	11,643,000
1642	1,649,012	10,764,000
1744	7,209,213	18,275,000
1843	6,703,684	16,632,000
1910		17,427,000

Source: Sin Yongha and Gwon Taehwan, "Joseon wangjo sidae ingu chujeong e gwanhan ilsiron," Donga munhwa 14 (1977).

Table 1 presents the findings of a study of population in the Joseon period based on household statistics. In 1393, shortly after Joseon's founding, the population was estimated to have been 5.5 million, and it exceeded ten million around the year 1511. In the early and mid-seventeenth century, the period of the Imjin War and the two Manchu invasions, the population dropped slightly to ten million, stagnating at that level for a time. It reached a peak of eighteen million people around 1744, but the population declined in the nineteenth century to 16.6 million in 1844. After the opening of Joseon's ports, the population began to recover, and it is estimated to have been 17.4 million in the 1910s. To answer the question posed at the beginning of the chapter, the population of Joseon exceeded ten million around the year 1500; i.e., the beginning of the sixteenth century.

Household Registers and Changes in the Social Status System

Household registers, the main source for household data, were created to help maintain the social status system and the dominance of the yangban class. They recorded the military service and statute labor (*jigyeok*) that each person had to perform. Even if a person's social status was not mentioned, it could be determined by looking at the *jigyeok* recorded in the household register. All commoners had to pay taxes and perform other duties for the state, while the yangban were exempt. The official position and rank would be recorded for a yangban serving in the government, while a yangban without an official position was classified as a scholar.

Table 2. Changes in Social Status in the Late Joseon Period.

Year	% Yangban	% Commoner	% Unfree
1729	26.29	59.78	13.93
1765	40.98	57.01	2.01
1804	53.47	45.61	0.92
1867	65.48	33.96	0.56

Source: Jeong Seokjong, *Joseon hugi sahoe byeondong yeongu* (Seoul: Iljogak, 1983), p. 249.

In the case of commoners, registers noted the type of their military service, such as infantry, cavalry, or a civilian whose taxes were used to support the military. Unfree people were clearly indicated with the terms *nomo* and *bimo*. To prevent people from falsely assuming a higher social status, household registers also recorded the names of a person's father, grandfather, great-grandfather, and maternal grandfather (collectively known as the *sajo*).

Since they were updated every three years, household registers are useful for tracing changes in the social status system. Registers have been found for the regions of Daegu, Ulsan, and Danseong. The Ulsan household register contains a relatively complete set of data for an almost two hundred year period (1708–1904). Table 2 presents an analysis of the changes in social structure based on its data.

According to Table 2, the number of yangban households rapidly increased toward the end of the Joseon period, while commoner households gradually decreased in number, and unfree households rapidly disappeared. These trends suggest that the dominance of the yangban class was gradually being undermined. This was not the result of natural population change; rather, commoners and the low-born were rising into the yangban class through the accumulation of wealth.

Population Growth and Commercial Development in Seoul

Analysis of household data indicates that population gradually increased during the Joseon period, but there was a brief period when the increase was particularly rapid in the seventeenth and early eighteenth centuries. At the time, the country was gradually recovering from the damage of the Imjin War and the Manchu invasions; the abnormal climatic conditions of the 'Little Ice Age,' which affected the whole world, were ending. Improvements in agricultural output helped to resolve food shortages, and advances in medicine improved the treatment of diseases. In 1525, the government established the Jinhyulcheong, an office that provided relief for starving farm families. It also passed a law to allow families to take in children abandoned due to a poor harvest or natural disaster and use them as slaves. The population gradually increased because of the resulting decrease in infant mortality. The social impact of population growth was significant, with the most striking change being the growing urbanization of the country from the eighteenth century. It mainly occurred in administrative centers, but commercial towns such as Ganggyeong, Songpa, and Wonsan also developed into cities. Of course, it was the city of Seoul that experienced the most change.

The population of Seoul grew rapidly from the late seventeenth century because of an influx of people from other regions. According to the government's official data, Seoul had a population of around 200,000 in the eighteenth and nineteenth centuries, with about thirty to forty thousand households. But, as mentioned earlier, the data seems to have significantly underestimated the actual size of the population. One contemporary record noted that there were about 10,000 households unaccounted for in the official data; another source mentioned that the number of households in Seoul totaled 50,000. These accounts suggest that the population

Map 10.1 Map of the Capital (*Doseongdo*), *Dongguk jeondo* (Complete Map of the Eastern Kingdom), early nineteenth century. (Kyujanggak Institute for Korean Studies)

of Seoul was at least 300,000 in the nineteenth century. Seoul was comparable in size to Japanese cities such as Osaka and Kyoto, whose population ranged between 300,000 to 500,000, while Tokyo's population exceeded one million. The population of Seoul was also comparable to that of European cities. Before the Industrial Revolution, most European cities had about 100,000 people. Thanks to industrialization, London's population reached 500,000 by the end of the seventeenth century.

Population growth brought about rapid change in Seoul. The boundaries of the city expanded as urban migrants started settling down outside the city walls. Most of them lived in areas along the Han River such as Mapo, Yongsan, Seogang, Mangwon, Hapjeong, and Ddukseom. These places underwent commercialization from the eighteenth century; they were hubs of water transport that linked Seoul to the rest of the country. The increased demand for day laborers generated by Seoul's commercial development was a major factor behind migration to the capital. Migrants earned a living by loading and unloading boats in these ports or by transporting goods to the city. Seoul expanded not just to the Han River but also to other areas outside of the city. By the late eighteenth century, Ui-dong, Beon-dong, Galhyeon-dong, Bulgwang-dong, and Nokbeon-dong had all been incorporated into Seoul. Ui-dong and Beon-dong were along the road to Hamgyeong province, and Galhyeon-dong, Bulgwang-dong, and Nokbeon-dong were all along the road to Pyongyang and Uiju, two of the cities on the overland route to China. By Jeongjo's reign in the late eighteenth century, Seoul had already expanded to include all the regions of Seoul today that lie north of the Han River.

Up to now, it has been thought that Seoul's transformation into a modern city began after the opening of Joseon's ports in 1876. According to this view, the capital was principally an administrative and military city where the monarch and his officials resided. However, Seoul was not simply a walled city; it was also a bustling commercial center that expanded by incorporating settlements and market areas beyond its walls. In actuality, the foundation for its later development into a modern city had already been laid in the late Joseon period.

Urban Problems and Urban Development

Population growth and urbanization has tended to lead to poverty, homelessness, and environmental problems, and Seoul in the eighteenth century was no exception. Since many of the migrants arriving in Seoul could not find housing, they lived in makeshift shanties built along Cheonggye Stream. Homeless people would sleep under one of the bridges that went over the stream, surviving by begging for food or working as day laborers. When beggars in Seoul were increasingly found dead of starvation or from the cold, the government established measures to provide relief. During Jeongjo's reign, it became customary in winter to provide straw bags to sleep on and clothes to wear to the homeless people sleeping under Hyogyeong and Gwangtong Bridges. Housing sometimes was a source of friction between the classes. If they did not have a proper residence, many yangban *sadaebu* would take advantage of their status and seize the house of a commoner. It was called *yeogatarip* and was clearly an illegal act. However, it was not until the late seventeenth century, during Sukjong's reign, that measures to punish such actions were implemented. The practice virtually disappeared by Jeongjo's reign in the late eighteenth century. Commoners who had lost their homes reasserted their rights and lodged protests with the city government and the Ministry of Punishments. If *yeogatarip* emerged because of the lack of housing in Seoul, its disappearance was a reflection of the commoners' growing consciousness of their rights to property.

Seoul's population growth also caused environmental problems. The increased use of firewood in winter led to deforestation in the mountains near Seoul, causing mountain soil to move down and settle at the bottom of streams. Even a moderate rain would cause Cheonggye Stream to flood. Many of the recently arrived migrants who lived along the stream suffered damage from floods every year. To solve this problem, King Yeongjo ordered a large-scale dredging of Cheonggye Stream in 1760. It was the largest project of its kind since Seoul became the capital of the country in 1394, and it brought about a complete transformation of the city. Cheonggye Stream was straightened out, and most of the makeshift houses built along its banks were torn down. During Jeongjo's reign, the government also carried out other urban improvements in Seoul such as the construction of a new road connecting the capital and Suwon.

with Won Kwang Park

PART TWO

SOCIETY

11. RURAL SOCIETY AND ZHU XI'S COMMUNITY COMPACT

Kwon Nae-Hyun

Toward the end of the Goryeo period, the government was increasingly unable to prevent the outbreak of rebellions and protect people along coastal areas from the intrusions of Japanese pirates. Underlying these problems were the economic decline of the peasantry and the financial crisis of the state. A group of powerful families had come to own vast estates of land, taking land from the peasants and depriving the government of badly needed revenue. Rural disorder was both a symptom and a cause of the decline of the Goryeo kingdom. After the founding of Joseon, the government undertook a reorganization of provincial administration in order to reestablish order. It divided the country into eight provinces, in contrast to the five provinces of the Goryeo state. Each province was further divided into counties (*gun*) and prefectures (*hyeon*), which were, in turn, subdivided into districts (*myeon*) and villages (*ri*). The system was meant to enable the government to exert more control over the countryside.

In the late Goryeo period, scholars began to reject Buddhism and turned to Neo-Confucianism as an ideology that could restore the social order. When it became the ruling ideology after the founding of Joseon in 1392, the country began to undergo a Neo-Confucian transformation that would affect all levels of society. Part of this effort involved the spread of its thought, rituals, and institutions to the countryside. One of the major institutions was the community compact (*hyangyak*). The seminal Neo-Confucian philosopher Zhu Xi (1130–1200) discussed his conception of the community compact in his emendation of the Lü Family Community Compact (Lushi xiangyue), which had originally been written by Lü Dajun (1031–1082). He saw it as a voluntary association in which people encouraged each other to lead a moral life and provided assistance to each other in times of difficulty. His text discussed the standards of virtue that were to govern communal life and had information on proper social etiquette, the ritual life of the family and of the community, and the procedures for holding meetings of its members. In Joseon, scholars belonging to the so-called *sarim* faction were enthusiastic advocates of the community compact and pushed for its widespread adoption. This chapter discusses how the community compact replaced the *yuhyangso* by the mid-Joseon period and how both came to serve as an instrument of class domination, despite their original intentions.

Yuhyangso – *The Organizations of the* Sajok

During the Joseon period, members of the yangban class were commonly called *sajok*. The term *sajok* referred to families that produced high-ranking government officials. They established their domination over the commoners by creating organizations and rules that served their interests; even in the late Joseon period, they enjoyed special privileges such as exemption from military service. The origins of the *sajok* can be traced back to the *hojang* class, the provincial ruling class of the Goryeo period. The *hojang* were the highest status group within the *hyangni* class (low or mid-level government functionaries). Some of them, particularly in the late Goryeo and early Joseon periods, raised their social status by passing the civil examinations or being awarded military honors, while others remained in the *hyangni* class in the Joseon period. By the early Joseon period, the former *hojang* class thus became differentiated into two groups, the *sajok* and the *hyangni* class. There were many prominent yangban lineages that originated as a *hyangni* family.

The *sajok* and the *hyangni* also came to live in separate areas. Until the early Joseon period, sons and daughters received equal shares of the family inheritance and shared responsibility for ancestral memorial rites. Through this custom, the *sajok* established new villages by moving into areas with a connection to their paternal families or with a connection to the families of their mothers or wives who had received an inheritance of land or slaves. Most of these villages were located on the outskirts of existing counties and prefectures. From the sixteenth century, these villages underwent development through the construction of levees and the introduction of new agricultural techniques. By contrast, the *hyangni* class continued to live near the town (*eup*) where they worked in the local government office.

The *sajok* were able to establish their authority over their regions through organizations called *yuhyangso*. They were self-governing associations of yangban in the early Joseon period. Its membership was restricted to *sajok* who were listed in the local register. The head of the organization was the *jwasu*, and below him were officers called *byeolgam*. All officials of the *yuhyangso* were chosen through an election.

> All of the prominent yangban in the region gathered for the meeting of the village assembly. Its purpose was to elect the people who would serve as *jwasu* and *byeolgam* of the *hyangso*. After examining their pedigrees and qualifications, candidates were selected. People over the age of thirty voted on the candidates for *byeolgam,* while those over the age of fifty voted on the *jwasu.*

By a majority vote, the yangban in a region selected a *hyangim*, who wielded considerable influence over regional administration.

Through the *yuhyangso*, the *sajok* were able to restrain the power of magistrates sent by the central government which was trying to strengthen its control over localities. In the early Joseon period, friction often existed between the two groups. Sometimes, the problems were caused by the incompetency of magistrates who were low in rank, but in many cases, the *sajok* were too greedy in pursuing gain and showed contempt toward the local magistrate. While the *yuhyangso* were successful in restraining arbitrary actions by the magistrates, they also served to maintain the power of the *sajok* over rural villages and advanced their economic interests. For instance, they tried to subordinate the *hyangni* to their authority.

The self-governing associations founded by the *sajok* were often in conflict with the authorities and could not fulfill their purpose properly, leading to a repeated cycle of establishment and abolition. The *yuhyangso* were abolished during Taejong's reign (r. 1400–1418) since they were an obstacle to the government's efforts to centralize authority. However, this had the unintended consequence of increasing the abuses and corruption of magistrates and *hyangni* officials. The government then revived the *yuhyangso* after it prepared regulations to deal with their abuses and established an office called the *gyeongjaeso* to supervise them. This time, however, many of the *sajok* joined forces with local magistrates to tyrannize the people. King Sejo used these developments as the pretext to abolish the *yuhyangso* again. They were reestablished during Seongjong's reign (1457–1494) when members of the *sarim* faction began to assume posts in the central government.

These *yuhyangso* were different in nature from earlier ones; they handled village rituals such as the archery (*hyangsarye*) and the wine-drinking (*hyangeum jurye*) rites and did not function as much to maintain the local autonomy of the *sajok*. Through these organizations, the *sajok* focused on supervising and instructing people who lacked filial piety or otherwise disrupted order in the villages. The goal of the *sarim* was to strengthen their authority over the people by reorganizing village life

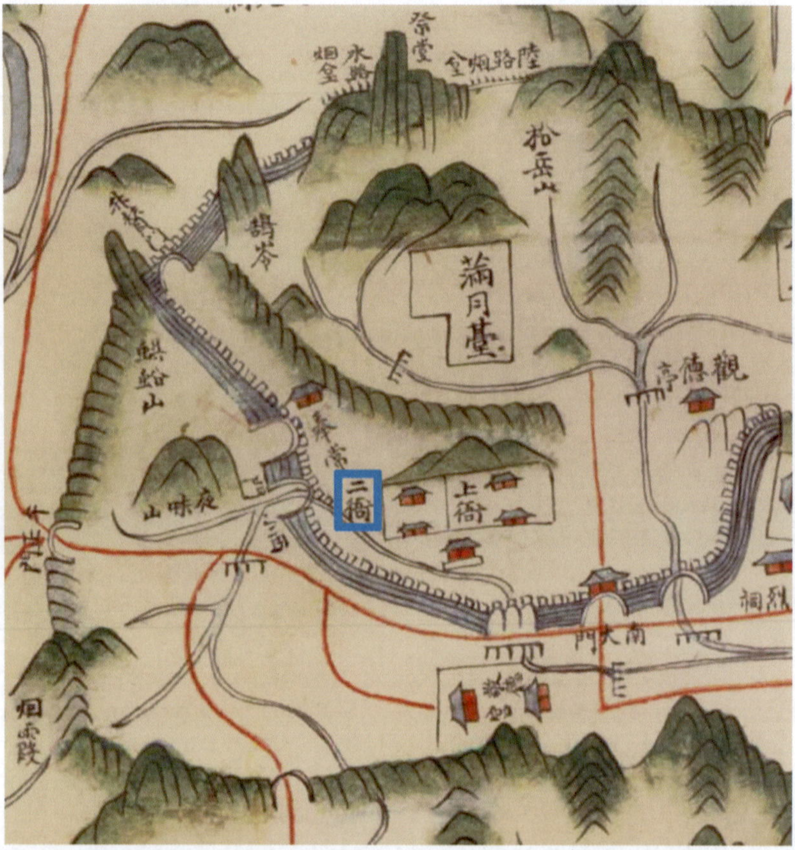

Map 11.1. Map of Gaeseong, *Haedong jido*, mid eighteenth century. After the Imjin War, *yuhyangso* were generally called *hyangcheong*. This map shows the location of a *hyangcheong* near Soseo Gate, indicated by the term 'ia' (inside the blue rectangle). (Kyujanggak Institute for Korean Studies)

according to Neo-Confucian principles. It was part of their effort to oppose the *hungu* faction[1] that was in power at the time. The lives of villagers were now strictly regulated under a hierarchical order based on Neo-Confucian values. The *sarim* achieved their goals in only a few regions in Gyeongsang province where they had strong roots. In most parts of the country, the

[1] The term '*hungu* faction' originally referred to officials who had served the king directly and performed many meritorious deeds. It later came to refer to the officials who helped King Sejo seize the throne and became the dominant power group. They were the political opponents of the *sarim* faction.

hungu faction had control over the *yuhyangso* because they controlled most of the *gyeongjaeso* which had the power to appoint members to the *yuhyangso* in their region. The autonomy of rural villages could easily be undermined by the politics at the center. The *sarim* now advocated the abolition of the *yuhyangso* that they had originally attempted to use as the base of their power. In its place, they sought to reorganize rural villages through the adoption of the community compact system.

Community Compacts and Rural Village Autonomy

Community compacts enabled rural villages to maintain autonomy over their affairs. Their implementation was initially tied to the fortunes of the *sarim* faction in the capital, as they would be abolished when they were in decline. Around the time of the Imjin War, however, the provincial *sajok* gradually implemented the community compact system, making adjustments in each region to suit its particular conditions. Examples include the community compact of Paju and those of the Confucian academies called *seowon*. Some were for units as large as a county or prefecture, and there were ones for small-scale units such as districts (*dong*). The *dong* of the Joseon era was about the same size as the units called *myeon* today. Districts already had a long-standing custom of mutual assistance among its members. The *sajok* formed community compacts in the villages where they resided, based on existing village regulations and the Lü family community compact created by Zhu Xi. After the Imjin War, they actively formed compacts and organizations that included commoners and united people of all classes.

How did the community compact system operate? All the residents of a region were supposed to be members of the community compact. Those who refused could be banished. Its main task was to manage all the affairs of the village such as providing mutual aid among its members, giving out punishments and rewards, and assisting the fulfillment of duties toward the state. It carried on long-standing traditions in the Korean peninsula of mutual aid, mutual regulation, and direct management of all large and small affairs of the community. Many matters in the village were handled according to the regulations of the community compact, and only very difficult issues would be brought to the authorities. Community compacts were supposed to be based on four main principles: mutual encouragement of virtue, mutual vigilance, maintenance of propriety, and mutual assistance in times of difficulty. Each of the virtues fulfilled a different function. For the *sajok*, these values provided legitimacy for the social order; for the commoners, they constituted the principles that governed their daily lives.

Now let's examine some of the terms associated with the community compact system. *Hyanggyu* refers to the regulations for the operation of the *yuhyangso* and the maintenance of registers (*hyangan*) that contained the names of members from prominent *sajok* families. *Hyangan* were a kind of list of local elites, and the *hyanggyu* can be seen as the rules used to manage the elites and govern local society. The provincial *sajok* strictly distinguished their status from that of the commoners, and they even limited the number of *sajok* who could be listed in the register. Since only people in the register could serve as the *hyangim* of a *yuhyangso*, they were key figures in their communities.

There were limitations to how much autonomy could be achieved because Joseon society was based on a hierarchical status system. Yangban held the highest positions in a community compact, maintaining a strict distinction from those of lower status. Those who failed to show respect to the yangban were disciplined, and even for the same crime, a yangban just had to appear at a court hearing while commoners were whipped. If a yangban did not show remorse, his unfree person would receive a whipping instead. The strict difference in treatment of the upper and lower classes shows that under the pretext of edification, the community compact functioned as a means for the yangban to establish their dominance and exert control over the rural population.

In later years, the community compact also came to be used by yangban as a tool for illegal exploitation of the peasantry. Jeong Yagyong (1762–1836) criticized their corruption in his treatise *Mongmin simseo* (A Book from the Heart on Governing the People).

> Wealthy landlords and local yangban are appointed as village leaders and call themselves the head of the community contract. They and other officials such as *yusa* and *jigwol* wield their power arbitrarily and threaten the people. They demand liquor and force them to pay them grain. Their demands are unending. Exposing unnoticed misdeeds by the people, they accept bribes or demand compensation. Everywhere they go, they are treated with liquor and meat, and their homes were noisy because of the complaints they had to deal with. Statute labor was required of ignorant peasants, and they forced them to engage in agriculture. Local magistrates file complaints with the community compact office and have them conduct investigations and make reports. There is no end to the wicked acts by people who are backed by powerful figures.

Though its original purpose was to promote mutual assistance and local autonomy, it actually functioned as a means to oppress the people. Its oppressive nature was rooted in the fact that local autonomy functioned to maintain the dominant position of the yangban ruling class, but there also was another factor involved. The local yangban, who should have restrained the power of the central government, now joined forces with them, increasing the suffering of the people.

Changes in Village Society

Through the *yuhyangso* and the community compact, the yangban served as the leading figures in rural society, but in the late Joseon period, their status underwent a general decline. Severe social and economic disparities were also emerging within the yangban class itself, even within the same family. For example, Yi Myeongyun, who had been involved in the Jinju peasant rebellion in 1862, was a prominent yangban in the region and had served in the central government as an official of the Office of Special Advisors. His second cousin, Yi Gyeyeol, was a leader of a rebel army whose life was no different from that of a peasant. On the other hand, some commoners were able to take advantage of developments in agriculture and commerce to accumulate great wealth. They then used their newfound economic power to obtain yangban status. These developments began to undermine the social order that had suppressed the commoner class.

The change in the nature of the *hyangim* also suggests that new forces were challenging the social order of the rural yangban. As mentioned above, the *hyangim* was a powerful figure that was selected in a village assembly where only yangban members whose names were in the village register could vote. In the late Joseon period, however, the local magistrate came to hold the power to appoint the *hyangim*. Rather than trying to curb the magistrate's power, the *yuhyangso* now provided support. In addition, the village assemblies of the yangban gradually became an advisory organ to the magistrate and focused on handling the payment of the region's taxes. In many cases, the magistrate was the one who initiated the founding of a community compact. The yangban became reluctant to serve as the *hyangim*, regarding its work to be drudgery that required taking care of small tasks. Now *hyangim* often came from new social groups and yangban who had been marginalized in the rural order. They took control of local offices and had their names recorded in the village registers.

Corruption involving the registers became widespread, with local magistrates even selling *hyangim* positions. They were valuable because once a person's name was recorded in the register, his descendants would maintain yangban status for generations.

Conflicts over inclusion in the registers led to incidents called *hyangjeon* in which they were burned or destroyed. The conflicts sometimes arose between yangban, but the ones between old and new social forces had more far-reaching consequences. They were struggles between the existing rural ruling class and a new social group challenging their hegemony. After their names were entered in the register, the new elites allied with the local magistrate and undermined the yangban's position in the rural order. Instead of trying to establish a new social order, however, they were content to enjoy the privileges of power; these developments contributed to the intensification of social contradictions in the late Joseon period.

The yangban were unable to prevent the decline of the autonomy of rural villages. Local yangban tried to unite and maintain their influence through the *seowon* and shrines that their families had established in their villages. But without any force powerful enough to counter them, the authority of local magistrates increased, as did that of the *hyangni* and the *hyangim*. Exploitation of the commoners became even more severe since this was also the time of rule by in-law families (*sedo jeongchi*). The combination of these developments was an important factor behind the outbreak of large-scale peasant rebellions in the nineteenth century. At the same time, commoners increasingly demanded a direct voice in the affairs of their villages. For instance, the nature of the village assembly changed during the period of peasant rebellions. Up to that point, these assemblies had been dominated by the yangban. Now, commoners became increasingly active in them, and some regions held separate people's assemblies (*minhoe*). In earlier periods, people did have informal forums to express their opinions on village matters; they would be organized more formally in times of emergency such as a rebellion. Commoners no longer accepted the restrictions of the social status system and were pushing for a system in which they would play a role in local politics.

with Philip Hong

12. WHY DID PEASANTS CREATE THE *DURE*?

Lee Hae Jun

Villages, the basic units of rural community, were the setting for a complex social life in which people engaged in daily rituals, communal events, and collective labor. Within them, there were organizations that managed these various activities; they developed over a long period of time and had long-standing traditions. Over the ages, they had different names and differed in nature according to the overall social structure. In the Joseon period, a variety of organizations existed at the village level such as the community compact and various kinds of *gye*. One of the most important was the *dure*, which organized the labor of the village and provided aid to its members. Many different kinds of organization can be classified as *dure*, such as the *hwangdu* in regions where dry-field cultivation was predominant, the *sunureum* of Jeju Island, and the *putgut* of Gyeongsang province. It originated as a communal labor organization in a few regions and then spread to the rest of the country as a result of changes in agricultural methods. It consisted of the able-bodied men of the village who managed the community's affairs. Among the various peasant organizations in Korean history, the *dure* were unique because of the social status of its members. They were created by the peasants themselves and operated at the level of the village. Rather than simply being a labor organization, they were involved in the entire life of the village. Its members worked together to organize the village's cultural activities such as communal rituals, music, and statute labor. This chapter examines their emergence and provides an overview of how they operated, including their involvement in seasonal rituals.

The Predecessors of the Dure

Village organizations have existed throughout Korean history, and they underwent changes as they remained somewhat beyond the reach of the ruling ideology and institutions. They can be seen as forming the deep structure of communal life in traditional society. One of the oldest types of organization was the *gye*, which is still common today. They were communal organizations that performed a variety of functions and whose exact origins are unclear. These organizations were so widespread in the mid-Joseon period that Yi Sugwang (1563–1628) observed in his *Jibung yuseol* that "in every part of the region, everyone is forming *gye* whose members provide aid to each other."

The predecessors of the *dure* included the *hyangdo* and the various *donggye* of the Goryeo and Joseon periods. First, the *hyangdo* was a traditional form of village organization that usually operated at the level of the natural village. Coming from the lower classes, its membership ranged from under ten to as many as 100 people. They organized events central to the life of the village, such as communal labor, weddings, funerals, folk customs, and rituals related to shamanistic beliefs. Rites focusing on natural deities had a long tradition, expressing the beliefs of a society that was primarily engaged in agricultural cultivation. It is entirely possible that such beliefs continued into the Joseon period in latent form since Joseon was an agrarian society. This also seems to be supported by the fact that peasant music and rituals have been passed down to the present.

Seong Hyeon (1439–1548) described *hyangdo* festivals as follows in *Yongjae chonghwa*:

> In most cases, the lowborn in the neighborhood gather together and hold a meeting. The number of people ranges from seven to nine to as many as about 100. They meet every month to drink, changing the site each time. If someone suffers a death in the family, the *hyangdo* would prepare the mourning clothes and make the coffin and food. Sometimes, they would help carry the funeral bier and prepare the gravesite. This is a truly good custom.

In the late Joseon period, Heo Mok (1595–1682) wrote in his work *Gieon* that "on days when rites were performed, [people] prayed and tried to divine the quality of the harvest as well as natural events of the new year such as droughts, floods, and epidemics." These texts provide a glance into how communities conducted their lives before the adoption of Neo-Confucian ideology and how traditional village organizations performed a variety of roles.

Second, *donggye* were communal organizations at the level of the village or the lowest units of provincial administrative such as the *dong* or *ri*. Also called *daedonggye* or *dongningye*, they managed communal property in order to provide aid to their members. They contained traces of earlier forms of peasant organization such as the *gye*. In Yeongam county, South Jeolla province, the village of Gurim had a *donggye* that held its meetings in a pavilion called the Hoesajeong. Its members "put on wooden shoes to harvest the rice and used it to help each other." Its origins show that the communal ties formed through the *hyangdo* in the early Joseon period were the basis for the later establishment of *donggye*. *Donggye* were formed by *sajok* families as Neo-Confucian ideology spread to rural areas. As the *sajok* established their hegemony, they gradually gained control over existing peasant organizations. This was accomplished through the landlord system, the restrictions of the social status system, and the institution of the community contract. Rural village organizations no longer operated at the level of the natural village and became a subordinate organization of the community compact or the *donggye*. As can be seen in the case of Hahoe village (North Gyeongsang province), *donggye* forced village organizations to join them and restricted their independence. After the Imjin War and Manchu invasions, they were revived; it is surmised that most villages and village organizations were absorbed into them with members coming from both the upper and lower classes.

Village organizations came to be dominated by the upper classes, and they enabled the *sajok* to use their position to appropriate privileges and influence. However, it could also be argued that the lower classes were taking a much more active role in the operation of the *donggye*. They grew in strength in the late Joseon period as a result of socioeconomic changes. Even within the restrictions of the social structure, they were able to take advantage of the opportunities brought about by these changes, and one of the most notable developments was the rise of the *dure*.

The Rise of Dure

Villages underwent significant change in the late Joseon period because of a number of political and economic factors. First, the government took a more direct role in the administration of rural villages. Feeling that the *sajok* were limited in their ability to establish control over the countryside, it implemented the *myeon-ri* system and required that villages pay their taxes collectively. Second, the adoption of the technique of rice transplantation increased both agricultural productivity and the amount of arable land, leading to an increase in population after the Imjin War and the Manchu invasions. These developments led to changes in the foundation of communal life and the leadership structure of villages. There was an increase in the number of villages, as well as the formation of single-clan villages. As the peasantry increasingly became economically independent, they formed *dure* in an effort to adapt to these changes in village life. Consisting of self-cultivators and tenant farmers, the *dure* became the main organization representing the interests of the villagers. Their formation was an effort to escape the restrictions of the social status system since they prevented landlords from interfering or being involved.

Another major development in the late Joseon period was the differentiation of villages; that is, some members would break off from the rest and form their own independent village. When the *sajok* were dominant, natural villages were placed under the administration of a *ri*. From the late eighteenth century, they developed into independent villages of substantial size and with their own organizations. There were villages that kept their original names when they split off. Others retained a connection to the original village by using a name that simply added one character to the original name – such as *sang* (upper), *ha* (lower), *nae* (inner), *oe* (outer), *won* (original), *gu* (old), *sin* (new), or *bon* (main).

As villages split and became independent, the *donggye* organizations led by the *sajok* remained in name only; it seems that their influence did not extend beyond the areas where the *sajok* resided. In other areas, village-level organizations came to handle the affairs of most villages; in the process, small communities played new roles in the lives of villagers. There were various signs that reflected the changes going on in rural villages. Shrines would split into larger and smaller shrines, or sometimes, people established a new, independent shrine. There were also instances when *dure* split, and there were differences in the composition and quality of music troupes. Groups within a village managed communal paddy land and prepared items for weddings and funerals separately. As villages became independent of the control of the *sajok*, communal organizations played a more active role. As the technique of rice transplantation spread, the role of *dure* as peasant labor organizations increased.

The Basic Characteristics of Dure

In general, each natural village had its own *dure*. There were very large villages that had multiple *dure* and small villages that had none or formed one with neighboring villages. Membership was open to all the able-bodied men living in the village, usually numbering ten to fifty members. Since it was made up of residents of the village, its hierarchy was determined by age rather than social status. The *dure* had a staff and officers who managed its affairs. The staff consisted of *munseo jaebi* and *gongwon* (clerks). There were two types of *gongwon*: the *non gongwon* who examined the fields and calculated the workers' wages and the *bab gongwon* who provided their meals. Sometimes, there was a person called a *soim* who was responsible for morale and carrying out punishments. There were also people called *sikhwaju* who brought meals to people working in the fields. Its officers included elderly supervisors and an advisor called the *yeongsang* and the *jwasang*; the *usang* provided advice and various kinds of assistance to the *jwasang*. The head of the *dure* was the *chonggak daejang*, but the exact title varied according to the region, including *chonggak, sumeoseum, chonggak daebang,* and *chonggak jwasang*. In some cases, the *chonggak daejang* was also in charge of the *sodongpae*, which consisted of young people who had not yet joined the *dure*. They were a reserve labor force that ran errands and did supporting tasks.

Potential members had to satisfy certain requirements and undergo an initiation in order to join the *dure*. Two of the most common types of evaluation and initiation were lifting stones and the *jinseteok*. When children turned sixteen or seventeen years of age, they were considered to be adults and could join a *dure*. They took a test that involved lifting stones (*deuldol*); in Jeolla province, these stones were called *deuldok*, and in Jeju Island, they were known as *ddungdol*. The stones were round and smooth and weighed a little more than the average person could handle. Lifting stones were generally kept under the guardian tree of the village or the main village pavilion. There were even villages that enshrined stones of varying sizes and treated them as objects of worship. If a person could lift the stone or hoist it above their shoulder, then he could become a member of the *dure*. It was a confirmation of his ability to do farming work. Lifting stones were sometimes used in the contests of strength that were held in villages to determine the strongest person on the day of the Ghost Festival (*Baekjung*) in the seventh lunar month. The winner would either become the head of the *dure* or would have his wages doubled as a prize.

An initiation ceremony was held for the new members of the *dure* in which they were treated to wine and a few light dishes. This ceremony was called the *jinseteok*. It acknowledged them as equal members of the *dure* and was also a coming-of-age ritual. Lifting stones and the *jinseteok* can be seen as playing a role in facilitating generational change in the *dure*, bringing about improvements in productivity, and promoting unity among its members.

Weeding Hoes and the Banner of the Dure

The weeding hoe (*homi*), one of the most basic farming tools, was used in events of symbolic importance to the *dure*. They included the *homi modeum*, the *homi geori*, and the *homi ssisi*. First, the *homi modeum* was held before the *dure* began its work in the farming season. It was a ritual in which the members of the *dure* hung their weeding hoes in the village hall. On that day, they gathered at the village hall to elect its officers democratically and to prepare for work. The custom was for the weeding hoes to be left there until the first day of work. The ritual was usually held on the first day of the second lunar month. Second, the *homi geori* was the largest festival of the *dure*. It was held around the fifteenth day of the seventh lunar month to celebrate the *de facto* end of the year's farming. In Jeolla province, it was called *homi ssisi*, a term referring to the washing of weeding hoes after the year's work was done. In Gyeonggi province, it was called *homi geori* since farmers would hang their weeding hoes on the ropes of the *dure*'s banner.

Banners were the symbols of the *dure* and the pride of their villages. They were attached to a long bamboo pole; at the very top, there was a decoration made of pheasant feathers, and below it were strands of peeled arrowroot plant. Three ropes were attached to the pole which was fixed to the ground by a stake. Banners were prominently displayed during ceremonies of the *dure*. Banners were commonly called *nonggi*, but there were a variety of terms for it that varied according to the region, such as *yongdanggi*, *yongdeokgi*, *deokseokgi*, *yongsulgi*, *seonanggi*, *daejanggi*, and *nongsanggi*. Banners often had a drawing of a dragon and a phrase in Chinese characters such as 'Farming is the Foundation of the World' or 'The Legacy of Shennong' (the Divine Farmer). Dragons were representations of water deities, and it was the custom to have drawings of them in regions engaged in wet-field farming. Banners were so big that only the strongest person in the village could lift it. They were placed in the fields where people worked, and when they moved to another place, the banner was held in front while music was played. When the *dure* moved, farmers played music and held a memorial rite in front of the banner.

The banners of the *dure* were an object of veneration both in rituals and in daily life. It was said that a yangban riding a horse had to stop and dismount when passing in front of a banner. This is an indication of how important the *dure* were in the late Joseon period and how they challenged existing status hierarchies. In some festivals, neighboring villages would play a game whose objective was to steal the other side's banner. When a troupe of entertainers came to perform at a village, they first had to bow before its banner. Some interesting customs also developed through the splitting of villages. One was the *gisebae nori*, in which a younger village used its banner to send new year's greetings to an older village.

Fig. 12.1. Various banners of *dure*.

Another custom was that when members of one *dure* met those of a neighboring village, they beat their drums to greet each other.

The Assemblies of the Dure

Though rituals for agricultural deities were important to the *dure*, selecting its officers and managing its finances were even more important. How did its members, who came from the peasantry, make decisions? Meetings of the *dure* were held on the same day as the memorial rites conducted as part of its shamanistic rituals, usually held while eating a meal after the rite. All affairs related to the village were discussed at these meetings. Studies have shown that in later eras, meetings were held in the house of the clerk, but originally, they were held at the village hall where the *dure* usually met.

Two general meetings were held each year, one before the farming season and one after. The first general meeting occurred in the second lunar month and settled all matters related to the year's farming. They reorganized the *dure*, selected its officers, and conducted initiations of new members. The meeting also set the order of farming work for the year, organized its finances, set wages for labor, and prepared weeding hoes and other tools. It even discussed the repair and purchase of musical instruments. At the second general meeting, the members settled accounts and decided how mutual aid should be distributed and what repairs and construction needed to be done (e.g., cleaning roads and weeding). They also discussed the general livelihood of the village and repaired musical instruments.

Decisions were made according to a completely democratic process. Though the *sajok* did provide assistance to villagers, it was ceremonial in nature with each household receiving an equal amount. By contrast, the *dure* handled mutual aid in a way that provided a more direct benefit. Its members would help farm the fields of a widow, elderly people, or someone with an illness or one with only children. They made sure to provide labor first for tasks that involved the entire village.

Dure *at the End of the Feudal Period*

Labor organizations in the late Joseon period were far more involved in the affairs of rural society than those in earlier eras. The *dure* was primarily a village-level organization whose members were commoners and the lowborn. The motivation for their formation was their desire to escape from the restrictions of the social status system. This put the *dure* in conflict with the government which served the interests of the ruling class. The social and economic changes of the seventeenth and eighteenth centuries created the conditions that enabled the rise of peasant organizations. *Dure* organizations existed within the existing rural village order, developing to the point that they could unite with those of other villages. The late Joseon period was a time when people's consciousness was undergoing significant development as markets developed and the circulation of commodities increased. The existence of the *homi ssisi* and *daedong dure*, which were discussed above, suggests that both a broad regional unity and a common consciousness were developing at the time. Though more research needs to be done on this topic, it seems clear that they had sufficient potential to develop into the leading force of resistance against the oppression of feudal society. If peasant organizations had combined into a single force, it is possible that the *dure* could have served as units for the peasant armies that fought in the peasant rebellions of the nineteenth century.

with Ellen Yuh

13. DID FAKE GENEALOGIES EXIST?

Jung Jin Young

In South Korea, almost every household these days has a family genealogy (*jokbo*). It can answer many of the questions a person may have about his or her family history. Genealogies from the Joseon period contained information about the career and lives of members of a clan beginning with the progenitor. For each individual, they recorded the name, the style, pen name, results of the civil service exam, government positions, notable achievements, date of birth, date of death, and the location of the grave. They also noted whether an individual had children and whether they were legitimate, distinguishing legitimate children from the offspring of concubines as well as sons from sons-in-law. People can use them to learn about their progenitors, the descendants of those progenitors, and their accomplishments. They feel pride at having eminent ancestors who achieved great deeds and enjoyed wealth and fame. Sometimes, they can find the name of a historical figure whom they read about in their school textbooks. People may even discover that they are the descendant of the royal family of Silla or of a famous figure from the Goryeo period. In some cases, they find out surprising facts; there are even some families whose ancestors are of Chinese origin.

Though most people trust the accuracy of Joseon-era genealogies, there are many aspects of them that are suspicious. If all the information they contain were true, then our ancestors must have lived in a strange world where the only people were a few thousand nobles and members of royal families. During the Silla and Goryeo periods, there were far more peasants than nobles, and those commoners must have had descendants. Furthermore, Koreans regard themselves as a homogeneous race who are the descendants of Dangun, but there are clans whose progenitor came from China. It is impossible to deny that genealogies are not completely accurate. Records in a genealogy could have been fabricated without any basis in historical fact. But even if all the information in a genealogy were correct, it is possible that a member of the clan is not a blood relation of the putative progenitor. This chapter examines the basic features of genealogies and discusses how they changed from the early to the late Joseon period, including the emergence of fake genealogies.

The Creation of Genealogies

Family genealogies became more common during the Joseon period. In the Goryeo era, there were similar documents such as the *ssijok* (family tree), *segyedo* (societal map), *gacheop* (family book) in addition to the *jokdo* (lineage map). Information about the royal family, members of the nobility, merit subjects, and children of high-level government officials were recorded in these documents to verify the succession of family lineage. The need for a more proper genealogy emerged with the gradual spread of Neo-Confucianism during the early Joseon period. The royal family began to compile systematic genealogies before private families did. At the beginning of the dynasty, it did not make distinctions among its many wives, concubines, and their children. There was frequent infighting among them over their lineages and the distribution of power. Taejong, who became king after two successive conflicts over the throne, believed that it was necessary to establish a strict hierarchy within the royal family. This was the reason that the royal family compiled a genealogy. Some of the first genealogies of the royal family were the *Seonwonnok* and *Jongchinnok* from Taejong's reign, as well as the *Dangdaeseonwonnok* from Sejong's reign. A genealogy established clear lines of pedigree and distinguished wives from concubines as well as legitimate children from illegitimate ones.

Yangban *sadaebu* families were in a similar situation to the royal household, though to a lesser degree. For private households, the compilation of genealogies became widespread in the sixteenth and seventeenth centuries, after the printing of the Andong Gwon family's *Seonghwabo* in 1476. During the Joseon period, having a genealogy in itself was a sign of belonging to the yangban class. Genealogies were also meant to facilitate ancestor worship which, for the yangban class, helped to maintain their social and political position. Through genealogies, the yangban class was able to strengthen the unity of their bloodlines and emphasize their differences with other classes. As is well known, the yangban were the elites who enjoyed power and privilege, while commoners and the lower classes were disadvantaged socially and economically. Every member of the lower class wanted to become a yangban, and one way to achieve such status was to obtain a genealogy. Thus, the use of genealogies became even more widespread in the late Joseon period.

There were many different kinds of genealogies in the Joseon period. Since they recorded the family lineage from a specific clan progenitor to the present day, they have also been called *sebo* (lineage records).

The two main types of *sebo* were *daedongbo* and *pabo*. *Daedongbo* recorded the information of the entire, extended family, and *pabo* were a record of a specific branch of a clan. Other types of *jokbo* included *gacheop*, *gaseung*, and *gabo*, which focused on the family lineage of a specific individual.

There Are No Daughters' Names in Genealogies

Genealogies were completely male-centered. The names of women were generally not recorded in genealogies in the Joseon period. The existence of daughters was only indicated through the names of sons-in-law. For wives, only the surname and ancestral seat of her birth family, her father's name, and the names of notable ancestors were recorded. Of course, the degree of detail of the information varied according to the individual and the genealogy. Genealogies were recompiled every thirty to forty years, every fifty to sixty years, or every 100 years. Even if multiple genealogies

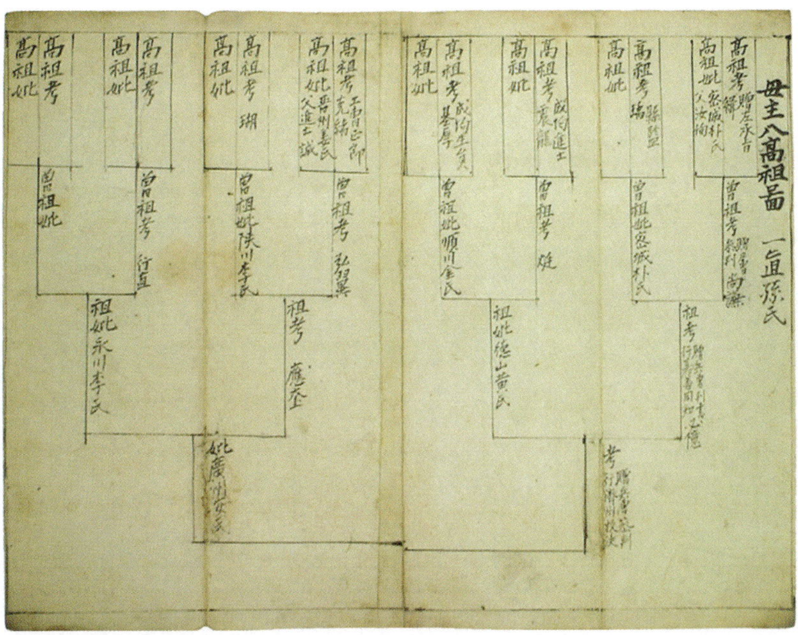

Fig. 13.1. *Palgojodo*, 1549. A type of genealogy compiled by the Gyeongju Choe family. This page shows that the genealogy listed maternal ancestors as the equal of paternal ones.

existed for the same family, their content differed depending on the period in which they were compiled. In general, there were significant differences in content and structure between genealogies of the early and the late Joseon periods.

Genealogies from the early Joseon period reflected the values of their time. Goryeo customs still prevailed, and the Confucian clan-based family system had not been established. It was common for a man to live with his wife's family after getting married. With no distinction between sons and daughters in matters of inheritance, it was not unusual for a son-in-law to carry on the family line or to take charge of the family's ancestral memorial rituals. Since families without a male child did not necessarily adopt, there were many cases of a family line ending because of a lack of descendants. Moreover, there was no prohibition against marriage between people with the same family name and the same ancestral seat. In genealogies from the early Joseon period, both sons and daughters, as well as their descendants, were recorded. Since the descendants of daughters were recorded for all succeeding generations, without any distinction with the descendants of sons, genealogies contained people of multiple surnames. Though the *Seonghwabo* was the genealogy of the Andong Gwon clan, only 867 of the 9,120 individuals listed in it had the surname Gwon. It recorded the family line of daughters down to the sixth or seventh generation. In fact, it was the descendants of daughters, such as Seo Geojeong (1420–1488), who completed the compilation of the *Seonghwabo*.

By the seventeenth century, Joseon gradually transformed into a Neo-Confucian society. This transformation was achieved, in part, through the influence of the *Elementary Learning* and the spread of Zhu Xi's *Family Rituals* (Zhu Xi jiali). A kinship system became established that was centered on the bloodline of the father. Wedding ceremonies that welcomed the bride into the husband's family, such as the *chinyeongnye*, became common. Families without an heir now felt the need to adopt a male child, and the eldest son began to receive most of the inheritance and take the responsibility for ancestral memorial rites. The genealogies of the late Joseon period changed to reflect these developments. The inclusion of adopted sons became common; as sons became the focus of genealogies, the presence of daughters' families gradually decreased. Their families were recorded only down to two or three generations or only the son-in-law's name would be listed. Earlier genealogies had recorded all children in the order of their birth, but now sons appeared first. Genealogies now included additional information such as the wife's family, the memorial days for ancestors, and the location of graves, adopting the form that is still in use today.

Fake Genealogies

Koreans originally did not keep genealogies, as Seo Geojeong mentioned in the *Seonghwabo*. It had been normal for people not to know the names of their forebears beyond a few generations, even in the most prominent families. In fact, the *Seonghwabo* only had brief records for the first twelve generations of the Andong Gwon clan. If the records were incomplete for such a powerful clan at court at the beginning of the Joseon era, they were even more so for clans that became prominent in later years and all the more so for those that did not begin compiling genealogies until the eighteenth or nineteenth centuries. Among later genealogies, some have well-organized and detailed entries for the clan founder and the earliest generations, but these records are likely fake or, at the very least, exaggerated or distorted.

In the Joseon period, only the yangban class kept genealogies, and there were many temptations to embellish or falsify them. The privileges of yangban status were legitimated by their noble bloodlines and the greatness of their ancestors. To claim that they had a prominent progenitor, some yangban families altered the location of their ancestral seat or fabricated and embellished an ancestor's lineage. One common method was to link the progenitor to China since it was the hegemonic power at the time. Families that rose to prominence in the mid and late Goryeo periods would claim that they were the descendants of merit subjects from the founding of Goryeo or of merit subjects of the Samhan confederations. If the genealogies are cross-checked with government records or information from stone inscriptions, it is possible to find many gaps and inconsistencies. From the Goryeo period, there were power groups in the central government that emerged from *hyangni* families in the countryside.[1] But when people began to look down on the *hyangni*, these families tried to hide their status or created a plausible explanation for it. They claimed that their ancestors had their status downgraded to that of *hyangni* when they refused to submit to the new dynasty after a dynastic change. As the importance of lineage increased in the Joseon period, a family without an

[1] The *hyangni* class were low-level government officials who handled administrative tasks in provincial offices.

eminent ancestor would change its ancestral seat in order to join a prominent existing clan.

A more fundamental factor behind the emergence of fake genealogies was the complicated system of family names in Korea. Although family names are purported to have existed before the Three Kingdoms period, their use actually began with the adoption of Chinese culture around the sixth to seventh centuries. With Silla's unification of the Three Kingdoms, Goguryeo and Baekje surnames disappeared. In the Later Three Kingdoms Period, Chinese-style surnames became common among provincial elites. After uniting the country and founding the state of Goryeo, Wang Geon, who became King Taejo, distributed surnames to local elites that were specific to their region. He thus established the institution of family names that were based on a surname and an ancestral seat. The ancestral seat (*bongwan*) was the region in which a clan was based. At the time, regions were organized into an administrative hierarchy. Counties (*gun*) and prefectures (*hyeon*) were autonomous administrative units; within them, there were districts such as *sokhyeon, chon, hyang, so,* and *bugok*. Each of these districts had different surnames.

During the Joseon period, surnames and ancestral seats were constantly being changed – leading to alterations of genealogies. After the founding of the country, the government undertook a large-scale reorganization of the *gun-hyeon* system. It placed more importance on the unit of *jueup*, which were counties or prefectures that had a magistrate sent from the central government. These changes led to a decrease in the number of ancestral seats. From the late fifteenth century, the various ancestral seats were gradually combined into *jueup*. The *sokhyeon, chon, hyang, so,* and *bugok* were either eliminated or absorbed into the county or prefecture that they belonged to. Family names associated with these districts changed their ancestral seat to the county or prefecture or used the *jueup* as a new ancestral seat. People with the same surname who originally had different ancestral seats now belonged to the same one. Of course, people who had only a surname in common were always blood relations, but with this change, their relations became closer.

While the number of ancestral seats decreased, the number of people with surnames increased even more rapidly in the late Joseon period. The main factor was the elevation of the low-born, who did not have family names, to commoner status. Up to the sixteenth century, about forty percent of the population did not have a family name. Despite the fact that the low-born began taking family names, there were hardly any new surnames. Since they chose to adopt existing family names, people with the surnames Gim, Yi, Bak, and Choe now could be found in all regions of the country. Today, genealogies of these well-known clans contain the descendants of these low-born people. Around forty percent of the names recorded in a genealogy are of people who have no blood relation to the clan. People with new surnames listed their place of residence as their ancestral seat on their household registers. Many new ancestral seats appeared, but people gradually changed them to one that was more

Fig. 13.2. *Threshing Rice*, Gim Hongdo, late eighteenth century. While commoners are busy threshing rice, a yangban is smoking a pipe and drinking alcohol. (National Museum of Korea)

renowned, enabling them to be smoothly incorporated into an existing family lineage. As a result, the number of surnames and ancestral seats decreased from over 4,500 in the early Joseon period to about 3,400 today.

In short, the system of surnames and ancestral seats underwent many changes in the Joseon era as a major shift occurred toward large clans and prominent ancestral seats. Most genealogies fabricated or embellished the clan progenitor and changed the surnames or ancestral seats of people in order to portray lineages as coming from a single bloodline. These genealogies can be regarded as fakes.

A World that Needed Fake Genealogies

Having a genealogy meant that a family had yangban status. In a hierarchical status society, a person who was not *yangban* was a commoner who had few social privileges and bore a disproportionately high economic burden. According to Jeong Yagyong, commoners made counterfeit genealogies or changed the names of their father and grandfather in order to avoid military service. They would become yangban by changing their surname or the name of an ancestor and by being added to the genealogy of another person. Many commoners, as soon as their names were recorded on a genealogy and they were exempted from military service, beat the *sinmungo* drum to lodge a complaint and ask the government to forbid commoners and the low-born from making fake genealogies.

Why did commoners and the low-born not have their own genealogies? They had no ancestor who could serve as a worthy progenitor; in many cases, they did not know the names of their ancestors beyond a few generations. They lacked both the financial resources and a sufficient number of blood relatives to make a genealogy. Moreover, their purpose in creating a genealogy was not to trace the true origins of their family; it was to become yangban. The only genealogy they could get was one of a family that was not a blood relation – in other words, a fake one.

The need for fake genealogies was not limited to the lower classes. They were also necessary for yangban who wanted to masquerade as members of an even more eminent family. There was also a hierarchy within the yangban class. Lower-level yangban wanted to reach a higher status, and higher-level yangban wanted to become even more prominent. Fake genealogies were the inevitable consequence of a society where a person could not lead a humane life without becoming a yangban – a society in which family status mattered more than a person's abilities. Today, all Koreans have a family name and a genealogy and believe that their ancestors had been yangban in the Joseon period. But the reality is that not everyone had family names from the beginning and that not everyone was yangban. This forces us to reevaluate our belief that the Gim and Yi clans had existed from the beginning of Korean history and that genealogies contain the absolute truth.

14. THE BAEKJEONG CLASS

Kwon Ki-jung

After the founding of Joseon in 1392, the government undertook a reorganization of the social status system based on Neo-Confucian principles. The main social group of the new kingdom was the so-called *sadaebu*, and they implemented a system now called the *yangcheonje* that classified people as either citizens (*yangin*) or lowborn (*cheonin*). All people, except for those of unfree status (*nobi*), were regarded as commoners, granted rights and privileges that were denied to the unfree. People whose status was difficult to determine were classified as commoners. Children born to a commoner father and lowborn mother were also deemed to be commoners. The purpose of this policy was to increase the number of taxpayers; in the process, the *baekjeong* class obtained the legal status of commoners.

In the early Joseon period, a wide range of classes belonged to the category of *yangin*. The majority of *yangin* were commoners; above them were the yangban, the civil and military officials who constituted the elite of the country, and below them were the so-called *sillyangyeokcheon*. Despite the fact that they all had the legal status of *yangin*, there were tremendous status differences between the yangban and the *sillyangyeokcheon* in actual social life. Since they worked at lowborn occupations, the *sillyangyeokcheon* were treated almost the same as the lowborn. Called *gan* or *cheok* in the early Joseon era, they generally worked at one of the so-called *chilbancheonyeok*, the seven occupations that were regarded as the most lowly at the time.[1] Though their work was arduous, they were respectable jobs that involved service to the state. People in these occupations lived together with commoners and also had opportunities to improve their social status. But among the *sillyangyeokcheon*, there were those who did not associate with the common people; they were called *baekjeong*.

---

[1] They included the *najang* (low-ranking soldier) of the State Tribunal (Uigeumbu), the *ilsu* of provincial government offices, the *joye* of government offices, the *jojol* who worked in boat transport and storehouses, the *yeokbo* (messengers) of the Yeokcham, sailors stationed at a regional naval base, and sentries who lit the fires at beacons.

Where Did the Baekjeong *Come From?*

The term *baekjeong* consists of two Chinese characters. The character *baek* (白) has the meanings of 'white,' 'clear,' 'ignorant,' and 'absent,' and the character *jeong* (丁) means 'able-bodied man.' When the character *baek* was used in a term indicating social status, it usually had the meaning of 'absent' or 'lacking.' Accordingly, the term seems to have originally referred to an ignorant, able-bodied man who possessed nothing. The meaning of the term changed from the Goryeo to the Joseon period. During the Goryeo period, all able-bodied males aged sixteen to sixty were required to perform certain duties for the state. In addition, there were specific types of physical labor and occupations that were hereditary such as soldiers, provincial clerks, and manual laborers. People required to perform these jobs were called *jeongho*, while all other peasants were known as *baekjeong*. The *jeongho* were exempted from the normal obligatory duties to the state and were provided with a certain amount of public land in return for their services, whereas the *baekjeong* received no land.

While the term *baekjeong* referred to the peasant class in the Goryeo era, the peasantry came to be called by other terms after the transition to Joseon, such as *pyeongmin*, *yangmin*, *baekseong*, or *chonmin*. This change was the result of a government measure in 1432 to reclassify *jaein* (entertainers) and *hwacheok* (butchers or wicker makers) as ordinary commoners – i.e., as *baekjeong*. The measure was part of the government's policy in the early Joseon period to increase the number of *yangin*. However, a legal measure could not force people to accept entertainers, butchers, or wickerwork makers – groups historically treated with contempt – as the equal of ordinary peasants. The term *sin baekjeong* (new *baekjeong*) was also used to distinguish between the *baekjeong* of the Goryeo and the Joseon periods. But ordinary commoners disliked being grouped together with entertainers and butchers and did not refer to themselves as *baekjeong*. In the Joseon era, the term *baekjeong* came to refer not to ordinary peasants but to entertainers, butchers, and wicker makers. There was no legal requirement that *baekjeong* had to inherit their occupations as was the case with people of unfree status. Their professions did become hereditary over time as a result of the government's discriminatory policies and their own traditional living patterns.

Another term for lowborn people was *yangsucheok*. It had been used in the Three Kingdoms period, continuing into the Goryeo period as well. One record from the late Goryeo period noted that "the *hwacheok* are none other than the *yangsucheok*." The term *yangsucheok* referred to the people

Fig. 14.1. *Performer on a Rope* (Gwangdae jultago), Gim Jungeun (aka Gisan), late nineteenth century. (Copyright: Museum fuer Voelkerkunde Hamburg)

engaging in low-born professions and the descendants of northern nomads and immigrants. A memorial from the early Joseon period by the scholar Yang Seongji briefly discussed their origins.

> The so-called *yangsucheok* existed at the beginning of the [Goryeo] dynasty and when the court moved to Ganghwa Island [because of the Mongol invasions]. The *jaein* and *hwacheok* also existed during the reign of King Chungryeol [1274–1308] and the reign of King Gongmin [1351–1374]. They existed as far back as 500–600 years ago, and they continued to exist for the next hundreds of years. Up to the present day, they continue to play the long-board zither [*geomungo*] and sing songs and to do the work of slaughtering animals.

This text demonstrates that the *yangsucheok, hwacheok,* and *jaein* had already become a part of Korean society long ago and that they made their living through butchery and making handicraft goods.

It is often thought that the *baekjeong* were descended from northern nomadic peoples who came to the Korean peninsula during the Goryeo era. Since some of the lowborn were called *yangsucheok* before the term *baekjeong* was used to refer to them in the Joseon era, this could mean that the term also meant the descendants of the northern peoples. However, the *baekjeong* class was not entirely composed of such people. At the beginning of the Joseon period, a sizable number of butchers, called *geogoljang,* existed throughout the country. But from the sixteenth century, the term *geogoljang* does not appear in any historical sources. This suggests that these people simply became absorbed into the *baekjeong* class since they worked in similar professions. Many people displaced from their land became part of the class for economic and other reasons. The incorporation of these groups into the *baekjeong* is further evidence that they were not just the descendants of northern nomads.

The Suffering of the Baekjeong

In the early Joseon period, the *baekjeong* were not targets of contempt as they were in the late Joseon period. Historical sources contain numerous examples of a relative lack of discrimination against them. For example, Choe Yundeok (1376–1445), a famous military official in Sejong's reign, was clearly of yangban status since his father was also a general. When he was young, he was sent to live with a *yangsucheok* (i.e., *baekjeong*) family who lived nearby. However, in the late Joseon period, the residential areas of the yangban and the *baekjeong* were strictly segregated to the point that it was unthinkable to raise a yangban in a *baekjeong* household. Another example was the case of a government slave of *baekjeong* status who petitioned to marry the widow of a man who died in exile in a remote area. The local magistrate forced the woman to marry the *baekjeong*. Yet another example can be found in the sixteenth-century text *Gimyorok boyu*, an unofficial historical chronicle. It mentioned that Yi Janggon, a yangban, took refuge in the house of a *yangsucheok* in order to avoid capture by King Yeonsangun and then married the daughter of a *baekjeong*. Though it was an act of desperation, the marriage would not have been possible in the late Joseon period.

A major factor behind the change in attitudes toward the *baekjeong* was the government's discriminatory policies. Fearing that they would wander around the country causing trouble, the government required *baekjeong* to carry travel documents when they went to another region. Despite the fact that they had the legal status of *yangin*, they rounded up *baekjeong* living in Seoul and other regions and forced them to live in specially designated areas called *bang* and *chon*. They also kept separate household registers for them. The government also kept track of births, deaths, and escapees among the *baekjeong*, recording this information in registers after it was reported to the king. At times, it used the degree of success at controlling the *baekjeong* as a key measure in evaluating the performance of village magistrates.

The severe discrimination that the *baekjeong* faced in the penal system was another measure of the oppression they suffered. If they slaughtered a cow or horse without proper authorization, the offenders would have a mark tattooed to their bodies and be sentenced to 100 blows and exile to a remote region 3,000 *ri* (roughly 1,200 km) away. Their families were forced to become servants in villages along major transportation routes or at *yeokcham* (government offices that handled matters related to communications and transportation). Thieves of *baekjeong* status were immediately beheaded, with their wife and children becoming the unfree people of merit subjects. The local government office seized their property, and their parents, siblings, and grandchildren were sent into exile to a location 2,000 *ri* (about 800km) away. These punishments were significantly harsher than those for other *yangin*, demonstrating that the situation of the *baekjeong* was hardly better than that of the unfree people.

The *baekjeong* faced even more severe contempt in society. They had to live in their own communities separate from ordinary commoners in specific areas outside of towns or on the outskirts of rural villages. When talking, they had to refer to themselves with the humble term *soin*, which literally meant 'small person.' They could not smoke or drink liquor in front of commoners and had to bow their heads even in front of children. The *baekjeong* were also distinguished by their clothing. Neither male nor female *baekjeong* were allowed to wear silk clothing or outer coats with large sleeves. They could not wear horsehair-woven headbands or leather shoes. For their hat, they could not use the *gat* worn by commoners, which was made of horsehair and colored with black lacquer; they were not even allowed to use silk for its chin-strings. Instead, they wore coarsely braided *gat* made of bamboo called *paeraengi* and used straw rope for its chin-string.

The prohibitions for *baekjeong* were not limited to everyday life but also extended to weddings, funerals, and religious ceremonies. Since chief mourners of commoner status wore *paeraengi*, the chief mourner for a *baekjeong* funeral had to use a long towel to cover his forehead. *Baekjeong* could not use funeral biers, their gravesites were in locations separate from those of commoners, and they could not build ancestral shrines. In wedding ceremonies, *baekjeong* grooms could not ride a horse; brides could not use a palanquin nor put their hair up with an ornamental hairpin. If a *baekjeong* violated one of these prohibitions, all the people in the community would band together to punish the transgressor. For example, in 1809, when a *baekjeong* wore the attire of a government official and used a large parasol in a wedding ceremony in Gaeseong, the local residents beat the offender and tore down his house.

Did the Baekjeong *Just Slaughter Animals?*

It is true that the *baekjeong*, who were treated not much better than animals themselves, were mainly engaged in occupations involving butchering or slaughtering animals. However, this does not mean that it was their only occupation. What their occupations had in common was the fact that commoners did not engage in them because they were regarded as lowly.

First, one of the major professions of *baekjeong* was wicker making; they wove baskets with willow branches and sold them in markets. Second, they worked as performers who wandered around the country and earned a living by playing instruments, singing, or doing simple dances. Third, there were executioners who worked for prisons or the Ministry of Punishments. Commonly called *mangnani* or *huigwang*, executioners were originally chosen from the military, but from the mid-Joseon period, *baekjeong* were used for this task. They were not given the status of jailers with the authority to enforce the law; rather, the *baekjeong* were made to carry out executions that other people could not bring themselves to do. Fourth, they worked as tanners, making shoes and other leather products. These *baekjeong* were called *gatbachi*; the character *gat* meant 'leather,' and *bachi* was an old term for 'craftsman.' Fifth, there also were *baekjeong* farmers. Though very small in number, some of the *baekjeong* were able to assimilate into agricultural society and engage in farming. In addition to these occupations, there were those who became owned by an official or a local gentry family, becoming a private unfree person.

Baekjeong tended to live frugally since they faced discrimination, and some of them became quite wealthy. Among the different types of *baekjeong*, the ones who slaughtered animals were the most well-off. They banded together, sharing the tools of their trade; they worked for meat sellers or were hired by private households. Some joined forces with figures in the ruling class or were be employed by them. As payment for their work, they usually received the blood, internal organs, and hide of cows. They then sold them in the market, making a considerable profit. They dried the hides or sold them to a tanner; some made simple goods from them for their own use. This is probably the reason that *baekjeong* villages were called *pichon* (hide villages) in the countryside. There were cases of butchers who cleaned their blades and gave up their professions for three years when their parents died. Not just an expression of filial piety, it also meant that they were sufficiently well off that they could afford not to work for three years. Slaughtering animals was so profitable that illegal butchers were common. However, only a small number of *baekjeong* butchers could amass such wealth; those in other professions did not lead such prosperous lives.

Hidden Discrimination

Though the social status system was abolished in 1894 in the Gabo Reforms, social discrimination against the *baekjeong* persisted. They could now register their names on household registers but had separate ones from other commoners. Since their occupation was listed as *dohan* (meaning *baekjeong*), their status as former *baekjeong* was evident. Despite legal revisions that later enabled them to use the same household registers as other people, it was still possible to identify them as *baekjeong* because of the continued use of the term *dohan* or because of the use of a telltale red mark. The *baekjeong* engaged in continual resistance against the persistence of discrimination despite rapid social change. Even at the end of the Joseon period, though they lived in separate communities scattered in various regions, they frequently engaged in collective action to submit petitions to the government. They pressed for a guarantee from the authorities to abolish low-born status and allow them to become commoners. They also asked to be allowed to wear a horsehair hat as commoners did. Their efforts continued into the Japanese occupation period and led to the Hyeongpyeong Movement in the 1920s whose goal was the liberation of the *baekjeong*. Today, the lowborn class, including *baekjeong* status, no longer exists, but there is still veiled discrimination in some parts of Korean society. It seems that a great deal of time and effort is needed for a class to become fully liberated from all forms of social discrimination.

15. THE REBELLION OF IM GGEOKJEONG

Han Sang Kwon

Im Ggeokjeong (?–1562) was one of a trio of legendary bandits, along with Hong Gildong and Jang Gilsan, who were active in the mid-sixteenth century during the reign of Myeongjong (r. 1545–1567). Unlike typical criminals, they were righteous heroes who were beloved and supported by the common people. Embodying the hopes and desires of the people, they were larger-than-life figures whose feats became the stuff of legend well beyond their deaths. Known for his smarts and valor, Im was born in the Yangju region into the *baekjeong* class. Though they were not as low in status as the unfree people (*nobi*), they were often treated worse because of their occupations. They did the jobs that violated Buddhist principles such as slaughtering, tanning, leatherworking, and meat-selling. The *baekjeong* were subjected to such severe discrimination that during the Gabo Peasants' War of 1894, one of the peasant army's demands was to eliminate discrimination against them and allow them to get rid of their *paeraengi*, the distinctive hats that they wore. Im Ggeokjeong, who came from the lowest segment of society, was a revolutionary who completely rejected the legitimacy of feudal society. His resolute resistance against the ruling class inspired Hong Myeonghui (1888–1968) to serialize the novel *Im Ggeokjeong* in an effort to give readers hope during the colonial period. The novel enabled a rediscovery of Im Ggeokjeong as the figure who best captured the sentiments of people during the Joseon era.

The Causes of Banditry

Im Ggeokjeong began his raids in the late 1550s at a time when people turned to thievery as a protest against society and in response to economic crisis. One of the main causes of banditry was continual crop failures and famine. Natural disasters precipitated crop failures and famine, pushing starving households to turn to stealing. A similar phenomenon can be observed in the West, when rampant piracy and marauding plagued the Mediterranean region throughout the latter part of the sixteenth century. In Korea, raids on wealthy landowners and government properties reflected declining economic and social conditions. It is not an

Fig. 15.1. Illustration from the serialization of the novel *Im Ggeokjeong* by Hong Myeonghui that appeared in the *Joseon ilbo* on November 21, 1928.

exaggeration to say that the chronic crop failures and famines of the mid-sixteenth century were a direct cause of the looting and pillaging.

Another factor was the excessive taxes levied on the people. The combination of a heavy tax burden and poor harvests brought farmers to the brink of ruin. In Hwanghae province, where Im's army was based, there were two severe problems with the tax system. The first was with the tribute tax. The amount of goods demanded by officials was in excess of what peasants could actually provide. Though Hwanghae province had far less land, population, and products than the three southern provinces, it was levied far more products, and the collection of tribute goods was much stricter. The second major problem concerned mandatory military service which was considered a form of taxation. Soldiers from Hwanghae province had to do sentry duty at strategic points in Pyeongan province along the frontier with China such as Uiju, Isan, and Ganggye, as well as tours of duty in Seoul. Popular sentiment in the province would turn against the government whenever it tried to raise an army. When Im Ggeokjeong's activities were at their height, the government temporarily suspended the draft, afraid that new recruits might join the bandits.

A third major factor behind the rise of banditry was the exploitation by local magistrates. The excessive tax burden was rooted in the corruption of powerful aristocratic families. By openly selling official posts, these families encouraged unscrupulous officials to exploit the people. They extracted all that they could from the peasantry, even seizing their livestock, in order to satisfy the endless greed of the ministers they served. This was the reason that Im Ggeokjeong's army targeted yangban, officials, and ministers as enemies of the people.

Guerrilla Raids

Im's raids began to develop into a rebellion when he attacked government offices and distributed the goods that he stole from the storehouses to the people. His forces consisted of peasants trapped in poverty, dispossessed farmers stripped of their land, criminals fleeing from conscripted labor, and those who feared oppression. There were also bankrupt farmers, runaway slaves, and *baekjeong* – the various disenfranchised elements of society. They had a support network of low-ranking civil servants who provided them with inside information and merchants who sold stolen goods for them. *The Veritable Records of King Myeongjong* contains the following description of Im's army and its tactics:

> Though the bandits in Hwanghae Province are said to be audacious, the main group consists of only eight or nine people. When they gather, they form a gang of bandits, and when they disperse, they become part of the populace. They hide themselves deep in the mountains and disappear without a trace. It is not a case where it is possible to set up a camp, launch an invasion, and engage in battle as if they were an enemy country.

The army was divided into eight or nine smaller units with Im Ggeokjeong as the supreme commander who directed the leader of each unit. The ideal size for a typical raid was no more than twenty men, and Im's army had a total of about 200 men. They were a well-trained, elite fighting force as shown in the battle of Pyeongsan when they conducted complex maneuvers to draw attacking government forces into a trap.

Im's forces used guerrilla tactics that utilized the terrain in mountainous areas. Their preference for quick strikes was largely a function of the level of their weapons. They were armed only with spears, swords, bows and arrows, and hatchets; they had no firearms or other weapons that used gunpowder. They could not engage in a direct battle with government troops since they were far inferior in both manpower and firepower. But Im's army had an advantage in maneuverability; they were a cavalry that had detailed knowledge of the local terrain. Their main bases were located in Hwanghae province in places such as Mount Guwol, Seoheung, and Singye; they had additional bases in rugged mountain areas such as Seongcheon, Yangdeok, and Maengsan in Pyeongan province and Icheon in Gangwon province.

Im Ggeokjeong's army also operated outside of mountain regions. When they scattered into private homes to escape from government forces, they were indistinguishable from ordinary people in their clothing and language. Even if a thousand soldiers were mobilized, there was no way to find the bandits unless someone informed on them. When they had to disperse, they went to highly populated areas where they could fend for themselves – mainly large cities such as Gaeseong, Pyongyang, and Seoul. Since bandits also had to eat and acquire weapons, they had to trade their stolen goods for things that they needed. They operated in commercial cities such as Gaeseong and Seoul and in trading centers such as Bongsan in Hwanghae province where it was easy to sell, purchase, and steal goods.

Eliminating Corrupt Officials

The ruling class condemned Im Ggeokjeong as a savage, lawless thief and plunderer.

> In the three years since the enemy began causing trouble, they injured five village magistrates. Soldiers from several provinces went after them but caught only one of them, and countless numbers of commoners have died.

Im was not simply a bandit who pillaged and plundered but a rebel who defied the authority of the government. Many of the attacks by his forces were bold and daring. They rescued captured comrades in broad daylight; first surrounding the gates of a government office, they killed the sentries and then broke through the prison gate. They also killed government soldiers who guarded official envoys and patrolled areas near Seoul in an effort to intimidate the heads of the police force.

The first official killed by Im's forces was Yi Eokgeun of Gaeseong in 1559. He was a police official with the city of Gaeseong who became a target because he had arrested dozens of Im's men. Receiving a report that Im's forces had entered the Gaeseong region, Yi set out with an army and surrounded them. In the middle of the night, he took a group of twenty men to attack their hideout and was killed, shot with seven arrows. The following year, government forces discovered that Im's men had snuck into central Seoul. The vice-chief of police Nam Chigeun pursued them, but they escaped after some fierce fighting. Battling government forces on the streets of Seoul, they shot an officer and broke through the police lines. To take responsibility for their failure to capture Im, Nam Chigeun and the other vice-chief of police, Yi Mongrin, were transferred to other posts, and the other soldiers and officers were sent to the State Tribunal to receive a severe punishment. Gaining confidence after their successful escape, Im's forces entered villages impersonating officials and received lavish treatment from the magistrates. They gained complete control over parts of Hwanghae province, making it impossible to enter those areas even in the daytime. They went to Seoul to sell the goods that they stole, openly impersonating court officials and their relatives.

When Im Ggeokjeong took control over parts of Hwanghae province, the government appointed Yi Heumnye as the magistrate of Bongsan county, where Im's base was located. This post was his reward for capturing many of Im's men years earlier when he was serving in Singye. Hearing the news of his appointment, Im planned to assassinate him. He felt that eliminating Yi would not only establish his authority but also stave off future complications. However, the plot was divulged when Im's chief tactician, Seo Rim, was captured, and Im's forces found themselves surrounded by government troops. Yi Heumrye and Jeong Suik took the troops stationed at Bongsan and headed to Pyeongsan, joined by troops led by Gang Ryeo and Jang Hyobeom. When five hundred government troops pursued Im's forces into the thick forests and deep gorges of Pyeongsan, they lured the troops into a valley and escaped through a gorge. Yeon Cheonnyeong, an officer with the government troops, took Gang Ryeo's horse and went with a soldier to cut off their escape at the base of the mountain, but he had the horse taken from him and was killed. After hearing the news of the officer's death, the king held a secret meeting with his key ministers and ordered them to come up with a new strategy to handle Im. The plan was to raise an army from the five provinces of Hamgyeong, Pyeongan, Hwanghae, Gangwon, and Gyeonggi for a large-scale suppression campaign. Worried that raising troops might cause the people to riot or instigate some kind of disturbance, the ministers proposed sending two high-ranking military envoys to recruit soldiers in just two provinces, Hwanghae and Gangwon.

The Capture of an Imposter

The news of the deaths of officials at the hands of Im Ggeokjeong and his forces shocked the king and the ruling class. Since they disgraced the country and undermined the authority of the king, they were viewed not as thieves or bandits but as treasonous insurgents who rebelled openly against the government. Well aware of the fighting abilities and tactical sophistication of Im's forces from the battle of Pyeongsan, the king advocated the dispatch of military envoys despite the risk of public outcry. He felt that a local magistrate or provincial governor would not have sufficient resources to catch him; it would be necessary for the central government to raise troops to suppress the insurgents. Those opposed to the plan feared that popular sentiment would turn against the government because of the severe famine and the high cost of supporting an army. But the hard-line stance of the king and some officials prevailed, claiming that it was necessary to annihilate the bandits in Hwanghae province.

In the twelfth lunar month of 1560, the government sent military envoys to Hwanghae and Gangwon provinces, along with fifty officers each to lead the troops, with an order to wipe out Im's forces. Soon afterwards, a report arrived at court with the news that Im Ggeokjeong had been captured. However, the captive turned out to be Im's older brother, Gadochi. The military envoy had used torture to extract a false confession from him. Officials had criticized the mission for failing to produce results though given much time. The envoys began catching suspicious individuals and subjecting them to severe torture. They went to such lengths to extract a confession, regardless of whether it was true, because they wanted to avoid blame and receive a commendation. When the captive's actual identity was revealed, criticism of the mission emerged again, leading to the dismissal of the envoys and the cancellation of further dispatches. In the ninth lunar month of the following year, an official in Uiju named Yi Sucheol reported that Im Ggeokjeong and Han On were captured, but this also proved to be false.

Turbulence in Seoul and the Capture of Im Ggeokjeong

The government's campaign to suppress Im's rebellion ended in failure. Meanwhile, the morale of Im's forces was high, and they continued to control large portions of Hwanghae province. They effectively turned those regions into an enemy state that had seceded from Joseon with Im Ggeokjeong as its leader. The Left State Councillor Yi Jungyeong proposed sending out military police officers to put down the rebellion. The plan was to surround Im's forces and coordinate an attack with authorities in the four provinces of Gyeonggi, Gangwon, Pyeongan, and Hamgyeong to cut off any possible escape routes.

Late in the tenth lunar month in 1561, about twenty days after the new campaign began, there was a rumor that a large number of Im's forces had snuck into Seoul. It was clearly a clever ruse by Im to confuse the court and get them to split up the army sent to capture him. Believing that Im was about to launch an all-out attack on Seoul, the king issued an order not to allow any more of Im's forces to enter the capital. The city gates were closed before their usual time and were not opened until after sunrise; during those hours, the government also imposed a curfew. Troops were also sent to stand guard at the four main mountains on the outskirts of Seoul – Mt. Mongmyeok, Mt. Inwang, Mt. Baegak, and Mt. Tarak – where bandits could enter. Concerned that those who evaded military service would join Im's army, the government temporarily suspended recruitment of soldiers until the rebellion settled down. It also increased the sentries at the gates of Gyeongbok and Changdeok Palaces to strengthen their defenses, and it quietly ordered the closure of all markets. When it was reported that Seoul was full of Im's men, the government ordered people in each of the city's five districts to patrol their neighborhoods. The king and the elites were terrified that Im was going to take over Seoul. With the capital in chaos, it appeared to people that the country was on the verge of collapse.

Nonetheless, Im Ggeokjeong's days were numbered. The government army's scorched-earth strategy severely weakened his forces. Though Im managed to break through the army's lines and escape from Mt. Guwol, he was eventually captured in an elderly woman's house in Seoheung in Hwanghae province in the first lunar month of 1562. King Myeongjong was happy to hear the news of his capture and said, "I did not take the outbreak of the rebellion seriously, but now that this tenacious foe has been captured, the people can lie on their pillows and sleep comfortably."

The government's campaign to suppress Im Ggeokjeong's rebellion was successful but at the cost of significant loss of life.

The Historical Significance of Im Ggeokjeong

After a three-year battle against government forces, Im was captured alive and executed in early 1562. His rebellion was a direct rejection of the authority of the feudal state. They did not hesitate to slay officials, local magistrates, and military officers, viewing the ruling class, including the prime minister, officials, and yangban, as their enemies. The rebellion was a tremendous shock to the ruling class. The government regarded Im's forces not just as a gang of bandits who stole for personal enrichment but as rebels who could undermine the foundations of the state. He created a separate government in Hwanghae province beyond the reach of the royal government. It mobilized an army to suppress them, despite much opposition and the high costs involved. Seoul, where the king resided, was filled with fear that it would soon fall. Many within the ruling class lamented the imminent ruin of the country and then expressed relief that a full-scale rebellion did not break out. These were signs of a crisis in the ruling order and of the necessity of reform.

Im Ggeokjeong's revolt contributed to a shift in power from the *hungu* to the *sarim* faction. It played an important role in removing existing political forces and bringing new social actors to the fore. However, it did not achieve liberation for the low-born class, an issue with direct personal relevance for Im. But it is unclear whether this issue was a key motivating factor for him. Though Im had an instinctive hostility towards the feudal ruling class, he lacked an objective understanding of the contradictions of his time, nor did he try to resolve them by uniting the peasant masses. As a result, his resistance was isolated from the sphere of production and focused on banditry; i.e, the seizure of its surplus goods. Resistance to feudal society initially started as sporadic and short-lived revolts led by socially marginalized people outside of agriculture. It later developed into a lasting movement of the peasant masses whose lives were rooted in farming. In this sense, the historical significance of Im Ggeokjeong was that his rebellion constituted an early stage of the movement to reform feudal society.

16. DID PEOPLE DIVORCE IN THE JOSEON PERIOD?

Kwon Soon-Hyung

During the Joseon period, family life underwent a transformation as the Confucian patriarchal system increasingly became dominant. Patrilineal descent became the norm as the authority of the patriarch became virtually absolute. While the husband provided for the family and handled its external affairs, the wife focused on the household. This division of gender roles was ingrained in language; for instance, a Korean term for a husband and wife was *naeoe*, a combination of the two Chinese characters for 'inside' and 'outside.' The relationship between husband and wife was one of the Five Relationships mentioned in the *Mencius* as well as one of the Three Bonds. This was an indication of how central the subordination of women was to the constitution of the Confucian family. In fact, a woman's life was to be completely governed by men; according to the notion of the 'three obediences,' she was to obey her father before marriage, her husband upon marriage, and her son after her husband's death. As long as the social opportunities for women were limited, they had no choice but to live within the family under the protection of men.

Initially, the Confucian family system was restricted to the yangban class. For the common people, there was no special education for girls, and the rules for the separation of husbands and wives were not strictly observed. Because the women had to work alongside men in the fields, it would have been ridiculous to follow these rules. Education for children was impossible; they were tied to a tree trunk or placed in the care of their older sisters while their mothers worked in the fields. Over the course of the Joseon period, institutions for the maintenance of the patriarchal family, such as ancestor worship, spread throughout society as it was increasingly seen as the basis for the social order. Gender distinctions were even evident in daily life. Houses were separated into inner and outer quarters with a gate in the middle that was used only on special occasions. It became natural for men not to discuss household affairs and for women not to mention external affairs. Married couples had separate wardrobes and wall shelves to prevent the mixing of clothes. Unable to leave the house freely, women could only go out at night with a candle for light and had to cover their faces. When walking on the street, men always walked on the right, and women on the left. In the process of these developments, the nature of marriage changed for women. This chapter is a brief examination of the status of women in the Confucian family system and the institution of divorce which served more to maintain patriarchy than to provide an escape from it.

Trained to be Dutiful Wives

The inequality of the sexes was ingrained in children's minds from birth. When a male child was born, his parents laid him on a table, and he was given beads to play with. But a female baby was laid on the ground and given spools as toys. This was to instill the idea that women were lower and weaker beings meant to exist under other people and that they needed to be diligent. As children grew older, boys were instructed to respond promptly to adults, whereas girls had to respond slowly. Belts for boys were made of leather, while those for girls were made with thread. Even the content of their education was completely different. At the age of six, boys were taught numbers and the four directions, and nine year-old boys learned about the principles of the calendar, such as the sexagenary cycle and the first and fifteenth days of the lunar month. Ten year-old boys were taught by a teacher who came from outside the household. On the other hand, when girls turned ten, they stayed at home and were taught cotton-spinning, sericulture, and silk-weaving by a female teacher. They also learned how to perform other duties of women, such as making clothes and helping to prepare the memorial rites.

During the Joseon period, the objective of marriage was to honor the ancestors and to ensure the continuation of the family line. Since a housewife had to live in her husband's house, women had many responsibilities, but her primary mission was to continue her husband's family line. Parents gave their daughters practical life lessons on adapting to married life, including sex education. The focus of practical education was mainly on proper speech, behavior, and other kinds of etiquette. Girls were taught to take steps no longer than the length of their foot when walking in the in-law's house and to walk backwards in front of adults without turning their back on them. They also practiced how to initiate and finish the chants at ancestor rituals and funeral rites and how to force themselves to cry whenever a situation called for tears.

The purpose of sex education was to bear sons. Young girls were taught to avoid food that negatively affected men's virility, such as buckwheat or

Fig. 16.1. *Woman Wearing a Long Hood*, Sin Yunbok, late eighteenth century. The *jangot* (long hood) was used by women to cover their faces when they went out. (National Museum of Korea)

fernbrake (*gosari*). They also learned how to calculate the day with the highest probability of becoming pregnant with a male child. A piece of clean cotton cloth was inserted into the vagina toward the end of the menstrual cycle. If the cotton stayed light in color, it meant that the prime impregnation period had already passed. If it was bright red, it signified the best time for impregnation had not yet arrived. If the cloth became golden in color, it indicated that the next four days were the optimal time. During this four-day period, insemination on even numbered days was believed to produce a male child while insemination on odd numbered days produced a girl. The sexagenary cycle was also thought to influence the gender of the child; impregnation on certain days during each season was believed to produce a male. In spring, it was the *gap* and *eul* days; in summer, it was the *byeong* and *jeong* days; in autumn, it was on the *gyeong* and *sin* days; and in winter, it was the *im* and *gye* days. The most difficult thing for women to learn was how to calculate these propitious days on their fingers, since the calculation had to be done within six days of menstruation.

The Status of Women

However, women in the Joseon period were not simply son-bearing machines who were inferior to men. Despite the wife's lower status, a balance had to be maintained with her husband. Each was recognized to have his or her own domain, and women were even given a certain level of status. Under the *buin bongjak* system, yangban women received specific social positions based on the official rank of their husbands. This included titles such as *jeongyeong buin*, *jeong buin*, and *suk buin*. *Bongjak* status could also be based on the ranks of their sons. Women were the center of the household. The husband could not interfere in domestic affairs, and the wife's authority within the household was absolute. The wife handled all household affairs, memorial rituals for ancestors, and children's education. A woman held rights as a mother as well. If her husband and father-in-law died, the wife took control of the family and became responsible for taking care of adoptions, marriage, and matters involving inheritance. These rights gave rise to the system of *suryeom cheongjeong* under which the queen mother would serve as regent and administer state affairs from behind a veil at court.

Finally, women had property rights. During the early Joseon period, sons and daughters received equal shares of the family inheritance, with the exception of the eldest son who received more because he had to take care of ancestral rituals. Even married daughters had the right to receive a share of the inheritance. Additionally, the property owned by a woman before marriage remained under her control afterward. If she died childless, the deceased wife's unfree people would be passed on to the husband, but if he remarried, they were returned to the wife's family. Women were allowed to own a significant level of property because remarriage for them was prohibited. Such guarantees were essential since a woman needed financial stability in order to remain faithful to her husband after his death. During the late Joseon era, however, property rights for women gradually declined. Because of the great emphasis on ancestral rites, eldest sons became more important, receiving most of the inheritance. Other sons now inherited far less property, with women receiving even less because of the growing preference for sons over daughters. Since married daughters were no longer considered to be part of their birth family, they increasingly received no inheritance from their own families.

The emphasis on a woman's fidelity gradually became extreme in this period. Before, a wife would be considered a virtuous woman (*yeollyeo*) if she did not remarry after her husband's death. But now she would have to join her husband in death or do something comparable in order to attain that title. In the late Joseon period, their numbers gradually increased among the commoner class. It can be seen as a reflection of the social and economic advances made by commoners at the time. The increase can also be explained by the spread of Neo-Confucian ideology from the yangban to the commoners through constant efforts to edify them such as the creation of Hangeul. As Confucian ethics spread throughout Joseon society, patriarchy and male dominance became even stronger, resulting in a gradual decline in the status of women.

The Seven Grounds for Divorce

Did people get divorced during the Joseon era? Since marriage is the union of a man and woman of their own free will, it is only natural that they must have been able to divorce as well. As with marriage, the institution of divorce was rooted in the patriarchal family system. This is demonstrated by the term *chilgeo jiak*; it refers to the seven evil acts for which a husband can abandon his wife. The seven acts (*chilgeo*) included things such as:

(1) not taking proper care of her in-laws
(2) not bearing a son
(3) being promiscuous and giving birth to possibly another man's child
(4) being overly jealous of a husband's concubines
(5) having a serious illness that prevents her from bearing a son
(6) engaging in gossip to the point of disrupting family life
(7) stealing

In practice, however, the criteria for the *chilgeo* were very ambiguous. Judgments could be very arbitrary in determining what constituted unfilial behavior toward the in-laws and how severe a disease had to be in order to be grounds for a divorce. If a family wanted to get rid of a daughter-in-law, they could always find something in her behavior that would fall under one of the seven categories. The only protection for women was the so-called *sambulgeo* – or the three exceptions to divorce. A wife could not be cast out of a family – even if she committed one of the *chilgeo* – if she had no place to return to, if she had observed the three-year mourning period for her in-laws, or if she got married before the husband's family became wealthy. Exceptions were not possible for women who had a serious illness or who had committed adultery. Unfilial behavior toward one's in-laws was also not tolerated since filial piety was one of the most important values in the Joseon period.

One would expect that women at the time lived in daily fear of divorce, but in actuality, divorces were rarely granted. The government did its utmost to prevent divorce because of the ideological importance of chastity. A woman was expected to remain chaste even after her husband died and not to remarry. In a society that prohibited remarriage, the potential existed for social problems to emerge if there were large numbers of divorced women. It was not possible to abandon one's wife except in extreme situations, and there were almost no grounds for divorce other than adultery and unfilial behavior toward one's in-laws. In the nineteenth century, during the reign of Gojong (r. 1864–1907), the 'seven evil acts' were reduced to five in number, as jealousy and the inability to bear a son were no longer considered legitimate reasons for divorce. The number of exceptions to divorce was also increased from three to four; it was prohibited under any circumstances if the couple had children.

The difficulty in obtaining a divorce had some benefits to women since it helped to secure the wife's position in her husband's household. But problems were unavoidable in marriages between two people who had not even seen each other's faces before the wedding. Husbands found all sorts of ways to fabricate reasons to divorce their wives. The most common was to accuse one's wife of infidelity since it guaranteed a divorce. During the reign of Sejong (r. 1418–1450), a man named Gim Dal, who had been married for three years, fell in love with his female unfree concubine. So Gim accused his wife of a relationship with another man prior to their marriage and kicked her out of the house. However, an investigation found her to be not guilty; after receiving a punishment, he was forced to live with his wife again.

There were also methods of separating from one's wife other than divorce. One was called *sobak*, which referred to a situation in which a husband and wife lived together but actually led separate lives. For instance, men would bring concubines into their homes, taking advantage of the fact that concubinage was accepted. Cases in which the husband abandoned the wife were called *oe sobak*. When a wife rejected her husband, it was known as *nae sobak*, but there were virtually no cases of this. Husbands were generally the ones who initiated *sobak*; women were more worried about *sobak* because it could occur without reasonable cause, in contrast to *chilgeo jiak*. The difficulties of obtaining a divorce and the practice of *sobak* were mainly limited to the yangban class. It was easier for commoners to divorce, and they had two methods for doing so – *sajeong paui* and *halgeub hyuseo*. In *sajeong paui*, when a couple was clearly incompatible with each other, the husband and wife would sit down to discuss their inability to live together and reach an agreement on a divorce. *Halgeub hyuseo* involved a simple ritual in which one person would cut the lower edge of the other's upper garment with a knife and give the piece of cloth to their spouse. These two methods were never used by the *sadaebu*.

Divorce, Sobak, *and Their Aftermath*

Were women in the Joseon period only the victims of divorce? Were they able to initiate a divorce themselves? A woman could demand a divorce only in two situations. The first was if her husband left the house and was missing for a period of three years. The second was if the husband committed a severe violation of their relationship. Examples of violations include beating the wife's parents or grandparents, killing a member of his wife's family, and committing adultery with his mother-in-law. In these cases, a woman could go to a government office and apply for a divorce. She could also get a divorce if her husband beat her, though it was only possible in instances when the women suffered a broken bone or worse and had the husband's consent. The fact that a man could divorce his wife if she beat him, regardless of the severity of his injuries, shows the degree of discrimination against women.

However, these were exceptional situations and rarely happened in everyday life; in reality, women had virtually no right to divorce their husbands. Women who wanted a divorce would threaten their husbands to get them to agree to a divorce, or they would simply run away. Such behavior ran afoul of the law; the punishment for a woman who abandoned her husband was a flogging of 100 lashes. If she remarried after running away, she would be executed by hanging. Even though divorce was permitted at the time, it was hardly a simple matter because remarriage was impossible and because women had little social or economic status outside of the family. Without any means to support themselves, they had to live their lives in fear of divorce or *sobak*.

What happened to women after a divorce? First, women lost custody of their children because they always remained with the father's family. Since remarriage was permitted until the early Joseon period, there were women who remarried. However, it was allowed only after their ex-husband remarried. For example, during the reign of Taejong (r. 1400–1418), the daughter of Son Heungjong and her second husband were sentenced to a flogging of 100 lashes because she remarried before her former husband did. During the reign of Seongjong (r. 1469–1494), remarriage was legally prohibited. The woman Eoudong, whose life has been the subject of a number of movies, called herself a prostitute and enjoyed a life of sexual freedom after being abandoned by her husband. Ultimately, her behavior scandalized society, and she was hung for her immoral deeds.

The victims of *sobak* also led lives of frustration. If the husband's family was from the upper class, a wife was able to find consolation by managing the household business. Even if her husband was madly in love with his concubine, it was not a major problem because they would live in separate houses. However, most commoner households could not afford a second residence; if a husband took a concubine, the wife returned to her family and led a sad life, scorned as an abandoned woman (*sobakdegi*). Alternately, she could choose to leave herself to the hands of fate by standing on the road leading to the shrine of a tutelary deity. During the Joseon era, there was a custom called *seupcheop*. If a woman who suffered from *sobak* stood on the road to a shrine early in the morning, the first man to find her had the duty to take her in and look after her. It did not matter if the man was married, single, a traveler, or a beggar; the woman had no say in the matter. She was required to follow the first man she met and share the rest of their lives together. The most common case was for older unmarried men and widowers to take these women as their spouses; if she were lucky, a woman would meet a nobleman or royal envoy returning to his hometown and would live as his favored concubine, changing her fortunes for the better. This custom was yet another example of how the lives of women in the Joseon period were completely controlled by men.

17. THE EDUCATIONAL SYSTEM

Jang Dong-Pyo

South Korea today is known for its highly educated populace, with a literacy rate of ninety-nine percent. Its success at creating a modern educational system is credited as a major factor behind its rapid industrial development. Nine years of schooling are compulsory, but over ninety percent of students continue their education. Competition is very intense to get into the top colleges. Students have to spend years preparing for the entrance exams, attending cram schools until late in the evening virtually every day of the week. This is routinely called 'examination hell.' Year after year, students subject themselves to such a pressure-filled, grueling schedule because they know that an elite college degree is the surest path to success. Though today's educational system differs greatly from that of the Joseon period, what they have in common is the fact that educational attainment was the key to gaining status and power.

At the beginning of the Joseon period, when Neo-Confucianism replaced Buddhism as the ruling ideology, the government undertook a reorganization of the educational system. The objective was to promote its new ideology and to assist the creation of a new social order based on Neo-Confucian principles. Mainly limited to the yangban class, education was meant to produce officials who were skilled at classical Chinese and thoroughly versed in the Confucian classics. It was not until the mid-Joseon period, when the adoption of Neo-Confucianism became complete, that a full educational system was established. Rather than a completely publicly funded system, there developed a dual structure of state and private schools. For the children of yangban families, the path to a high-ranking government position began at the local *seodang* (village schools), the equivalent of a primary school. Students who continued their education then enrolled at either a *hyanggyo* or a *seowon* in the provinces. *Hyanggyo* were schools established by the government; *seowon* were private Confucian academies that were established by provincial Neo-Confucian scholars called *sarim* and local yangban elites. After completing their studies at a *hyanggyo* or *seowon,* students then went to the capital to study in one of two government-run institutions. Most enrolled in one of the Sahak (literally, 'the four schools') that were located in eastern, western, southern, and central districts of Seoul. The most promising students entered the Seonggyungwan, the highest educational institution in the country. They finished their education when they passed the civil service examination, assuming official posts in the government. This chapter provides an overview of the three main provincial schools in the Joseon period: the *seodang*, the *hyanggyo*, and the *seowon*. It examines their organization and curriculum and discusses how private schools gradually came to play a larger role in education than state schools.

Seodang: *The Primary Schools of the Joseon Period*

Some scholars claim that the origins of the *seodang* can be traced back several centuries to the Goguryeo kingdom where there were schools called *gyeongdang*, but this has not been proven definitively. In the Joseon period, they began to spread throughout the country during the reign of Jungjong (r. 1506–1544). Their growth was the result of the community compact movement led by the *sarim* faction and of structural changes in rural society at the time. *Seodang* were preparatory schools for students whose ambition was to obtain an official post. They entered the school at age seven or eight and finished their studies at age fifteen or sixteen. They were built in villages by commoners and yangban families in the provinces. Families belonging to a rotating credit association (*gye*) jointly contributed the funds for its operation.

In contrast to *hyanggyo* and *seowon*, the types of *seodang* varied according to the region and the period. First, there was the *sasuk* or *dokseodang*. Established by powerful families, they employed a teacher and provided all the funds for their operation. Second, another type of *seodang* was the *donggye seodang*, schools built to educate the children of a specific clan. A yangban or wealthy family would raise money for a school by forming a local credit union or devoting a portion of their harvest to it. The school building was also used for other purposes such as family or clan meetings. Teachers were selected among educated village elders and itinerant intellectuals who taught for a living. The parents of students did not pay tuition, but they compensated teachers in other ways, providing them rice, firewood, and clothing as salary. When their children graduated, they held a simple celebration for the teacher called a *chaekgeori*. They also prepared special seasonal delicacies for the teacher to eat. When the summer study session called *hagwa* began, each household paid a separate fee. Third, there were *seodang* that were established jointly by several families and were thus larger in scale than those for a single family. They were advanced schools where the best students in each village were educated. Their purpose was to strengthen relations among families already connected by marriage ties and to continue the scholarly lineage of a particular teacher.

The staff of *seodang* consisted simply of the *hunjang* (headteacher) and *jeopjang*. The scholarly level of the headteacher varied since their qualifications differed greatly from region to region. The *jeopjang* was a kind of assistant teacher. The position originated from the custom in large *seodang* of selecting two or three of the top older students to help the headteacher. They were in charge of teaching and disciplining the younger students, taking care of them as if they were their older brothers. The curriculum at *seodang* was meant to prepare students to continue their studies at a *seowon* and consisted of three subjects: reading, composition, and calligraphy. The main textbooks were the *Thousand-Character Classic*, *Zizhi Tongjian*, and the Four Books and the Three Classics of Confucianism, as well as a Korean text from the sixteenth century, the *Dongmong seonseub*. Sometimes, additional texts were used such as the *Records of the Grand Historian* and prose texts from the Tang and Song dynasties, but in most cases, *seodang* only covered up to the *Zizhi Tongjian*. Classes were not held throughout the year; they were taught in special periods such as *hagwa*. The principal method of teaching was the *gang*; students read aloud from texts that they had already studied and then answered questions about their meaning. There were two types of *gang*: *baegang* in which students recited texts from memory and *myeongang* in which students used a book to recite. There were *gang* that were held every ten days, every fifteen days, or every month, but in *seodang*, it was common to have class every day. Classes also focused on teaching the principles of composition. The curriculum differed according to the season, and *seodang* even used games appropriate to the students' ages to facilitate learning.

The government tried a variety of measures to promote *seodang* education, but by the end of the Joseon period, it became ossified and empty. In the nineteenth century, the educational system underwent a fundamental decline because of disorder and corruption in the civil service examination system and because of the practice of selling official positions. Eventually, *seodang* did little more than teach students basic literacy, undergoing tremendous change at the end of the nineteenth century.

Hyanggyo: *The Secondary Schools of the Joseon Period*

Hyanggyo were public schools that were one level below the Seonggyungwan and had two main functions – education and the promotion of Confucianism in the local community. To carry out these functions, the Joseon government established one in each county and prefecture in the country. A *hyanggyo* was also built in all townships that were ruled by a magistrate sent from the central government under the policy of one *hyanggyo* for every township. With the spread of *seowon* beginning in the mid-Joseon period, *hyanggyo* focused more of their efforts on promoting Confucianism.

The staff of *hyanggyo* were called *gyoim*, and the types of *gyoim* consisted of the *doyusa, jangui,* and *saekjang*. The *doyusa*, who was appointed for a term of one year, was in charge of all administrative affairs. Below them were the *jangui* and *saekjang*, who took care of the students and their living quarters. Selected according to strict criteria, the *gyoim* performed a variety of roles in both the *hyanggyo* and the community. They prevented the authorities from interfering in the *hyanggyo*'s affairs and supervised the conduct of various rituals, including the memorial rites for Confucius. They advised local magistrates on their policies and *yuhyangso* on the selection of their members. In the early Joseon period, the government sent out instructors to teach in the *hyanggyo*. When this practice ended in the late Joseon period, local yangban from prominent families served as *gyoim* and ran the *hyanggyo*. Occasionally, there were instances when a person of middle status or a son of a concubine became a *gyoim*, but they were not regarded as the equals of yangban and were not able to assume leadership of the school.

Students over the age of sixteen at the *hyanggyo* were called *gyosaeng*, and their number was set according to the size of the village. The social status system structured life within the school. Students were distinguished according to their class; those from the yangban class were called *aengnae gyosaeng*, and those of commoner status and the offspring of concubines were *aegoe gyosaeng*. There were differences between two groups in where and what they studied as well as in their role in rituals. The fact that *gyosaeng* were exempt from military service gave rise to many social problems as the children of commoners tried all means possible to get a place in order to avoid their required duty. From the early seventeenth century, yangban tried to distinguish themselves from regular *gyosaeng* by calling themselves *dongjae yusaeng* rather than *aengnae gyosaeng*. The term derived from the fact that the dormitory for yangban was located on the east side of the school compound (*dong* meaning 'east'). Commoners and the children of concubines were then able to enter *hyanggyo* as *aengnae gyosaeng*, and they came to be called *seojae yusaeng*. Similarly, the term referred the location of their dormitory on the school's west side (*seo* meaning 'west'). In the late Joseon period, *gyosaeng* had the same status as commoners or *jungin*, and these changes reflected changes in the social status system at the time.

In the mid to late Joseon period, the *hyanggyo* gradually functioned less as an educational institution and more as an organ that served the interests of provincial yangban. In response, the government first tried measures to restore its focus on education. It dispatched instructors and supervisors, and in the eighteenth century, during the reigns of Yeongjo and Jeongjo, counties and prefectures selected teachers to educate both yangban and commoners. However, yangban students did not support these policies. As the educational function of the *hyanggyo* declined, the government put more emphasis on its ideological role by trying to increase the *hyanggyo*'s role in their communities through rituals such as the memorial rites performed at Confucian shrines. Their concern was to maintain order in a time of the social change by putting more emphasis on obedience and indoctrination. Local magistrates increasingly utilized the *hyanggyo* as an instrument of their rule; provincial yangban families used the schools to maintain their influence and promote their class interests. They held meetings in its building where they debated governmental policies and drafted documents to send to the local government office to protest a policy or push for a particular initiative. Though the nature of *hyanggyo* deviated from their original purpose in the late Joseon era, they continued to exist until the fall of the kingdom because of their importance to yangban families in the provinces.

Seowon: *The Private Secondary Schools of the Joseon Period*

The driving force behind the establishment of *seowon* were the provincial Neo-Confucian scholars known as the *sarim*.[1] In the early Joseon period, they devoted much effort to expanding their influence in their localities.

---

[1] The *sarim* were originally Neo-Confucian scholars located in the provinces who devoted themselves to their studies and did not initially pursue careers in government. They moved into politics and became a significant force in the late fifteenth century, becoming the political opponents of the so-called *hungu* faction.

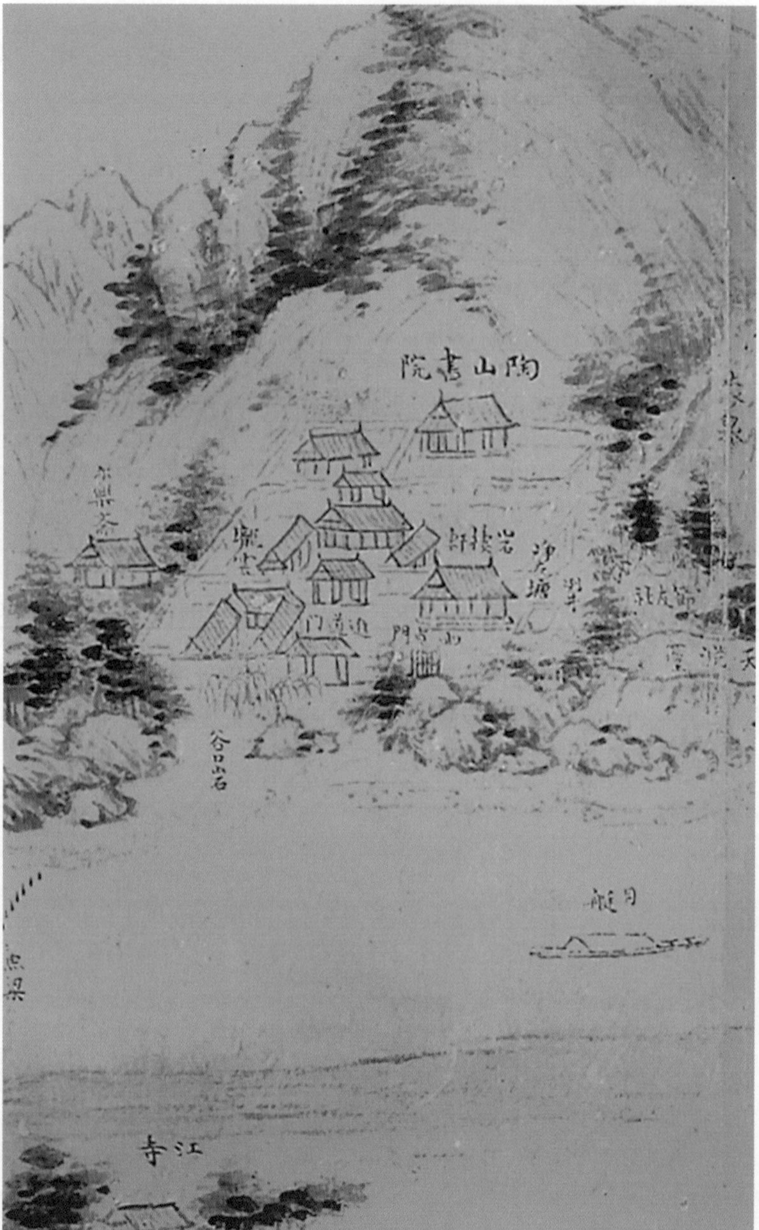

Fig. 17.1. *Dosan Seowon* (*Dosan seowondo*) (detail), Gang Sehwang, mid eighteenth century. The painting is National Cultural Treasure no. 522. (National Museum of Korea)

The first *seowon* was the Baegundong seowon established by Ju Sebung (1495–1554), the magistrate of Punggi county, North Gyeongsang province. From the mid-sixteenth century, their number increased as *sarim* scholars began to assume positions in the government. The *sarim* felt that education needed to shift its focus to training people to carry out an ethical politics. Education should be a more self-reflective form of study that enabled students to have a sincere appreciation of the devotion of earlier scholarly role models. These scholars also organized a movement to enshrine their intellectual forebears in Confucian shrines in order to claim the superiority of their scholarly lineage and thus to strengthen their political standing.

One of the main leaders of the *seowon* movement was Yi Hwang (Toegye, 1501–1570), one of the most prominent Neo-Confucian intellectuals of his age. He studied at the Seonggyungwan and passed the civil service examination in 1534. At the end of Jungjong's reign, he returned to his hometown in North Gyeongsang province and resigned from all positions in 1546. He spent almost all of the rest of his life far from Seoul, devoting most of his time to his studies. One of his major achievements was to provide a clear exposition of the role of *seowon*. *Sarim* scholars were to be the leaders of the *seowon*, with commoners seen as targets for enlightenment. Believing that it was first necessary to elucidate the principles of moral philosophy, Toegye felt that the *sarim* should take charge of this task and begin by rectifying their ways and setting a proper direction for their scholarship. Critical of the official scholarship taught at *hyanggyo*, Toegye organized the establishment of many *seowon*. Most were built in quiet, scenic, and isolated places where students could devote themselves entirely to study, in former temple sites or run-down temples, or in places with a connection to the sages enshrined within its grounds.

The curriculum of the *seowon* focused on Neo-Confucianism and the study of ethics. In contrast to governmental schools, *seowon* stressed the autonomy and unique benefits of private education. The regulations that Toegye drew up for the Isan seowon in North Gyeongsang province served as the prototype for the curriculum. The order in which students learned the Confucian texts was as follows: the *Elementary Learning*, the *Great Learning*, the *Analects*, the *Mencius*, *Doctrine of the Mean*, *Classic of Poetry*, *Classic of History*, the *Book of Changes*, and the *Spring and Autumn Annals*. Instruction involved a combination of self-study and the methods prescribed in Toegye's regulations. The most basic type of class was the *gang*, in which a student read aloud from a text he had prepared and then answered questions about it. Just like *seodang*, there were two kinds of *gang* – *baegang* and *myeongang*, that were held once every ten days, every fifteen days, or every lunar month. The performance of students was judged on a scale of either four or five grades.[2] *Seowon* kept records of students' attendance and grades, as well as of what they read. They also functioned as a library in rural society; as the characters of the term *seowon* suggest (*seo* meaning 'writing' or 'book' and *won* meaning 'house'), it was a place for collecting, storing, and lending books.

The *seowon*'s role in communal rituals was just as important as its role in education. Memorial rites were conducted in the spring and autumn in which sages from the past were enshrined at the school. They were occasions to present sages as ideal role models for their communities. Only people whose scholarship and morality were superior or whose loyalty and integrity were exemplary could have their tablets enshrined at a *seowon*. Some *seodang* were built when a famous scholar was still alive, and there were cases where they developed into a *seowon* with a shrine dedicated to that scholar. Compared to other regions, there were relatively more *seowon* in Gyeongsang province since it produced many scholars who belonged to an orthodox Neo-Confucian lineage that included Jeong Mongju (1337–1392), Gil Jae (1353–1419), and Yi Hwang.[3] The Joseon government began to provide support for the establishment of *seowon* as part of its policy to promote Confucianism. However, when factional conflicts became severe from the seventeenth century, the schools began to function as the base for a particular faction. They now enshrined eminent figures who could help raise the political profile of its associated faction.

The number of *seowon* increased rapidly from the mid-Joseon period, leading to the decline of *hyanggyo*. Political, economic, and social changes all contributed to the rapid growth. First, the growth of *seowon* was connected to the emergence of factional politics. Factional struggle dominated politics after the *sarim* faction gained power at court, intensifying in the seventeenth century after the Imjin War and the Manchu invasions. Political dominance now involved gaining the support of the *sarim* whose views were shaped through the *seowon* in the provinces. *Seowon* gradually increased in importance as they became the primary institution through which the *sarim* sought to gain broader support for their political agenda. In addition to their roles in education and ritual life, they also functioned as public forums in their regions where yangban gathered and discussed

---

2 The four grades were *tong*, *yak*, *jo*, or *bul* (from high to low); the five grades were, from high to low, *daetong* (大通), *tong* (通), *yaktong* (略通), *jotong* (組通), and *bultong* (不通).

3 The lineage also included scholars such as Gim Jongjik (1431–1492), Gim Goengpil (1454–1504), Jeong Yeochang (1450–1504), and Yi Eonjeok (1491–1553).

various issues. Second, with the rise of factional conflict, family and scholarly lineage gradually became more important. One of the *sarim*'s motivations in establishing *seowon* and shrines was to enhance the prestige of these lineages. Third, the emergence of the *seowon* also reflected the rise of provincial yangban clans. They were the leading figures behind the formation of institutions such as the *yuhyangso* and the community compact,[4] as well as *seowon*. As these schools became established in rural society, they provided the foundation for the hegemony of provincial yangban.

Many kinds of corruption emerged as *seowon* gradually focused more on cultural indoctrination of the rural populace. One source of corruption was *mukpae*, the documents issued by *seowon* to summon commoners or raise funds from them. Some of its staff took advantage of their status to use these documents to extort money from the lower classes. Another source was the exemption from military service granted to students. Under the pretense of rectifying customs and fostering communal spirit, these abuses functioned to resist social change and benefitted the yangban class. *Seowon* displayed their ability to mobilize the yangban class during the debate over the mourning rites for King Hyojong in the seventeenth century. Yangban families in Gyeongsang province utilized them to build support for their positions and even to organize protests.

The increase in the number of *seowon* and shrines led to their being centered on a particular clan. These were the so-called *munjung seowon*. Their numbers grew rapidly as *seowon* became more active in communal ritual life from the seventeenth century. Enshrining a famous scholar from one's family in a *seowon* was an effective way to enhance its prestige. Rather than working for the benefit of the entire village, the local yangban elites began to focus more on protecting the interests of their families. Their influence now extended only over their villages rather than an entire county or prefecture. The decline of their influence from the late eighteenth century and their lack of unity stemmed from their inability to articulate interests common to all members of the community. Problems with the *seowon* had already begun to be seriously debated in the government in the early eighteenth century, and King Yeongjo (r. 1724–1776) ordered nineteen of them to be torn down in 1741. In the mid-nineteenth century, the Daewongun abolished all but forty-seven of them in an effort to undermine the yangban and strengthen the authority of the monarchy.

with Nari Been

[4] The *yuhyangso* and community compact are discussed in chapter eleven by Kwon Nae-Hyun.

18. MILITARY LIFE

Seo Tae-Won

The Korean peninsula is one of the most militarized regions of the world. Two large armies have been standing off against each other for over fifty years since the two Koreas remain technically at war. South Korea has the sixth largest army in the world, while North Korea has the fourth largest. In both Koreas, all men are required to serve in the military; as of the year 2010, the length of mandatory service in the South is twenty-one months for the army, slightly longer for the navy and the air force. Virtually all young men in South Korea are concerned about their mandatory military service, particularly after they turn nineteen, the first year of their eligibility. Although protecting the country's borders is considered a sacred duty, they feel a psychological burden because of the stresses of military life and a separation from their normal lives. Several methods have emerged to avoid military service; occasionally, a celebrity or other public figure will cause a controversy because of the extreme lengths he is willing to go. In South Korea, a man's duty to the state does not end with his discharge from the military; men must serve in the reserves until they are thirty-five years of age.

The military was one of the main groups behind the founding of the Joseon kingdom. All Korean school children are taught the story of Yi Seonggye, the founder of the country. He was a general at the end of the Goryeo era who was sent to fight against Ming China; however, he turned back and overthrew the government to found a new kingdom. Though Joseon is often associated with the literati, the military also loomed large over social and political life. This was especially true for commoners who had to pay the military tax and bore most of the cost of supporting the military. This chapter examines the differences between the military of the Joseon period and that of today and the ways that people at the time tried to avoid military service.

The Basics of Military Life

Military life during the Joseon period was very different from that of today. Information about the basics of military life can be found in texts such as the *Gyeongguk daejeon*, the code of laws of the Joseon era. First, the length of military service was long. In principle, commoner men were eligible for military duty between the ages of sixteen and sixty, serving far longer than they do now. In contrast to today, men in the Joseon period served for two to six months each year before being replaced. Service was regarded as an onerous duty since it lasted for so long. Second, the government generally did not give a salary to rank-and-file soldiers. In the Joseon period, *bo* were assigned only to the main army, varying in amount according to the type of soldier. The term *bo* referred to the men who fulfilled their military service by tending to the material needs of the armed forces. The government did not give a separate salary to regular soldiers until the formation of the Hullyeon Dogam army during the Imjin War (1592–1598). Today, all active soldiers receive at least a small salary, including full-time reservists and those who fulfill their military service by working in government offices, but in the Joseon period, most low-ranking soldiers did not receive any direct benefits from the government. Instead, soldiers had to depend on each other for support.

Third, soldiers in the Joseon period had to provide their own uniforms and weapons. They did so in order to avoid punishment during inspections by their commanders. One example can be found in a passage about the Sogo Army in the *Veritable Records of King Hyojong* for the year 1657:

> If the army's weapons were even a little dull or if their uniforms were slightly dirty, the commander beat the soldiers severely. So they pawned their cows and horses or sold their fields to procure weapons, uniforms, and military supplies.

Soldiers used their families' entire wealth to obtain weapons and uniforms themselves since their commanders would have punished them severely if they were below standard. The government did give tax exemptions to soldiers who purchased expensive weapons with their own money, such as rifles.

Fourth, armies in the Joseon period were organized according to social status. Armies made up of yangban included the Gapsa, Byeolsiwi, Naegeumwi, Chunguiwi, Chungchanwi, Chungsunwi, Doseongwi, and the Hoikwi. Commoners served in the regular army, and the Japsaek Army and the Sogo Army were made up of people of lowborn status. There were times when existing armies were disbanded, and new ones were formed. There were also cases such as the Sogo Army, which originally consisted of both commoners and lowborn and was later reorganized to have only

Fig. 18.1. *The King's Blessings Extend to the North* (*Buksaeseoneundo*) (detail), Han Sigak, c. seventeenth century. This part of the painting shows a military examination being conducted in the town of Gilju in Hamgyeong province in the year 1664. (National Museum of Korea)

private unfree people (*sacheon*). Thus, these distinctions did not apply throughout the Joseon period. The treatment of armies in the Joseon period also varied according to social status. Yangban serving in the military were granted the special privilege of being guaranteed a government position. During the Imjin War, the Sogo Army was formed with the objective of strengthening provincial defenses. Since it mainly consisted of lowborn, it received inferior treatment despite the fact that it received training and fought in battles like other armies. However, the Sogo Army did play an important role in social history; in contrast to the past, the government regarded the lowborn as a matter of importance to state policy, acknowledging that they were human. Selected through meritorious service and through examinations, they also gained opportunities to elevate their social status. Fifth, in the late Joseon period, the government levied taxes on those performing military service in an effort to improve the country's finances. However, the heavy taxes led to corruption and were an important factor in the deterioration of the condition of the peasantry.

In sum, there were many differences between the military in the Joseon era and that of today. Whereas yangban gained official positions through their service, military life was a burden to the commoners who constituted the majority of soldiers. Military service was long, and there was no salary for low-ranking soldiers. Occasionally, soldiers even had to bear the considerable financial cost of providing their own weapons and uniforms. The treatment of soldiers and the organization of armies differed according to social status, and those in military service also had to pay the military tax. These were the reasons that soldiers in the Joseon period tried to evade military service through official exemptions as well as by various other means.

Official Exemptions from Military Service

Military service in the Joseon era lasted, in principle, until old age. Joseon's code of laws, such as the *Gyeongguk daejeon* and the *Daejeon hoetong*, specified cases in which a person would be eligible for an exemption, and the criteria were based on Confucian values, such as loyalty and filial piety. Exemptions were frequently granted to the descendants of soldiers killed in battle and to the children of parents who were very old, handicapped, or suffering from an incurable disease. People with incurable conditions such as epileptics, the blind, the mute, the mentally ill, dwarfs, hunchbacks, and those missing a limb also received exemptions. Special consideration was also given to people in education and those already engaged in service to the state. Officials on active duty, students in the Seonggyungwan, Sahak, or *hyanggyo*, and former officials of rank two and above were also not required to serve in the military. Officials and clerks in *hyanggyo* and *yuhyangso* did not have to pay the military cloth tax.

Today, by contrast, exemptions in South Korea are determined by the economic situation of the family, as befits a capitalist society. They are not necessarily granted to only children or people living with their parents, reflecting changes in the nature of the family in the modern period. Nuclear families are now more common than extended families, and in recent decades, people are having fewer children. As a result, only children are relatively common these days. Table 1 is a comparison of the regulations in the Joseon period and those of today.

Table 1.

	Joseon Period	South Korea (2004)
Length of Military Service	Until age sixty	– Army and marines – discharged after 26 months, navy – after 28 months, air force – after 30 months; – National Guard – discharged after commuting from home for 24 months; – Those fulfilling military service in public offices: government offices – discharged after 26 months; international cooperation – after 30 months; arts and athletics – after 34 months
Naturalized foreigners	In some cases, they served in the military	Enlisted in the civil defense force
Benefits for the families of deceased or wounded soldiers	Exemption from military service for three generations for those who belong to the Chungjangwi as the child of a fallen soldier	One brother or son of deceased or wounded soldiers of 6th rank or higher is allowed to work in public service for six months
Only sons or those who have old parents	– One son is exempted if his parents are over 70 years of age or if taking care of parents with an incurable illness or disability. – All sons are exempted if parents are older than 90. – If the son is dead, then one patrilineal grandson is exempted; if there is no grandson, then one matrilineal grandson is exempted.	A person without whom the family cannot survive can do military service with the civil defense corps, if the proportion of support for the family, wealth, and income falls within the regulations set by law

Evasion of Military Service

During the Joseon period, there were many ways to evade military service illegally. First, there was the practice of 'substitution' in which wealthy people hired 'part-time' soldiers to serve in the military for them. It originated with wealthy individuals reluctant to serve and merchants whose businesses were affected by their military service. It was commonly done with soldiers serving in the central army. There were brokers who arranged substitutions, and some soldiers even served in the military for an entire year. Although photographs did not exist at the time, documents that recorded the facial features of soldiers allowed easy identification of fake soldiers. People paid commanders money to turn a blind eye to the substitute soldiers. Later, more severe forms of corruption emerged. Since commanders could not get money if the real person came, some forced soldiers to use a substitute. The corruption brought about by the practice of substitution was an important factor behind the decline of the military. Another factor was the fact that military commanders in provincial regions accepted bribes for exemptions from military service since the government did not pay them a regular salary.

Another way to avoid military service was to attain yangban status. In the early Joseon period, everyone except the lowborn had to serve in the military, regardless of their social status. The sons of both commoners and high officials were placed into an army if they could not enter a school. However, when yangban became exempt from compulsory military service in the late Joseon period, commoners used a variety of ways to attain yangban status, such as buying or forging a genealogy or by pretending to be the descendant of the king or a powerful official. There were many other methods of evading military service. Some took advantage of the fact that students were exempt and faked the credentials necessary to enter a *hyanggyo* or a *seowon*. Another method was to become a clerk or temporary official in a local government office or an officer at a provincial office or military base. Others became monks, servants in a yangban household, or members of a *hyanggyo* or *yuhyangso*.

With large numbers of people evading military service, the burden increased on the remaining soldiers. It was a common sight for families to fall into ruin because the costs were difficult to bear. Examples can be found throughout the Joseon period, such as this passage in the *Veritable Records of King Jungjong* for the year 1538.

> Before, infantry had to pay seven to eight rolls of military cloth a month [as tax]. However, because of continual bad harvests, grain was precious, and

> the value of military cloth dropped. So [the government] demanded up to ten times more cloth than before. Therefore, when providers became unable to bear the burden and left their villages, soldiers deserted one after another. Then the relatives of relatives and the neighbors of neighbors became responsible for the military cloth tax…As a result, because of continual flight from villages, they became completely empty.

However, since magistrates were punished if they did not secure their quota of soldiers, they fabricated documents to show that deserters still resided in the village. They then transferred the tax burden onto the relatives and neighbors of deserters, as well as doubling or tripling the tax on children, the deceased, and people over sixty years of age. As evasion of military duty became widespread, it had the dual effect of increasing the suffering of the commoners and worsening the state of government finances.

The government adopted various measures to rectify the problems caused by the corruption in the military. It implemented an identification tag system in order to track down deserters and those evading military service and a registration system for monks to restrict people's ability to become one. The government also tracked down people who tried to get an exemption from military service by taking an examination to become a student at a *hyanggyo*. Able-bodied men who did not have to perform statute labor were now required to serve in the military, and it reduced the military service requirement in order to prevent men from enlisting as soldiers at provincial government offices. To reduce the burden on commoners, the government let the lowborn enlist in the military. Silhak scholars advocated conducting a land reform that would give land to soldiers in order to secure their livelihoods and requiring the yangban, whose numbers had increased tremendously in the late Joseon period, to serve in the military. However, since the government did not attempt a more fundamental solution to the evasion of military service, it became one of the main causes of the decline of commoners and the outbreak of peasant rebellions.

Volunteer Soldiers

Despite the arduous nature of military life, there were some people who voluntarily became soldiers in the Joseon era. Except for the armies consisting of yangban, there were very few volunteer soldiers in the early Joseon period. They belonged to the Paengbae and Daejol, units that strong young commoners could join by taking an examination. They provided a way for commoners without the time or wealth to learn the military arts and become low-ranking soldiers. Since the Paengbae and Daejol were often used for construction projects, soldiers gradually began to avoid these units, making it difficult to maintain them at full strength. But these units still had 8,000 soldiers at the end of the fifteenth century, when the total strength of the armed forces was 150,000.

Serving in the Hullyeon Dogam army, which was established during the Imjin War, was a good career for poor young men. During a lull of more than a year after the beginning of the war, the government recruited soldiers for the army, promising two *doe* of rice per day as pay. Unable to eat regularly, the poor in Seoul rushed to join the army in order to obtain grain. Among them were many young men of unfree status, but the government accepted them all as soldiers since it was in no position to be selective. When problems at the beginning of the war, such as food supply issues, were resolved and the economic conditions of the people became stabilized, around half of the Hullyeon Dogam deserted because it was now necessary to serve for long periods as professional soldiers and because of their harsh treatment by the commanders. It became difficult for the army to maintain its troop levels. People were now reluctant to enlist in the Hullyeon Dogam, and they could no longer accept private unfree people as soldiers because of an incident in which a person murdered his own unfree person who had joined the army. In response, the government improved its treatment of soldiers by establishing a system of rewards and creating opportunities to be promoted to low-ranking officers. It also attempted to stabilize troops levels by toughening punishments for deserters and by recruiting soldiers for the Hullyeon Dogam from every province of the country.

In the late Joseon period, the majority of soldiers served in the army because it was compulsory. As time passed, however, the number of people only paying the military cloth tax began to exceed the number actually serving in the military. Before the Equal Service Law (Gyunyeokbeop) was implemented in 1750, the amount of military cloth tax differed according to the army and government office to which one belonged. There were cases of people flocking to ones where the tax burden was light. The actual number of people on active duty was small since people took turns doing their military service. As a result, most of the active-duty soldiers in Seoul were in the Hullyeon Dogam, which was made up of professional soldiers. Because of the increased importance of firearms in this period, soldiers had to serve in the army all year round, as did those in the Hullyeon Dogam, in order to become skilled at using those weapons. In both numbers and fighting capability, the Hullyeon Dogam played a key role in the central army. Later, as part of the Gabo Reforms in the mid-1890s, existing armies were abolished, and new central and provincial armies were founded, both composed of only professional soldiers. At the end of the Joseon period, the military was mainly composed of professional soldiers.

with Jung Y. Lee

19. THE PENAL SYSTEM

Sim Jae-woo

Historical dramas in South Korea often contain scenes of a prisoner, clothes dirty and hair unkempt, being tortured while screaming in agony. Suspected criminals are tied to a bench or chair and beaten with a stick or club, usually protesting their innocence. Many of the punishments in the Joseon period involved inflicting bodily pain, unlike today, but this was true throughout the world in pre-modern times. When we think of the penal system in Joseon, we usually think of harsh torture. This view is not entirely inaccurate; the transition to a more rational penal system was possible only after the advent of modern society. However, it is a mistake to think that the administration of laws and punishments was completely arbitrary and without any underlying principle. This chapter takes a look at the types of punishment that existed during the Joseon period, ranging from corporal punishment to exile, and also the rationality behind their application.

What Kinds of Punishment Existed?

Criminal law in Joseon was mainly based on *The Great Ming Code* (*Da Ming lü*), which listed five kinds of punishment: beating with a light stick (*tae*), beating with a heavy stick (*jang*), penal servitude (*do*), banishment (*ryu*), and execution (*sa*). Beating with a light or heavy stick was the punishment for minor crimes, with the offender being struck on the buttocks. There were five grades of punishment; for a light stick, a sentence could be for ten, twenty, thirty, forty, or fifty blows, and for a heavy stick, it could be sixty, seventy, eighty, ninety, or one hundred blows. *The Great Ming Code* specified the use of wooden sticks made of white oak, but in Joseon, people generally used ash or some other wood if ash were unavailable.

Penal servitude was for criminals who committed a relatively serious crime; it involved putting the captured person in a large building and making him do hard labor, similar to imprisonment today. There were five types of sentence that varied according to the length of confinement – one year, one and a half years, two years, two and a half years, and three years; for each, criminals were beaten a corresponding number of blows

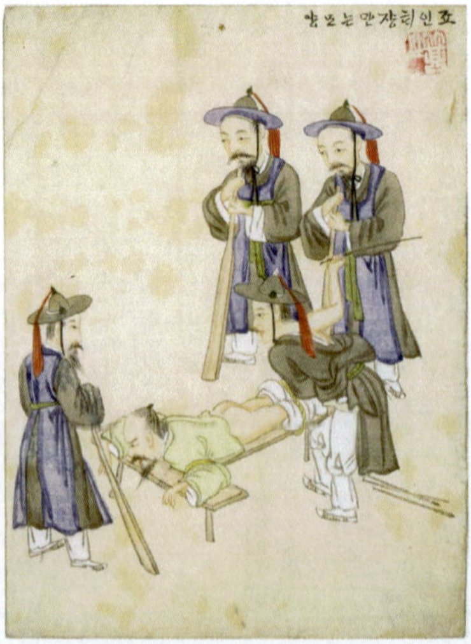

Fig. 19.1. Beating a Prisoner, Gim Jungeun (aka Kisan), late nineteenth century. (© Musée Guimet, Paris, Dist. RMN-Grand Palais)

with a heavy stick – sixty, seventy, eighty, ninety, or one hundred. Banishment was for the most serious crimes that could not be punished by execution; a criminal would be sent into exile to live in a far-off region until his or her death. There were three degrees of banishment varying according to the distance of the location: 2000 *ri*, 2500 *ri*, and 3000 *ri*; in each case, criminals were also beaten one hundred times with a heavy stick.

Execution, the harshest form of punishment, was carried out by hanging or beheading. Today, we consider all executions to be similar regardless of the method, but at that time, there were distinctions according to the crime. Since hanging left the body whole, beheading was considered a more grave punishment. After a beheading, the head was displayed in public for the people to see; this was called *hyosu*. Traitors suffered an even more cruel form of execution called *neungjicheosa* or *neungjicheocham*. Their heads would be cut off; their bodies would be cut into pieces, and burial was not permitted. One example is the treatment of Gim Okgyun (1851–1894), the leader of the Gapsin Coup, who was assassinated in Shanghai in 1894. His corpse was brought back to Joseon, and he was labeled as a traitor. After his body was drawn and quartered, his head was suspended for display in Seoul near where the Yanghwa Bridge is located today.

The main organs of law enforcement in the Joseon period were the Ministry of Punishments, the Seoul city government, and the Office of the Inspector-General – the so-called *sambeopsa*. The duties of provincial governors and local magistrates also included law enforcement. In reality, however, a number of government offices could lock up criminals and interrogate them, including the Ministry of Military Affairs, the Royal Secretariat, the Agency for Unfree People, the Jongbusi, the Border Defense Command, and the Agency for the Arrest of Thieves. The Ministry of Punishments handled matters of justice and also was in charge of processing petitions from provincial offices and holding hearings before trials.

Not all government offices had the authority to sentence criminals and carry out punishments. The final decision on death sentences rested solely with the king, and a limited number of government offices could administer punishments. For example, in the provinces, the local magistrates could render judgments only on minor crimes that would be punished by a beating with a light stick. More serious crimes had to be handled according to instructions from the provincial governor's office. The provincial governor reported to the king crimes that were punishable by execution. Except in special situations, executions were carried out at the end of the year after three rounds of hearings were held at court.

Corporal Punishment and Harsh Torture

Criminal cases in the Joseon era were handled differently than they are today. In principle, they had to be settled within a fixed period of time. Death penalty cases were decided within thirty days. For penal servitude and exile, the period was twenty days, and it was ten days for beating with a light or heavy stick. Suspects were supposed to be kept in prison for crimes to be punished by beating with a heavy stick or worse. But at a time when there was no formalized system or regulations, not every case was handled within the prescribed time limit. Only unconvicted suspects were put in prisons since sentences were carried out immediately after they were handed down. Prisons took on the role of reforming criminals only in modern times, but prison life was full of hardship both then and now. In his treatise *Mongmin simseo*, Silhak scholar Jeong Yagyong (1762–1836) called prison the hell of the earthly world. He mentioned the five kinds of agony of being in prison: the interrogation chair, harassment, disease, cold and hunger, and long-term confinement. He felt that a long confinement was the worst of the five kinds of agony, emphasizing that careful consideration was necessary before confining a suspect, particularly during the farming season. Jeong's comments suggest that the settlement of cases was often delayed.

Unlike today, torture was used in interrogations. During the Joseon period, it was permitted for suspects of serious crimes. Koreans today mistakenly believe that only clubs were used for beatings. In actuality, three kinds of implements were used for punishment in the Joseon era: light and heavy sticks, paddles, and clubs. Light and heavy sticks were two of the five punishments mentioned earlier. Clubs were used for punishments in the military, and paddles were used for torture. Paddles were supposed to be made of white oak; similar to long and short sticks, they had

Map 19.1. Jeollado mujang hyeondo, nineteenth century. The map indicates the location of a jail (orange rectangle) in the southwest of the town. (National Museum of Korea)

round handles, but the ends were flat so that it could strike a person's buttocks and thighs. A suspect could be beaten up to thirty times in cases of a serious crime in which he did not confess despite the existence of sufficient evidence. Made from willow trees, clubs were only used in the military since they were far more painful than light and heavy sticks. Local magistrates were not allowed to use either paddles or clubs for carrying out punishments; however, they used clubs illegally. They also made large, round implements called *wonjang* for use in beatings.

Magistrates used harsh forms of torture as well, which became a problem when used excessively. Two of the main forms of torture were *nanjang* and *juri*, which were used in military bases in the late Joseon period. *Nanjang* involved pulling out a person's toe. In *juri*, two pieces of wood were placed between the legs at the shins as the suspect sat in a chair, and then they were pulled downward to twist the legs. Injuries from *juri* would be so severe that people would no longer be able to bow properly at their parents' memorial rites. There were other harsh forms of torture used for interrogating traitors. *Apseul* involved pressing down on a person's knees with a heavy piece of wood; *nak* was the branding of a person's body with a hot iron; in *jujangdangmyun*, the body was pummeled with several red cudgels.

The use of torture and corporal punishment differed according to social class. For minor offenses, the government preferred to avoid using physical punishment on the upper classes; *sadaebu* and civil and military officials could instead pay a fine as a penalty. Women of *sajok* families would not be beaten if the crime was not serious, and to be beaten on the buttocks was considered to be especially shameful for women. Torture was forbidden for children and the elderly; such thinking was only natural given the strong influence of Confucian values.

Changes to the Justice System

The penal system did not undergo fundamental change until the late Joseon period. Many changes occurred in the eighteenth century during the reigns of Yeongjo and Jeongjo when abuses in the system became a political and social issue. First, severe physical torture was forbidden, and the government took steps to prevent the illegal punishment of commoners. There were many cruel punishments that had been in use until the late Joseon period. If a thief was captured, pincers made of wood were used on vulnerable spots to extract a confession. The edge of a cudgel was used to strike

Fig. 19.2. *Apseul,* Gim Jungeun (aka Kisan), late nineteenth century. (© Musée Guimet, Paris, Dist. RMN-Grand Palais)

the shins or the heels, and there were cases where prisoners were restrained and then hit on the buttocks until their skin peeled off. Local elites captured runaway people of unfree status and put lit matches between their toes, or they would hang them upside down and pour lye into their nostrils. In extreme cases, they were hung upside down after their toes would be bound with cord, and then the elites would hit the cords to cause pain or even sever their hands and feet. In the same period in the West, Enlightenment thought gave rise to a movement opposing torture.

Second, when a new legal code was compiled, the penal system was revised and expanded. Both Yeongjo and Jeongjo made great efforts to revise the section on criminal law. To reduce the problems caused by officials' ignorance of the law, they promoted the publication and distribution of legal books. These books included *Muwonnok* (1796), a forensic text on examining corpses; *The Great Ming Code*; *Jeollyul tongbo* (1786), a guide to the criminal law sections of the country's legal code; and the *Heumhyul jeonchik* (1777), which detailed the standards and usage of instruments of punishment. These books enabled accurate assessments of and objective standards for causes of death. The government also increased its supervision over the penal system. One of the duties of secret royal inspectors (*amhaengeosa*), who were dispatched more frequently in the late Joseon period, was to observe whether local officials were administering the law and punishments fairly. It became easier to petition the king directly about unjust imprisonment. King Jeongjo repeatedly reviewed reports on murder cases, as if poring over the Confucian classics, to ensure that there

Fig. 19.3. *Lighting Matches between the Toes as Punishment,* Gim Jungeun (aka Kisan), late nineteenth century. (© Musée Guimet, Paris, Dist. RMN-Grand Palais)

was no room for doubt in how they were handled. Both Yeongjo and Jeongjo criticized the fact that powerful people could escape punishment for serious crimes while the powerless were punished even for minor offenses. Though these changes did not mean that the penal system of the Joseon period became modernized, they can be seen as a step in that direction.

The Ordeal of Exile

There were various kinds of banishment, one of the five basic categories of punishment in the penal code. Both ordinary criminals and high-ranking officials could be sentenced to banishment; some people were banished because they were the relative of a criminal. Many eminent scholars were sent into exile because they belonged to a faction that was on the losing side of a political battle; some of them influenced their localities, leaving behind a distinct exile culture. For the royal family and high-ranking officials, there was another form of banishment called *anchi* in which they would be sent to a specific location within a region. A variation on this was *wiri anchi*; the thorny trifoliate orange tree was planted all around the house so that the person could not leave. For this, criminals were generally sent to southern islands where trifoliate orange trees were plentiful. An example of *wiri anchi* is the Purge of 1722 during Gyeongjong's reign, in which high-ranking officials were sent into exile and later executed. Chief

State Councillor Gim Changjip (1648–1722) was sent to Goje Island; Yi Imyeong, to Namhae; and Jo Taechae, to Jin Island.

The law stipulated that a sentence of banishment had to involve both exile and a beating. According to Chinese law, criminals had to be exiled to a location 2,000 *ri*, 2,500 *ri*, or 3,000 *ri* away, but Joseon could not follow Chinese practice since its territory was smaller than China's. In the early Joseon period, the region of exile was selected based on the location of the criminal's residence. In the late Joseon period, criminals did not take a direct path to their exile location but went on a winding route in order to conform to the distance stipulated by law. The most common exile regions were areas along the northern border in Hamgyeong and Pyeongan provinces such as Samsu and Gapsan and southern islands such as Goje, Jin, and Chuja. During Yeongjo's reign, it was forbidden to send criminals to uninhabited islands or places where survival was difficult such as Heuksan Island, except in exceptional circumstances. Did high-ranking officials sentenced to exile actually receive one hundred blows with a heavy stick as required by law? In most cases, they paid a penalty and avoided physical punishment. King Yeongjo ordered that officials above the rank of *jinsa* were not to be beaten when they were sent into exile, thus reducing the severity of their sentence. Without that protection, many would have died before reaching their destination.

The experience of exile differed according to the person and to the region of exile. In some places, a site was selected for a residence, and the people took turns sending things to eat. In other cases, all the people in the village would prepare some food and give it to the owner of the house where the exile lived. In general, no more than ten exiles lived in a single village. During the reign of Yeongjo, however, the governor of Jeolla province once requested that exiles be moved to another region since there were so many of them in the province that both exiles and residents were starving. Exiles were a significant burden in regions where they were numerous. When Jeong Yagyong was magistrate of Goksan, he bought a tile-roofed house to house all the exiles, and he collected 500 *nyang* every year from the local populace to cover their food and other expenses. During the eighteen years he spent in exile in Gangjin in Jeolla province, Jeong wrote a poem that expressed the frustration he felt: "if you are a little poor, there are people who pity you, but if you are very poor, there is no one who will sympathize." If the exile had no chance of a political comeback, people looked down upon them, no matter how high a position he had held in the past.

with Arjun Mehra

20. EATING CULTURE

Chung Yeon-sik

The typical Korean meal consists of a main course and side dishes called *banchan*. Though tastes have become very westernized in the South in recent decades, rice remains the main staple of the Korean diet. Koreans eat short-grain rice, as do the Japanese, in contrast to China and Southeast Asia where long-grain rice is preferred. Another staple is kimchi, whose unique spiciness is one of the defining flavors of Korean cuisine. It may seem as if Koreans have eaten these foods since ancient times; in fact, garlic, a key ingredient in kimchi, appears in the legend of Dangun, the mythical founder of the first Korean kingdom. In actuality, much of what constitutes Korean cuisine and eating culture today developed in the Joseon period.

There were obviously great differences in cuisine according to social class. Food ranged from the simple dishes of commoners to the elaborately prepared tables of palace cuisine. Since people tend to see the lives of the commoners as poverty-stricken, they may view palace cuisine as being more vibrant and dynamic than that of the peasantry. However, Korea was not particularly poorer than other countries. According to British travel writer Isabella Bird Bishop, author of *Korea and Her Neighbours*, and British journalist Frederick A. McKenzie, the life of Koreans was not that impoverished. In fact, Koreans in general were known for their large appetites in Ryukyu (today's Okinawa) in the Joseon period. Westerners who came to Korea in the late nineteenth century also noted how much Koreans ate. If people were poor, how were they able to eat so much? It seems that food culture was just as vibrant among the commoners as it was among the upper classes.

Koreans seem to have even more interest in food than other people; in fact, one way that Koreans greet each other is to ask if they have eaten. Despite the importance they placed on eating, people in the Joseon era hardly left any comprehensive accounts about their food culture, perhaps because they took it for granted. We can only piece together Joseon's food culture through the fragments of information that remain. This chapter attempts to answer some basic questions about eating habits of the time and explores two of the staples of Korean cuisine, rice and kimchi.

How Many Meals Did Koreans Eat a Day?

Today, in both the East and the West, it is normal for people to eat three meals a day. But in the past, Koreans usually had only two daily meals. In fact, another term for a meal was *joseok*, a word that combined the Chinese characters for 'morning' and 'evening.' In the late eighteenth century, Yi Deokmu (1741–1793) noted in his collected works *Cheongjanggwan jeonseo* that Koreans ate five *hop* at each meal, totaling one *doe* a day.[1]

Does this mean that people did not eat lunch? The word for lunch – *jeomsim* (dim sum or *dianxin* in Chinese) – already existed in the early Joseon period. Originally, the term referred to the simple food that monks in China ate before their early morning and evening offerings to Buddha. It was literally, as its characters indicated, 'a spot in the stomach.' A record from the beginning of the fifteenth century noted that teachers at Seoul's major academies were worse off than those at provincial *hyanggyo* since they had to teach all day without eating lunch. Clearly, lunch was a snack that was not necessarily eaten on a daily basis. *Swaemirok*, a diary written during the Imjin War, used the term *jeomsim* to refer to a light meal, and a full meal was called *natbap*. Even in the palace, full meals were prepared only in the morning and evening; at midday, a light snack or noodles were served. Gradually, the meaning of the term *jeomsim* changed, as it evolved from a snack to a light meal and ultimately into a regular meal.

The number of meals also varied with the season. The *Oju yeonmun jangjeon sango*, written by Yi Gyugyeong (1788–1856) in the mid-nineteenth century, stated that people ate three meals a day from the second to the eighth lunar month. During the five months from the ninth month to the first month of the following year, people ate two meals a day. In the late eighteenth century, lunch was eaten in the Seonggyungwan, the highest educational institution in Joseon, in the months between the spring and autumn ceremonies for Confucius – from the second to the eighth lunar month. Lunch consisted of just a few spoonfuls of rice and a few pieces of seaweed. Thus, during the long days of summer, people ate three meals, including a simple lunch; during the winter, when the days were short, they ate two.

The amount of labor done was another important factor in determining the number of meals. In rural villages, people ate five meals a day, including light meals, during the rice transplantation season. Since travel

---

1 In the Joseon period, one *hop* = 180 ml; 10 *hop* = one *doe*. Five *hop* in the Joseon period would be equivalent to 1.5 *hop* according to today's units of measurement.

Fig. 20.1. *Farmers Eating a Meal* (Nongbu bab meokgo), Gim Jungeun (aka Gisan), late nineteenth century. (Copyright: Museum fuer Voelkerkunde Hamburg)

required a lot of energy, travelers had to eat a midday meal, even in the days before three meals a day became the norm. Travelers would eat a midway meal called *junghwa* in taverns. When they ventured far from the palace, kings would take a rest and eat a lavishly prepared midday meal. It seems that people ate only two meals in winter not so much because the days were shorter but more because no farming work was done.

A few historical sources note that the poor ate only two meals a day while wealthy people ate three meals or more. *Opisaniie Korei* (A Description of Korea), published by the Russian Ministry of Finance in 1900, mentioned that Koreans ate three or four meals a day. The book seems to have counted *joban*, a simple meal of something like rice porridge that was eaten before breakfast. If the nighttime meal is included, then the total would be five meals a day. But it was usual to have two meals a day. *Chosenjin no ishokuju*, a 1916 report by medical officers of the Japanese army on life in northern Korea, wrote that the number of meals Koreans ate varied by region, season, and earning power, but in general, they had two meals a day. Lunch, which originally was a simple snack, gradually developed into a full meal, but even at the end of the Joseon era, eating three meals a day was not widespread. It was not until the latter half of the twentieth century that it became usual for most Koreans to have meals three times a day.

Did Koreans Eat White Rice or Barley Rice?

What did Koreans eat at their meals in the past? Rice has been the main course in most Korean meals, but it was not necessarily white rice. The grain used for cooking rice varied according to the region. It is commonly thought that the main staple in the north was millet, but in the south, families with a certain level of wealth ate white rice. For instance, Seo Yugu's *Imwon gyeongjeji*, written in 1827, noted that people in the south cooked white rice while people in the north mixed rice with millet. However, in actuality, the situation was more complex. In the countryside, people must have eaten barley rice or multi-grain rice during the period from the spring to the fall harvest when rice stores were low. But wealthy elites were not the only ones who consumed white rice. According to numerous Korean sources and accounts by foreigners, Koreans had white rice except in the north where people ate rice with millet. During the Joseon period, people in the south ate white rice with barley or mixed grains; people in the north ate rice with millet, with variations according to a family's economic situation.

This goes against conventional wisdom in Korea. The older generation has vivid memories of eating only boiled barley during the spring when rice was scarce. During the Japanese occupation (1910–1945), the colonial government exported rice and beans from Korea, virtually to the point of plundering, in order to secure supplies for its military and to keep domestic wages low. Though Korean farmers cultivated rice, they had none to eat for themselves; instead, they had to eat barley, Annam rice, and mixed grains from Manchuria. There were so many families that could not eat even those grains that the faces of their children became swollen and yellowish in color. The Japanese occupation period thus represented a break with the past for Korea's food culture.

Why did Koreans, as well as Indians and Southeast Asians, eat white rice? It was not a matter of choice but a matter of survival, since rice cultivation was suited for areas with high population density. Though it is a very labor-intensive crop, rice is able to feed large numbers of people. The usage of farmland and productivity per unit of land are higher for rice than for wheat. In mid-eighteenth century Europe, one seed of wheat would yield six grains. By comparison, one seed of rice would yield an average of twenty-five or thirty grains.[2] It was not necessary to let rice fields lay fallow for one or two years like wheat; in fact, double and even triple cropping was possible in regions with favorable conditions. Since wheat lacks essential amino acids, it is necessary to supplement a wheat diet with meat. Rice is nutritionally balanced, so it is only necessary to add a few nutrients to have a complete diet. If a plot of land planted with

---

[2] In his work *Taengniji*, Yi Junghwan (1690–1756) wrote that a good place to live was one where one *mal* of rice seeds yielded sixty *mal* of rice; the next best was one that produced forty to fifty *mal*, while it would be difficult to live in a place that yielded thirty *mal*.

Fig. 20.2. *Chaemi* (detail), Gim Hongdo, late eighteenth century. The painting depicts people cutting royal ferns which peasants ate during the 'barley hump.' (National Museum of Korea)

wheat could support seventy-five people, then the same plot, planted with rice, could feed 100 people. If it were used for pastureland, then the meat produced could feed only nine people.[3]

Kimchi and Pepper, the Symbols of Korean Food

Kimchi is another essential part of the Korean diet. Korean meal tables are distinguished by the number of side dishes in bowls with lids – e.g., three *cheop*, five *cheop*, or seven *cheop*. The higher the number of *cheop*, the

[3] Some anthropologists claim that India's ancient religions of Buddhism, Jainism, and Hinduism prohibited the eating of beef because population density at the time exceeded sustainable levels in which it would have been feasible.

more lavish the meal. But rice, soup, and kimchi are part of every meal and so are not included in the number of *cheop*. The term kimchi, in a broad sense, refers to vegetables pickled with salt, vinegar, or soy sauce. The word that kimchi is derived from – *dimchae* – also means 'preserved vegetables.' Thus, *ggakdugi* (kimchi made with daikon radish), *oiji*, *oisobagi* (stuffed pickled cucumbers), *danmuji* (*takuan* in Japanese), and *jangajji* can all be considered types of kimchi. Another term for kimchi was *ji*. Certain types of kimchi, such as *jjanji*, *singgeonji*, and *oiji* all have the character *ji* in their names. The earliest forms of kimchi were probably pickled vegetables without pepper, similar to *jangajji* or *danmuji*. In other countries, foods similar to kimchi include Japanese *tsukemono* such as *takuan*, Western pickles, Chinese *pao cai*, German sauerkraut, and Indonesian *acar*; all are vegetables pickled with vinegar or salt.

Originally similar to pickles, kimchi developed into a food completely different in appearance and taste with the use of red pepper powder and *jeotgal*, a salted fermented food made with seafood. Made first in the eighteenth century, this kind of kimchi was initially made with daikon radishes or cucumbers. The kimchi that Koreans eat today is made with napa cabbage, which was introduced into Korea from China at the end of the eighteenth century. It was not until the twentieth century that it became more popular than kimchi made with daikon radish.

Though chili pepper is the primary spice used today in Korean cuisine, it did not exist in the country in the early Joseon period. The spices available at that time included black pepper, Sichuan pepper (*chuan jiao* in Chinese), and ginger. Introduced to Korea in the Goryeo period, black pepper was so expensive that it was used as medicine and hardly used in food. In the West, black pepper, which eliminated the smell of meat, was so expensive that it would be recorded in ledgers of personal property. Sometimes, it was even sold by the grain. One purpose of European exploration was to acquire new, cheap sources of black pepper and thus eliminate the need to purchase it through Arab merchants. In the early Joseon period, kings would bestow gifts of black pepper. An account in the *Jingbirok* by Yu Seongryong (1542–1607) mentioned an incident involving pepper caused by Japanese envoys before the Imjin War. When they sprinkled a handful of pepper on a table at a banquet, musicians and *gisaeng* (female entertainers) fought each other to get some, causing a commotion. Sichuan pepper, ginger, and mustard were more commonly used than black pepper in the early Joseon period.

Things changed with the introduction of chili peppers. Native to Mexico, they were introduced to Korea at the end of the sixteenth century.

At the time, they were called *nammancho* or *waegyeoja*. They gradually spread throughout the country in the seventeenth century, and red pepper powder began to be used in kimchi by the end of the century. When chili pepper became the predominant spice in Korea in the nineteenth century, the price of black pepper decreased, and the use of Sichuan pepper declined to the point that today, it is only used in dishes such as *chueotang* (loach stew). Compared to other chili peppers, Korean ones are relatively sweet and intense in color and have a high concentration of vitamin C. When mixed with salt and *jeotgal*, it produces an enzyme that is good for one's health, and it oxidizes fat cells to warm up the body and help it endure the cold in winter. This seems to be the reason that people began to use chili pepper to make kimchi.

Subsisting on Roots and Tree Bark

Another important development in the late Joseon period was the emergence of foods for famine relief. In the early Joseon period, people ate things such as pine needles, pine tree bark, elm bark, acorns, arrowroot, and mugwort in times of famine. Pine needles, in particular, were eaten throughout the Joseon era. There were many ways of eating pine needles, and one method was to steam, dry, and ground pine needles into a powder that was then mixed with bean powder to create porridge. Bean powder was added to prevent constipation. In fact, the phrase 'poverty tearing us apart' was derived from the fact that poor people would eat so many pine needles that they would become constipated.

Many new foods were introduced to Korea in the late Joseon period. Spain and Portugal had established colonies in Central and South America, and when they came into contact with East Asia, they brought with them several products native to that region to China and Japan. Between the seventeenth and nineteenth centuries, these new foods began to be introduced to Joseon as well. They included potatoes, sweet potatoes, corn, squash, and tomatoes. In particular, potatoes and sweet potatoes were viewed as useful for famine relief since they were easy to grow and resistant to drought. An envoy brought sweet potatoes over to Korea from Tsushima in the mid-eighteenth century. Originally grown in Gyeongsang province, they gradually spread to Gyeonggi province, Chungcheong province, and then to Jeolla province during the nineteenth century. Sweet potatoes were first called *gamjeo*, and it is believed that the term *goguma* was derived from the Tsushima pronunciation of an alternate Japanese word for sweet potato – *kokoimo*. After potatoes were introduced to Spain from Central America in the second half of the sixteenth century, they spread throughout Europe in the eighteenth and nineteenth centuries, becoming a primary staple of the poor. Potatoes came to Korea in the early nineteenth century, decades after the sweet potato. They were called *maryeongseo*, since they resembled the bells hung around a horse's neck (*mar* meaning 'horse'), or *bukgamjeo*, which meant 'potatoes from the north.' Since potatoes were resistant to drought, floods, and cold weather, they quickly spread to Gangwon province and the northern regions, becoming preferred to sweet potatoes soon after their introduction.

Spoons and Meal Trays for Everyone

A unique feature of Korea's food culture is that people use both spoons and chopsticks. Today, about forty percent of the world's population eat with their bare hands, thirty percent with forks and knives, and thirty percent with chopsticks. Of course, all people originally ate with their hands. Forks were first used around the tenth century in Byzantium in the Eastern Roman Empire. Spreading to elite society in Italy in the sixteenth century, they brought about a significant change in European eating culture in the seventeenth century. But it was not until the eighteenth century that forks were widely used throughout Europe – in all regions and by all classes. The practice of eating with one's hands disappeared much earlier in East Asia than it did in the West. People began to use spoons instead of their fingers; then they made chopsticks and used them together with spoons. Around the time of the late Goryeo period in Korea, the Chinese and Japanese stopped using spoons and began using only chopsticks to eat. During the reign of Seonjo, Yun Gukhyeong (1543–1611) wrote that he thought it was unusual that the Chinese, both upper and lower class, who came to Joseon during the Imjin War did not use spoons. Sin Sukju (1417–1475), who had traveled to Japan as an envoy, once specifically mentioned that there were only chopsticks in Japan and no spoons. For Koreans, spoons also have a special function in a meal. Even today, placing a spoon on the table is a sign that one is finished eating.

Koreans have continued to use spoons because soups are always served at meals. Japanese cuisine also includes soup, but spoons are not necessary since the soups are more like broth and can be drunk from small handheld bowls held with one's hand. Korean soups also have broth, but they usually contain a good amount of meat, fish, or vegetables and are

Fig. 20.3. *Wedding Banquet* (Hoehollyedo), eighteenth century. Each guest has an individual tray of food. (National Museum of Korea)

meant to be mixed with rice. Almost all Korean soups are like this, such as seaweed soup, *doenjang* soup, and oxblood soup. Stews (*jjigae*) and rice with hot water also require spoons to eat. The introduction of Mongolian cuisine in the late Goryeo period led to the development of dishes such as today's *seolleongtang* and *gomtang*, both of which involve cooking meat in boiling broth. *Gukbap* comes with rice already in the soup, and this kind of dish is said to be unique in the world. Thus, Koreans have become the only people in the world who use both chopsticks and spoons regularly at meals.

Dining tables in Joseon were different from those of the West. Several people would sit together for a meal in Western societies, and two or three people would share a dish. It was not until the seventeenth century that the use of individual plates became standard. Another factor was the early tradition of sharing even forks and plates. In Korea, however, everyone had his or her own meal table, regardless of social status. Today, a family may use a large table for a banquet, but in the past, individual tables were used even at banquets, as shown in historical records and paintings from the time. That is why every family had a few small tables in their house. Children ate together at their own table or occasionally ate with their grandfather, but the general rule was for adult males to have their own tables. Housewives of the commoner class did not have their own individual tables. They usually had a simple meal in the kitchen by the fireplace or ate next to a table with their rice and soup bowls on the floor. It has not been long since these customs disappeared. Since each person had his or her own table, they had their own bowls and utensils. When children reached their first birthday, it was customary to give them their own spoon, chopsticks, and rice and soup bowls.

with Yoojin Ma

21. LIQUOR AND TAVERNS

Chung Yeon-sik

Koreans are truly a people who love to drink. Drinking is an integral part of social life in South Korea, and alcohol consumption is high. Per capita consumption reached its peak in the mid-1970s with an average of more than fifteen liters per person. It has since declined but remains relatively high at 7.9 liters per person in 2003. The Korean people's love of song, dance, and drink goes back to ancient times; it was even mentioned in the ancient Chinese text *The Book of the Later Han* from the fifth century. In the Joseon period, liquor was not something drunk only on special occasions but was virtually an everyday beverage. It was used as a tonic to give energy and pleasure to people whose lives were filled with arduous labor. The *Geumyang jamnok*, a fifteenth-century book on agriculture, advised farmers to take a jug of liquor when they went out to weed their fields. Liquor, rather than tea, was served to guests and used in ancestral memorial rites.

Although Koreans enjoy drinking, Korea does not have its own liquor as China does with maotai and Great Britain does with whisky. Nor does Korea have many kinds of liquor. There were over 200 kinds of liquor mentioned in records from the Joseon period; however, they began to disappear in the Hanmal period, hardly any remaining today. After turning Korea into a de facto colony with the Protectorate Treaty in 1905, Japan implemented the Liquor Tax Law in 1909, which required liquor producers to pay a tax. After its takeover of the country, Japan passed the Liquor Tax Ordinance in the year 1916. It forbade brewers without a permit from making liquor and cracked down on bootlegging. Since these policies have continued up to the present, the only liquors remaining are those mass-produced in factories.

The Types of Liquor

Though there were many different kinds of liquor in the Joseon period, they can be classified into three general types: *takju*, *cheongju*, and *soju*. Popular among commoners, *takju* were cloudy liquors such as *makgeolli*.

Fig. 21.1. *Lunch* (Jeomsim), Gim Hongdo, late eighteenth century. Farmers are drinking liquor as they eat lunch. (National Museum of Korea)

In fact, the term *makgeolli* itself means 'liquor brewed carelessly.' To make *takju*, wheat flour was kneaded into dough, placed in a round or square frame, and stepped on until it became a mash. As the mash mold grew, fermentation would begin. Next, rice was put in a steamer to make hard-boiled rice. It was dried and mixed with mash that was grounded into a powder; then, it was placed in a jar into which warm water was added. If it was maintained at the proper temperature, a bubbling sound emerged from the jar, and fermentation produced wort. Water was added little by little to the wort, and the resulting liquor was strained to produce *takju*.

The method of making *cheongju* was almost the same as that for *takju*. Instead of straining out the wort, a strainer was put in the jar, and the clear liquor that collected inside it was *cheongju*. *Cheongju* was also called *yakju*. According to the *Imwon gyeongjeji* by Seo Yugu (1764–1845), the term came from the fact that there was a master *cheongju* brewer named Seo Seong in the district of Yak during the reign of Injo (r. 1623–1649). But the origins of the term are unclear. In the Joseon era, the main type of *cheongju* was *samhaeju*. Since it was made in the winter and drunk in the spring when the willow trees bloomed, it was also called *chunju* (*chun* meaning 'spring') or *yuseoju* (*yu* meaning 'willow'). Such a large quantity of rice was used to brew *samhaeju* that from the eighteenth century, the government occasionally considered prohibiting its production.

The Chinese characters for *soju* mean 'burnt liquor.' Similarly, the term 'brandy' is derived from the Dutch word 'brandewijn,' which also means 'burnt wine.' It would be more accurate to say that the liquor was distilled rather than burned. First, an iron pot was filled with wort, and a distilling device called a *sojutgori* was placed on top. After the pot was sealed tightly, it was put over a fire. Alcohol, having a higher volatility, evaporates faster than water. The vapor condensed like dew because of the cold water at the top of the distiller, and the liquor that was collected was *soju*. This is the reason that it was also called *noju*, the character *no* meaning 'dew.' The taste of *soju* in the Joseon era was very different from that of *soju* produced today. Made in factories, *soju* is now diluted with water and mixed with various additives; originally, it was a distilled liquor with a very high alcohol content, such as *Andong soju* from Andong, *hongju* from Jin Island, and *gamhongno* from Pyongyang.

Soju is thought to have originated in Arabia, where chemistry was highly developed at the time. In Chinese texts, the terms for *soju* were *aciji* and *aliqi* (pronounced *aragil* and *arigeol* in Korean). In Korea, the smell of *soju* being distilled was called the *aragi* smell; in the city of Gaeseong, *soju* was called *arakju*. These terms were all derived from the Arabic word *araq* (or arak) meaning 'distilled liquor.' *Soju* was introduced to Korea through Yuan China at the end of the Goryeo period. It is no coincidence that places famous for its *soju* such as Gaeseong, Andong, and Jeju Island were regions involved in the Mongol invasions of the late thirteenth century. *Soju* was already widespread throughout Korea by the end of Goryeo period and the beginning of the Joseon period. For instance, Gim Jin was appointed as a military commander in Gyeongsang province at the end of the Goryeo era to defend the area against Japanese pirates. According to the *History of Goryeo*, he ignored his military duties and only drank *soju*, leading the people to call him and his troops *sojupae* (gang of *soju* drinkers). The *Veritable Records of King Taejo* mentioned that Yi Seonggye's oldest son, Bangu, was a heavy drinker and that he got sick and died after drinking *soju*. As early as the late Goryeo period, the government once banned the drinking of *soju*. Records from Seongjong's reign noted that *soju*, which had been used only by the *sadaebu* in King Sejong's time, was now served in banquets of the common people as well. This was taken as a sign that extravagance had become extreme and that the consumption of *soju* needed to be prohibited.

Soju was expensive because it used more grain than *takju* or *cheongju* and because its production process was complicated. It was not a liquor that everyone could afford to drink. *Jibong yuseol*, a text from the early seventeenth century, noted that *soju* was so expensive and so strong that it was drunk using small cups that were called *sojujan*. *Soju* was mainly drunk in the northern regions of the country. Commoners generally drank low-quality *soju* even in the north. In the south, commoners drank *takju* while the upper class drank *cheongju*. *Soju* was so common that there were several distillers in Seoul located in the neighborhood of Gongdeok-ri; there were also a few places famous for their *soju* in Gyeongsang and Jeolla provinces. Yangban officials seem to have drunk *soju* occasionally. As mentioned in Charles Dallet's *Histoire de l'Église de Corée* (1874), the yangban drank a lot of honey water and *soju* during the summer. It was drunk primarily in summer because its high alcohol content enabled it to withstand the heat for a long time without spoiling. Yi Yulgok even suggested using *soju* rather than *cheongju*, which spoiled more easily, for ancestor memorial rites held during the summer.

Soju was often used as medicine, as mentioned in diaries from the Joseon era. Suffering from a stomachache caused by the summer heat, O Huimun (1539–1613) claimed that his condition improved after he drank three cups of *soju* one after another. Admiral Yi Sunsin (1545–1598) once woke up in the middle of the night with acute gastric pain; when he tried to cure it with *soju*, he felt worse and almost lost consciousness. A patient on the verge of death because of a parasite was cured after drinking two cups of *soju* and vomiting up the parasite. Whether or not these stories are true, it is clear that people at the time thought of *soju* as medicine. Among the types of *soju*, there were two that were well known for their medicinal properties: *juknyeokgo*, which was made with bamboo sap, and *iganggo*, which was made with pear and ginger extract.

The Prohibition of Alcohol

In the Joseon period, the term *samgeum* referred to the three kinds of prohibitions that the government would enact to maintain levels of important resources: *songgeum*, *ugeum*, and *jugeum*. *Songgeum* was a ban on the cutting down of pine trees in order to make houses or boats, and *ugeum* prohibited the arbitrary killing of cows that were important in farming. *Jugeum* forbade the selling and drinking of liquor for a fixed period of time; usually, a ban would be enacted during a spring drought and lifted in the autumn during the harvest. Its purpose was to conserve grain in years of bad harvests because brewing one drink of liquor used enough grain to feed ten people. Brewing *soju* was punished more severely than brewing *cheongju* since *soju* required more grain for its production. Another reason for prohibiting the production of liquor was its potential to disturb the social order. Liquor was regarded as good for honoring the gods, treating guests, and taking care of the elderly. But excessive drinking could lead to fights, acts of disrespect toward one's superiors, and the undermining of gender distinctions.

The prohibition on alcohol was not always enforced strictly. It was customary to make exceptions for the king and all palaces, for foreign envoys, for ancestral memorial rites, for weddings, and for medicinal purposes. There were also times when the prohibition was relaxed in the winter when the cold became severe. Even so, the king would occasionally refrain from drinking in order to set an example for the people. For instance, even though he was often ill and needed treatment, King Sejong (r. 1418–1450) refused all medicinal liquors offered by his ministers after he ordered a ban on liquor, so they were forced to offer saltwater instead. The prohibition of liquor was sometimes implemented differently according to social status. Once, the regulations for ancestral memorial rites required that the royal family and high-ranking officials use *cheongju*, scholars use honey water, and commoners use plain water. When the use of liquor was forbidden at the Royal Shrine (Jongmyo), even the king refrained from drinking, and the punishment of infractions was more severe.

The punishment for violating the prohibition of liquor differed according to the quantity, use, and situation. The punishments were diverse, ranging from receiving a warning to receiving 100 blows and then being sent into exile. It is clear that the punishment was generally heavy, especially during Yeongjo's reign (1724–1776) because he was very concerned about establishing his authority. The list of punishments for the year 1756 shows that people who brewed liquor illegally were exiled to an island.

Scholars who drank liquor were exiled to a faraway place; *jungin* and the sons of concubines were sentenced to serve in the navy just as the low-born were; and commoners were reduced to unfree status in a small village. As noted in the *Hanjungnok*, the memoirs of the Lady Hyegyeong, Crown Prince Sado was so angry at his father for scolding him when he was falsely accused of drinking that he set fire to the palace and threatened to commit suicide by throwing himself into a well.

Many officials lost their positions or were exiled because they neglected to enforce the prohibition of liquor or violated it themselves. One example was O Doil, who had loved liquor from his youth; he said that even exile would not be bad if he could drink, eventually dying in exile in Jangseong. When King Sukjong (r. 1674–1720) himself performed the rain-praying ritual at the Sajikdan, O Doil was one of the officials supervising the ritual. Although a ban on liquor was in effect, he was drunk and fell down, knocking over the liquor for the ritual. He was interrogated at the State Tribunal and was dismissed as Vice-Minister of Rites. In rare instances, the government sentenced high-ranking officials to death to make an example out of them. King Yeongjo once threatened to behead any violators of the liquor ban on the sandy riverbank in Nodeul (today's Noryangjin). When it was discovered that Yun Guyeon, a military official in Pyeongan province, had secretly brewed liquor, the king had him brought to Seoul and went to Sungnye Gate (Namdaemun) himself to watch him be beheaded and his head be placed on a pole for public display.

However, the prohibition of alcohol was not enforced equally on all social classes. When the authorities cracked down on commoners, the liquor law became a target of their grievances. But people of influence could easily buy and drink liquor by taking advantage of their positions and legal exemptions. *Cheongju* came to be called *yakju* because yangban would drink it during a ban, claiming that it was used as medicine. Since so many of the brewers were *sadaebu*, it was not easy for low-ranking officials to stop them. Even if they were caught, they usually escaped prosecution by claiming that their servants or slaves were selling liquor without their knowledge. Some village magistrates even used the liquor ban to make tremendous profits by monopolizing liquor sales. There was also a group of officials who could ignore the law and drink liquor openly. They were the five people who served as *eongwan* in the Office of the Censor-General. According to the *Pilwon japgi* by Seo Geojeong (1420–1488), they had the special privilege of being able to drink while on duty, even during a liquor ban. Since they had the difficult task of exposing and rectifying the errors of the king, it was necessary to keep their spirits up if they were to risk their careers and lives by speaking candidly to him.

Jumak – *Taverns for Drinkers and Travelers*

Jumak, also called *sulmak* and *sutmak*, were places where liquor was sold; most also sold food, and some provided lodgings. *Jumak* in large cities such as Seoul and Pyongyang only sold liquor, but in the countryside, they also served as restaurants and inns. *Yeok* and *won* were also places that provided food and lodgings to travelers; their main customers were officials and people traveling on official business. Commoners mainly frequented the *jumak*, many of which were located at key transportation hubs. When Jeong Yagyong and his brother Jeong Yagjeon were traveling south to their respective places of exile, they spent their last night together at Yuljeongjeom, a *jumak* located at the place where the main road split into two, one leading to Mokpo and the other to Haenam. They were concentrated in places along the route taken by the high-ranking government official traveling to Namwon in 'The Tale of Chunhyang.' These places included the street of rice cake shops in Suwon (Byeongjeom), Saesulmak in Cheonan (Sinjumak), Mungyeongsaejae, a checkpoint on the route from Gyeongsang province to Seoul (Joryeong), and the ferry port along the Seomjin River on the way to Jeolla province. But in general, few *jumak* seem to have existed in the country. Hendrick Hamel, a Dutchman detained in Joseon for fourteen years in the mid-seventeenth century, noted that there were hardly any lodgings for travelers. Travelers carried rice with them and stayed in private residences; if they provided their own rice, the owner would prepare a full meal for them. This was the situation for travelers until the end of the nineteenth century.

The service provided by a *jumak* was simple. In the Joseon period, if a customer drank a cup of liquor, the *jumak* would serve a side dish such as tofu or a fried dish. If a customer had a meal, it would provide a place to sleep in a room with a heated floor to be shared with other guests. However, *jumak* in the countryside, while cheap, did not offer anything more than a meal and a place to sleep. In the *Gapjin mannok*, Yun Gukhyeong (1543–1611) noted that there were few *jumak* in Joseon and that even *jumak* along the main roads of Gyeongsang and Jeolla provinces had only liquor, fodder for horses, and firewood. Travelers had to use two or three horses to carry food and other necessary supplies. Yun advocated the circulation of paper currency and the establishment of inns and restaurants. Travelers took

Fig. 21.2. *Tavern* (Jumak), Gim Hongdo, late eighteenth century. (National Museum of Korea)

small meals with them made of things like fish or fried *doenjang* pancakes, and some took dried rice. Further evidence can be found in other historical sources. For example, Bak Manjeong was a secret royal inspector during Sukjong's reign who was sent to Hwanghae province. In his report, he mentioned that before departing, he received cotton cloth, rice, and beans, as well as three croaker and three strings of twenty yellow corvina each, from the Ministry of Taxation. Written by Bak Duse in 1678, the novel

Yorowon yahwagi contains a scene in which a traveler arrives at a *jumak* and takes out dried bean paste and half of a herring to eat with dinner. The situation was little changed for travelers in the late nineteenth century. The main difference with a commoner's house was that *jumak* provided feed for horses and had a stable for them to sleep in. There were no *jumak* that had individual rooms for guests, and since they did not provide bedding, wealthier travelers had a horse carry their own.

Jumak were the Joseon-period equivalent of a rest area. Paintings from the Joseon era provide a glimpse into what they looked like. One of Sin Yunbok's (b. 1758) paintings depicted a *jumak* with a woman sitting behind a stove and serving liquor and hot soup. She wore fine clothes and had a male servant to handle chores, and the interior was neat and clean. It was clearly an urban *jumak* frequented by officials and the upper class. A painting by Yi Insang (1710–1760) depicted the Beodeunae Jumak with several guestrooms and a stable to put up horses or change a horseshoe, suggesting what a *jumak* on a main thoroughfare probably looked like. On the other hand, the *jumak* in Gim Deuksin's (1754–1822) drawings and Gim Hongdo's (1745–1806?) folding screen looked quite run-down. A woman was sitting inside a room with a child, placing a jar of liquor and some bowls in front to welcome passers-by. Travelers sat on the ground without a seat or roof over their heads and ate lunch from a tray.

with Eric Min Kweon

22. TEA AND TOBACCO

O Jong-rok

In Korea, there is a special word for products, such as alcohol, cigarettes, and coffee, that have little or no nutritional value but are consumed principally for pleasure – *gihopum*. Unlike sweets or seasonings, the pleasure comes from the presence of a depressant such as alcohol or a stimulant such as nicotine or caffeine. In modern societies, these products remain popular despite concerns about the health and social problems they can cause when consumed to excess. South Koreans are known for their relatively high consumption of alcohol (see the previous chapter) and cigarettes. South Korea ranked twenty-first in the world in cigarette consumption with 1,733 cigarettes per adult per year in 2007, higher than the United States (#39) and the United Kingdom (#65) but lower than Japan (#12). Coffee consumption has been increasing steadily in the South since the 1970s. It ranks fifty-seventh in the world, behind the United Kingdom (#47), Japan (#41), and the United States (#27). Starbucks entered South Korea in 1999, and now there are hundreds of stores in cities throughout the country. In fact, at one point, the largest Starbucks coffeehouse in the world was located in Seoul. Koreans have drunk alcohol since ancient times, and tobacco was introduced in the Joseon period. But coffee was not introduced to Korea until the late nineteenth century; similar to other Asian countries, they drank tea. This chapter examines two of the main *gihopum* of the Joseon period, tea and tobacco, and the relation of tobacco to the social status system.

Tea

Geographically, the peninsula is located in a climate suitable for tea cultivation, situated between China and Japan, two of the world's major tea producers. Thus, there was potential for tea culture to spread among the commoner class as well. The Chinese character for tea can be pronounced either 'cha' or 'da' in Korean because its pronunciation differs in northern and southern China. The existence of two differing pronunciations shows that the tea cultures of both northern and southern China existed in Korea; it is also a sign that tea culture had once been widespread.

It is not known when tea was introduced to the Korean peninsula, but tea drinking was common among Buddhist priests during the Unified Silla period. Evidence can be found in passages from the *Memorabilia of the Three Kingdoms*:

> The monk Chungdamsa prepared tea on Jungsamil [the third day of the third lunar month] and Jungguil [the ninth day of the ninth lunar month] every year. He offered it to the Maitreya Buddha at Sahwaryeong on Mount Nam in Gyeongju. At the request of King Gyeongseok, he also served tea to the king.

Since several Korean monks and scholars studied in China around the time of Silla's unification of the Three Kingdoms, it is likely that tea culture was introduced to Silla from China in this period. Tea drinking became widespread among the aristocracy in the Goryeo period. According to the *Goryeo dogyeong* (An Illustrated Account of Goryeo), aristocrats drank tea imported from China because native tea was of inferior quality. Tea utensils were all imitations of Chinese ones, but it seems that tea culture had already secured a place in Korea's culinary culture. Just as people drink water after drinking coffee today, people in the Goryeo era drank tea after each meal and then would also drink *sungnyung* (scorched rice tea). For the Goryeo aristocracy, tea was not an everyday drink but a *gihopum* with a distinctive place in its eating culture.

Tea culture, however, declined in the Joseon era, as the yangban class did not drink it often; monks were the main drinkers of tea. Travelogues written by Westerners in the late nineteenth century noted that Koreans did not drink tea at all. One explanation is that other satisfying beverages could be found throughout the country; some point to the suppression of Buddhist culture during the Joseon period. However, these explanations are not very convincing since tea was enjoyed as a *gihopum* rather than an everyday drink and since Buddhism remains a powerful religion today. It seems that tea was no longer enjoyed as a *gihopum* in the Joseon period because of the potential for severe exploitation under the tribute tax system. When the government requested an unreasonable amount of tangerines as tribute, people would damage the base of tangerine trees and ruin the harvest in order to avoid paying the taxes. Similarly, it is probable that farmers dried the seeds of tea plants in an effort to avoid being exploited by having to cultivate tea to pay the tribute tax. By the late Joseon period, terms such as *charye* (ancestor memorial rites), *dasik* (a kind of rice cake), and *dabang* (tea room) – all of which use the Chinese character for 'tea' – were the only reminders of the past existence of a tea culture. The term *damo* originally referred to the government slave in every office whose job was to make tea; in the late Joseon period, they became undercover female detectives in the Agency for the Arrest of Thieves (Podocheong).

The Introduction of Tobacco

As tea drinking declined, tobacco became popular as a *gihopum*. Tobacco spread throughout Europe after its introduction in the sixteenth century. In 1558, Philip II of Spain obtained tobacco seeds from the central plateaus of South America and cultivated them for trade and for medicinal uses. Today, tobacco is cultivated throughout the world between latitude sixty degrees North and latitude forty degrees South. It is thought that tobacco was introduced to Korea in the late sixteenth or early seventeenth century, soon after the end of the Imjin War – i.e., about a half century after it was first cultivated in Europe. It was initially called *dambago* or *namryeongcho*. The term *dambago* was derived from the pronunciation of 'tobacco;' the term *namryeongcho* meant 'a divine plant from the southern countries.' Later, it was commonly called *namcho* or *yeoncho*. In the early seventeenth century, tobacco was regarded as a medicinal plant. It continued to be used as medicine even after it became a *gihopum* and the number of smokers increased. Legends about its origins reveal what people thought of tobacco in the early years after its introduction. According to one tale,

> nasal diseases were common a long time ago in China, but they could be cured by plugging the nose with a tobacco leaf. Since it was not possible to get tobacco leaves in the winter, people would dry the leaves and smoke them to prevent nasal diseases.

According to another,

> There was a *gisaeng* who loved the company of men. She wanted to be able to kiss the men she would not be able to meet after her death. So her soul transformed, making tobacco grow on her tomb. That is why people can smoke tobacco only through their mouths.

There was some truth to the claims about the medicinal properties of tobacco. Farmers soaked tobacco in water and then used the water to spray their crops since nicotine can act as an insecticide.

Despite lacking a scientific basis for their views, people were also becoming aware of the dangers of smoking. The scholar Yi Ik (1681–1763) thought that they outweighed its benefits. Smoking tobacco was helpful when one's throat was full of phlegm, when one salivated after eating something disagreeable, and when it was difficult to lie down due to indigestion. It was also useful in treating excessive salivation because of heartburn and in warming the body against the winter cold. On the other hand, it had ten harmful effects, according to Yi. He was concerned that people – both high and low, young and old – would waste their time and wealth on tobacco, even though they had a lot of work to do. Fires were another problem, and government officials also thought that a food shortage might arise if fields used to cultivate grain and vegetables were converted into tobacco fields. Yi was even worried about its negative effects on

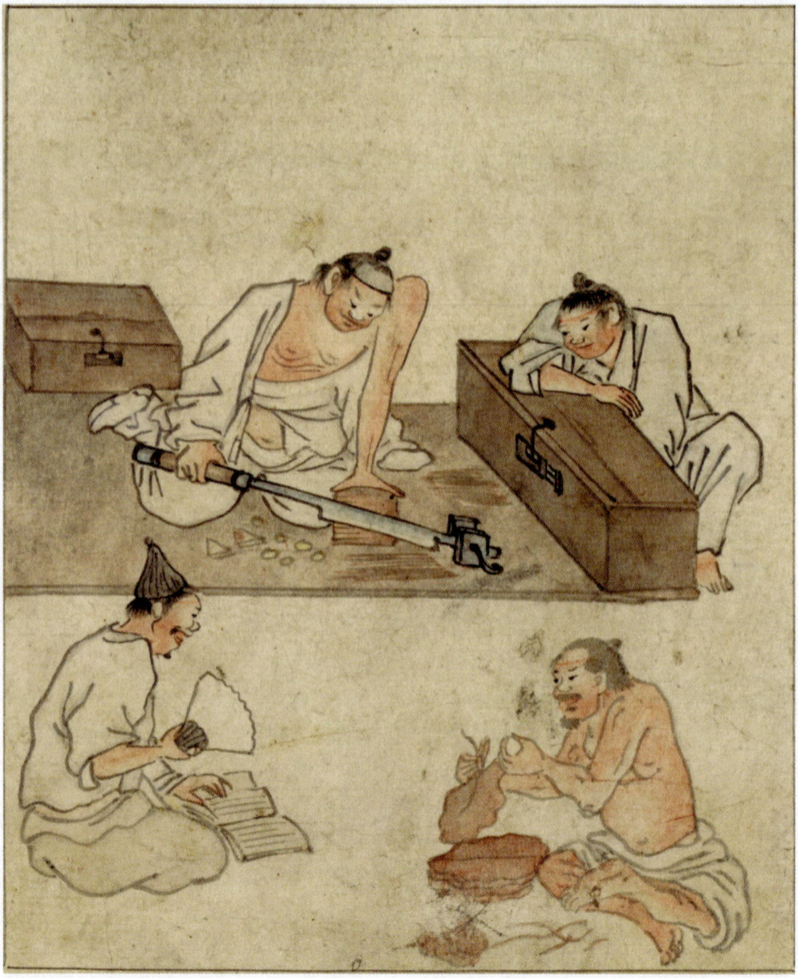

Fig. 22.1. *Making Cigarettes* (Dambae sseolgi), Gim Hongdo, late eighteenth century. (National Museum of Korea)

spiritual health, claiming that the smell was so bad that smokers would be unable to become purified and approach the gods.

As Yi Ik's comments indicate, the spread of tobacco was rapid. After being shipwrecked at Jeju Island in 1653, a foreigner named Hendrick Hamel lived in Joseon for fourteen years. According to his journals, tobacco was so popular among Koreans that children began to learn how to smoke at four or five years of age and that there were very few people – male or female – who did not smoke. Tobacco was very expensive at the time; one *geun* of tobacco (0.6 kilogram) cost one *nyang* of silver. Considering its cost, Hamel's account seems to be an exaggeration, but it is true that its spread was quite rapid. In the Joseon era, Koreans of all ages, genders, and classes became such habitual smokers that it was said that tigers must have smoked tobacco a long, long time ago. It also became common for stories about the distant past to begin with the line 'when tigers smoked pipes.'

Social Class and the Length of Tobacco Pipes

Smoking etiquette developed as the use of tobacco spread throughout society. In the late Joseon period, it became the norm for commoners not to smoke in front of yangban and for children not to smoke in front of adults. According to *Gyeongdo japji* by Yu Deukgong (1749–1807), a text probably written in the late eighteenth century, "people of low birth cannot smoke in the presence of someone of high status." It also stated that the authorities strictly enforced the prohibition against smoking when officials were out in the streets. If someone smoked when state councillors or officials of the Office of Special Advisors passed by, that person was locked up in a house along the street and later punished. Smoking became closely associated with a person's social authority. For instance, the sounds of a grandfather smoking in the drawing room of the house came to signify his authority within the family. The regulations on smoking were part of the yangban class' efforts to strengthen the Neo-Confucian social order in the seventeenth century. Scholars emphasized the study of ritual, worried that the social status system was in disorder as a result of the invasions of the Japanese and of the Manchus. In addition, King Injo and his supporters seized the throne in 1623, criticizing King Gwanghaegun for abandoning Ming China, pursuing a policy of neutrality, and failing to show filiality toward Queen Inmok.

Over time, the length of a person's pipe came to represent his or her social status. Tobacco pipes consisted of three parts: the *dambaetong*, which held the tobacco; the *mulburi*, which was placed in the mouth, and the *seoldae*, which connected the other two parts. A pipe with a long *seoldae* was called a *jangjuk*; one with a short *seoldae* or none at all was called a *gombangdae*. Since tobacco was introduced from Japan, the first pipes were Japanese in style with a small *dambaetong* and a short *seoldae*. These were the pipes that the commoners used. However, genre paintings from the eighteenth century show that *jangjuk* with a larger *dambaetong* became popular in Korea. When using a *jangguk*, it was difficult to light the tobacco while puffing on the *mulburi*. It became usual to have a servant light the pipe; in other words, the only people able to smoke a *jangjuk* pipe were people of means, such as the yangban class. Wealthier yangban used *jangjuk* decorated in gold and silver with a *dambaetong* made of white brass or copper.

Commoners believed that the prohibition from smoking in front of adults originated in the distant past 'when tigers smoked tobacco.' One story about its origins is a folk tale about King Munjong (r. 1450–1452). One day, he was talking with Jiphyeonjeon scholars when the edge of his garment caught fire from a pipe; this incident led him to urge people to be careful when smoking. This tale placed the origins of the prohibition about 150 years before tobacco was even introduced to Korea. According to another folk tale, officials at court often smoked when debate stalled on state affairs. The smoke would rise, gathering around the king who was seated above them. Unable to stand it, the king forbade people from smoking in front of their superiors. Both tales suggest that officials were initially able to smoke in front of the king. The phrase 'when tigers smoked pipes' expresses a nostalgia for the days when even animals could smoke freely. It was a longing for the times before the social rules for smoking became established.

Tobacco and Commoner Life

Tobacco was one of the new crops introduced in the mid-Joseon period that brought about many changes to the lives of the peasantry. It is well known that potatoes, sweet potatoes, and later corn played a large role in helping people avoid starvation. By contrast, tobacco helped to improve the earning power of peasant households since it was a cash crop. Its cultivation was an important factor in the development of the agricultural economy. The economic impact of tobacco was similar to that of cotton. Brought to the peninsula at the end of the Goryeo period, cotton spread rapidly after the founding of Joseon, bringing about a revolution in Korean clothing. It also helped to stimulate the emergence of markets in the provinces. Similar to cotton, tobacco was cultivated in many regions throughout the country. Selling their crops as far as China, tobacco producers helped to increase the earning power of the peasantry and to improve the government's finances. Tobacco helped agriculture to reach the stage of commercialization in the late Joseon period.

From the time of its introduction, strong demand made tobacco a very expensive product.

> Co, Co, Tobacco –
> Tobacco from Dongnae and Ulsan.
> Have you come to give me silver?
> Or have you come to give me gold?
> I have no silver nor gold,
> But I brought a tobacco seed.

These lines are from the 'Ballad of Tobacco,' a folk song from Gyeongsang province. It shows that tobacco was first cultivated in the Dongnae and Ulsan regions after its introduction from Japan and that its value was comparable to that of gold and silver. Even after the cultivation of tobacco expanded tremendously in the eighteenth century, it remained a profitable crop since demand continued to grow among the people.

Tobacco became widely used among the commoner class in the eighteenth century, quickly becoming an important part of their daily lives. Along with alcohol, it enabled them to endure long hours of work. In the southern regions of Korea, farming work was coordinated by organizations called *dure*, and in the northern regions, there were similar organizations called the *hwangdu*. When it was time for the *dure* or *hwangdu* to weed the fields, people gathered early in the morning, and after reaching the field, they took a short break called a *dambaecham* (tobacco break). Whether working individually or with a group, it was usual for the peasantry to have a smoke at the beginning of the workday or in the middle of the day. It was in this period that smoking became popular among adult males and that the length of the tobacco pipe came to represent one's social status.

with Ellen Yuh

23. THE OUTHOUSES OF THE ROYAL PALACES

Hong Soon Min

Soon after the founding of Joseon, King Taejo decided that Gaeseong, the capital of Goryeo, was no longer suitable to serve as the capital of his new kingdom. He moved the capital in the year 1394, choosing the location based on the principles of feng shui. It was surrounded by four mountains which acted as a natural defense barrier, and it was just north of the Han River, giving the capital access to the western coast and inland regions. Construction of the first royal palace began that year, and the layout of the capital followed Chinese practice. The main palace compound was on the northern edge of the city, with the main gate facing south, and it was between two of the country's most important spiritual sites. To the west was Sajikdan, the altar for the ceremonies for the deities of the land and grain; to the east was the Royal Shrine (Jongmyo), the shrine for the former kings and queens of the dynasty. Over the course of the Joseon era, there were several palaces built in Seoul. At the time, the Chinese character for palace, *gung*, was not just used for royal residences. It also appeared in the name of buildings with a significant connection to the king, such as the building where he was born if it was outside the palace. It was also used for members of the royal family who were comparable in status as the king, such as the king's father; one example is Unhyeon Palace, the residence of the Daewongun, the father of King Gojong. Seoul is mainly known for the five main palaces that remain today – Gyeongbok, Changdeok, Changgyeong, Deoksu, and Gyeonghui Palaces. The first three were located just south of Mt. Baegak and the other mountains on the capital's northern border; the last two were built near Mt. Inwang in the northwest. These five palaces were the main residences of Joseon-era kings. They were also the site of nearly all public activities and affairs of the state; in other words, they were the country's highest government office. This chapter provides an overview of the palaces in Seoul and their internal workings, concluding with a section on perhaps their least dignified areas – their outhouses.

The Palaces of Seoul

A dual-palace system developed in the capital by the late fifteenth century. The main palace (*beopgung*) was where government business was conducted and where the king and queen lived. The secondary palace (*igung*) was to be used if the main palace was damaged by fire or some other event or if the king wanted to live in an alternate residence. Despite the fact that it was lower in status in the hierarchy of official buildings, both had the facilities necessary to be fully working palaces. Though the destruction of palaces in times of war or invasion necessitated the construction of new ones, the dual-palace system remained in effect until the year 1896. Initially, the main palace was Gyeongbok Palace, and the secondary palace was the combined Changdeok and Changgyeong Palaces. Gyeongbok Palace was completed in 1395, and the royal family officially moved in at the end of the year. During the first few years, the kingdom focused on building the foundation of its government, and moving into the palace marked the completion of this process. King Taejong ordered the construction of a secondary palace in the tenth lunar month of 1404, and Changdeok Palace was completed about a year later. Changgyeong Palace was established in Seongjong's reign through the reconstruction of Sugang Palace, which started in 1482 and was completed in 1484. Sugang Palace had been built in 1419 as a residence for Taejong after he abdicated the throne to his son, King Sejong. Though Changgyeong Palace was technically an independent palace, it was actually a compound attached to Changdeok Palace, which lacked sufficient space for living quarters.

The dual-palace system had to be reorganized after the end of the Imjin War because all the palaces were burned down in 1592. The Changdeok-Changgyeong Palace complex became the main palace, while two new palaces were built as secondary palaces. When he returned to Seoul in 1593, King Seonjo used the former residence of Seongjong's older brother as a temporary palace. In 1604, reconstruction began on the Royal Shrine and the royal palaces, but by the end of his reign, little had been done because of a lack of labor and materials. When Gwanghaegun became king in 1608, work on the buildings resumed once again. By the end of the fifth lunar month of that year, the restoration of the Royal Shrine was finished, and Changdeok Palace was almost completely rebuilt by the end of 1609. The temporary palace was renamed Gyeongun Palace in 1611; the smallest of the five royal palaces, it remained empty for over two hundred years after Gwanghaegun officially took residence in Changdeok Palace in 1615. The adjacent Changgyeong Palace also underwent a large-scale restoration, and Joseon built two new palaces – Gyeongdeok Palace and Ingyeong Palace – that served as the new secondary palaces. The new arrangement was revised during the reign of Injo (r. 1623–1649) because most of the buildings in Changdeok and Changgyeong Palaces were

Fig. 23.1. *Palace Celebration at Sungjeongjeon* (Sungjeongjeon jinyeondo), early eighteenth century. This is a painting of a banquet for King Sukjong in 1710 that was held in Gyeonghui Palace. (National Museum of Korea)

destroyed in the rebellion of Yi Gwal and the two Manchu invasions. Ingyeong Palace was torn down for material to rebuild the two palaces, leaving only Gyeongdeok Palace for use as a secondary palace. In 1647, the grounds of Gyeongbok Palace stood empty, and Changdeok Palace and Changgyeong Palace were regarded as a single palace area called the Eastern Palace. It became the official primary residence of the king, while Gyeongdeok Palace (i.e., the Western Palace) served as the secondary palace. The latter was renamed Gyeonghui Palace during the Yeongjo's reign in the eighteenth century.

The original dual-palace structure was restored during the reign of Gojong in the mid-nineteenth century. After he took the throne in 1864, the Queen Regent Sinjeong proposed the restoration of Gyeongbok Palace in the fourth lunar month of 1865. Work progressed rapidly once the Daewongun took control of the government, and Gojong was able to take residence there officially in 1868. The restored palace was thus able to reclaim its past position as the main palace, with the Changdeok-Changgyeong Palace complex as a secondary palace once again and Gyeonghui Palace now left unused. The dual-palace system ended after Gojong moved the court to the Russian legation in February 1896 and then took residence in Gyeongun Palace, which was renamed Deoksu Palace in 1907.

The Inner Structure of the Palace

A large number of buildings filled the grounds of the palace. According to the 'Palace Gazette' written around 1908, the total area of Gyeongbok Palace was about 9,240 *gan*, while the buildings of Changdeok-Changgyeong Palaces covered about 6,200 *gan* (1 *gan* = the area between two columns). Given that a large yangban house was usually called a '99-*gan*' house, the palaces could easily hold fifty to seventy such houses on their grounds. By today's standards, Gyeongbok Palace could hold almost 500 modern homes with an area of thirty-*pyeong* (100 sq. m) each. Just the scale of the buildings shows that the palaces were bigger than a large village, comparable in size to a small city.

The layout of the palace was generally based on the principles given in the *Kaogongji* (Record of Trades) in the ancient Chinese text *Rites of Zhou*. Along the palace's central axis, there were the main gate and two compounds called the *oejeon* and the *naejeon*. The main gate usually faced south, part of a high wall that surrounded the palace. The walls were a display of royal authority and prevented unwanted people from entering, with doors and gates located at strategic places. In front of the main gate were the country's main government offices; this area was known as the *gwoloegaksa*. The *oejeon* was the area where officials could meet with the king. The center of the *oejeon* was the *beopjeon*, the large hall where official functions were held, and the *pyeonjeon*, the king's official office where the king and officials conducted meetings. The *naejeon* was the living quarters of the king and the queen. Located further inside the palace from the *oejeon*, it contained the *yeongeojiso*, the buildings where he could meet with officials individually. The queen's residence was located in the innermost part of the *naejeon*, the palace's central and most restricted area. Called the *jungjeon* or *junggungjeon*, it was where she carried out her official duties such as supervising her ladies-in-waiting.

Though the Six Ministries of the government were located in front of Gyeongbok Palace, there was an area near the *naejeon* and *oejeon* called

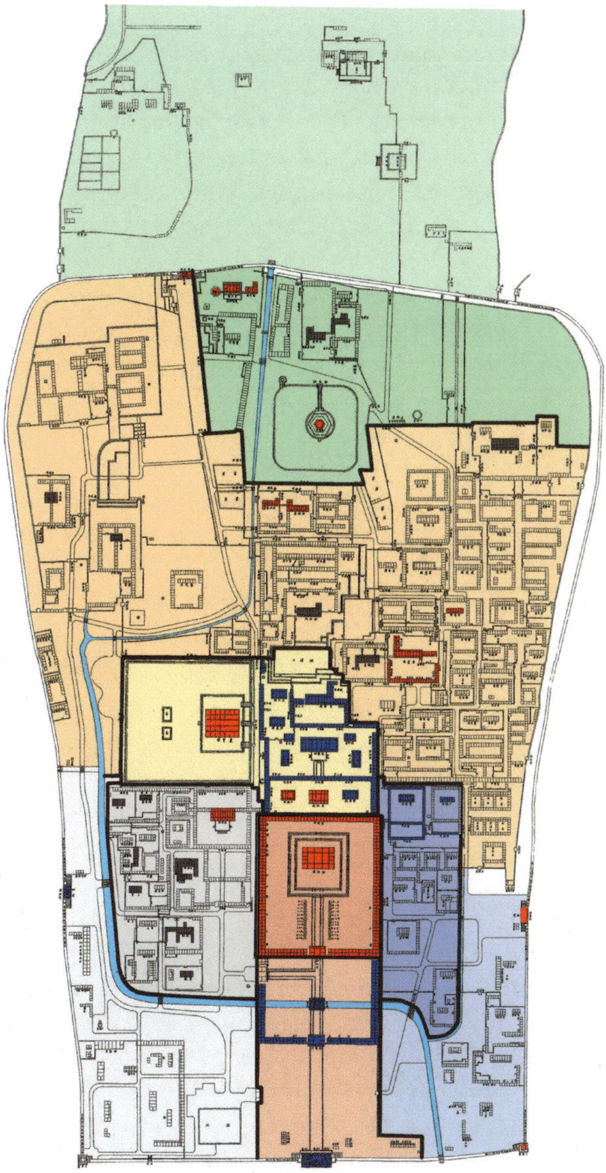

Map 23.1. Map of Gyeongbok Palace, *Bukgwol dohyeong*, late nineteenth or early twentieth century.

Legend: [gray] = Gwollae gaksa [pink] = Oejeon
[purple] = Eastern Palace [yellow] = Naejeon
[orange] = residential areas [green] = Rear Garden

the *gwollaegaksa* that had many important offices. First, there were offices that handled matters requiring direct contact with the king. The Bincheong was the building where state ministers gathered before or after a meeting with the king, and the Daecheong had offices for officials of the Office of the Inspector-General and Office of the Censor-General. The Yemungwan was responsible for producing diplomatic documents, and the Jeongcheong was the building where officials from the Ministries of Personnel and Military Affairs handled personnel matters. This part of the palace also had the Office of Special Advisers, whose scholars gave lectures on the classics to the king, and the Royal Secretariat. There were offices such as the Chunchugwan, where historical records were kept, and the Royal Library, which was responsible for overseeing royal documents and general publications, along with scholarly research and supervision. Second, there were also offices that directly attended to the daily needs of the king. The Naeuiwon was responsible for preparing medicine for the king and the court, and the Saongwon was where meals were prepared. The grounds also had many areas for the various military offices whose duty was to protect the king and the palace, such as the Inner Royal Guard.

To the east of the *naejeon and oejeon* was the Eastern Palace, which was the residence of the crown prince. Located near the prince's quarters was the Seja Sigangwon, where he received lessons, and the Seja Ikwisa, his personal guards. The living area for the king's relatives and their servants was located behind the *naejeon*, and further back were leisure areas such as the Geumwon, Rear Garden (Huwon), and North Garden (Bugwon).

The size and rank of palace buildings varied according to their function and the status of the people who used them. The differences were roughly indicated by the final character in their names; most ended with one of the following Chinese characters: *jeon, dang, hab, gak, jae, heon, nu,* or *jeong*. The character *jeon* was for residences of the king, the queen, or the king's mother or grandmother. The next level in the hierarchy was the *dang*; a king could live in a *dang*, but a crown prince could not live in a *jeon*. The *hab* or *gak* were buildings a level or more below the *jeon* or *dang* and often had a supplementary role to other buildings. The *jae* or *heon* were used either as living areas for royal relatives or as work areas for government officials. Two-story structures had separate names for each floor; the character *gak* was used for the first floor, and the character *nu* was for the second. *Nu* was also for buildings with raised floors several meters above the ground. The character *jeong* referred to small leisure structures built in scenic settings. Although the terms *cheon-dang-hab-gak-jae-heon-nu-jeong* were not strictly defined, they gave a general indication of a building's relative stature.

In the palace, there were many secondary buildings or structures that had no name. These included the servants' quarters surrounding the main palace buildings, the passageways between buildings, the gates in the walls sectioning the palace grounds, and storage areas. Of course, a palace also had more than buildings. It needed wells and rice fields since many people lived there. Its grounds were landscaped with lotus ponds, islands, brooks, bridges, sluices, heights, platforms, springs, streams, and terraces. The diversity of its environment was an indication of how lively and variegated were the lives of people within the palace. An examination of outhouses, designed for one of the most basic human physiological needs, can provide an interesting perspective on life in the palace.

The Outhouses of the Palace

The Korean language has many words that mean 'toilet' or 'outhouse.' These days, people mainly use the word *hwajangsil*; not long ago, the word *byeonso* was used commonly but is hardly heard now. In the past, there were many more words for outhouse such as *seogak*, *jeongbang*, *cheongcheuk*, *cheongbang*, *cheonghon*, *cheukgan*, *cheuksil*, *cheukcheong*, *honcheuk*, *honheon*, and *hoechijang*. The large number of terms may be a reflection of the fact that outhouses were relatively advanced from early on in Korean history. In commoner houses, they were built in the courtyard, far away from the main building. There was even a saying that went: "the farther away the in-laws' house and the outhouse, the better." Its placement was for hygienic purposes and was also meant to keep the odors away from the rest of the house. This was usual in the commoner class whose houses were spacious and among whom the separation between men and women were not so strictly enforced. The situation was different in yangban households. Living spaces for males and females were strictly separated, particularly in urban yangban houses. There was an inner toilet for women and an outdoor toilet for men. The inner toilet was usually located away from the main building in an isolated spot; it was part of the inner servants' quarters or an independent structure. The outdoor toilet was located in the outer servants' quarters or in a separate structure outside the main door. Sometimes, there were two outdoor toilets, one for the owner and guests and one for people of lower status.

Though Koreans generally believe that there were no outhouses in the palaces, if individual houses had them, it would be likely that palaces did too. The residents of the palace did use the term *cheukgan* for 'outhouse' as well as euphemisms such as 'the urgent place,' 'the unclean place,' or 'small house.' The fact that the palace used the same term as did people outside of it shows that palaces did indeed have outhouses. Where were the outhouses of Gyeongbok Palace? There are two large maps, the *Bukgwol dohyeong* and the *Donggwol dohyeong*, that were produced at the same time as the 'Palace Gazette.' They contain detailed information on the layout of the palace. According to these maps, Gyeongbok Palace had toilets in twenty-eight locations, with a combined total area of 51.5 *gan*, while the Eastern Palace had twenty-one toilets with an area of 36 *gan*. Most of the toilets were one *gan* in size, with the largest being seven *gan*. The smallest possible house was a one-*gan* house – a simple structure with four pillars. Since the smallest commoner residences were straw houses three-*gan* in area, a seven-*gan* toilet was a building of considerable size.

How did the king go to the bathroom? Palace maps show that there were no toilets in the palace's central areas such as the *naejeon*, the *oejeon*, and the living quarters of the royal family. This means that the royal family

Fig. 23.2. Reconstruction of an outhouse in the Eastern Palace.

used chamberpots rather than outhouses. In palace terminology, feces were referred to as *maeu*; in Chinese characters, it was called *maehwa*, which was sometimes pronounced *maeu*. The king's chamberpot, called a *maeuteul*, looked like a Western-style toilet; it was made of wood and shaped like the letter 'u.' The seat was covered with red velvet, and under the frame was a copper dish to receive the urine and feces. In the Neo-Confucian value system, people of high status were not supposed to work with their hands. Since the king was the person of the highest status in the country, servants assisted him with his basic physiological needs. A female servant working for a court lady was in charge of looking after the *maeuteul*. She put finely cut chaff inside the *maeuteul* and brought it to the king when he wanted to relieve himself. After the king was finished, his servant would add more chaff and take it away. At times, the *maeuteul* would be taken to the Naeuiwon to enable the king's physicians to examine it and check the status of his health.

Though the king and the queen did not need an outhouse, hundreds of other people resided within its walls, and hundreds more entered the palace on a regular basis. How did these people go to the bathroom? It was not possible for all of them to use a *maeuteul*. If people had no access to an outhouse, some would have relieved themselves anywhere, making the palace foul-smelling. The outhouses of the palace were mainly located in its outer areas. They were for people living in the palace such as court ladies and eunuchs and for people who worked there such as officials and soldiers. They were separate buildings in remote parts of the palace or in the servants' quarters. Even those built in the servants' quarters were located far from the main building and close to an entrance, providing easy access to the outside. Because of their remote location, young children could not go by themselves and had to go in pairs or groups of three. The fact that the outhouses were located in such areas is evidence that there were people who stayed in the palace for long periods of time and took their meals there. The palace was not just the stage of politics and administration but also a living community with a vibrant culture.

The palaces of the Joseon period survived foreign occupation and the Korean War in the twentieth century. Despite much restoration work, only a quarter of the original buildings remain. Wide grassy lawns exist in places where buildings once stood. People no longer live in the palaces, and there are no outhouses there. Instead, they have public restrooms with modern flush toilets. Today, palaces are no longer the center of politics or living communities but have been turned into tourist attractions or parks. Just by walking around a palace, it is difficult to discover the history of its time and to visualize its original layout and the lives of the people who worked there. Examining the toilets of the palace is not some pointless, eccentric pursuit but an opportunity to discover the history and culture of the time when it was truly a living community.

ABOUT THE AUTHORS

Founded in 1988, the Organization of Korean Historians (Hanguk yeoksa yeonguhoe, 한국역사연구회) is one of the largest and most active historical associations in South Korea today. Its purpose is to promote an objective and systematic understanding of Korean history by training researchers and educating the general public. With a membership of around 600, it operates joint research projects and study sessions and holds a series of academic talks and discussions where historical issues are debated in depth. Among its many publications are the journal *Quarterly Review of Korean History* (*Yeoksa wa hyeonsil*), the general history *Korean History* (*Hanguk yeoksa*), and books such as *Lectures on Korean History* (*Hanguksa gangui*) and *Introduction to Korean History* (*Hanguk yeoksa immun*), as well as an assortment of books for a general readership. Its current President is Professor Ha Ilsik of Yonsei University.

APPENDIX – MONARCHS OF THE JOSEON PERIOD

(1)	1392~1398	Taejo	太祖	태조
(2)	1398~1400	Jeongjong	定宗	정종
(3)	1400~1418	Taejong	太宗	태종
(4)	1418~1450	Sejong	世宗	세종
(5)	1450~1452	Munjong	文宗	문종
(6)	1452~1455	Danjong	端宗	단종
(7)	1455~1468	Sejo	世祖	세조
(8)	1468~1469	Yejong	睿宗	예종
(9)	1469~1494	Seongjong	成宗	성종
(10)	1494~1506	Yeonsangun	燕山君	연산군
(11)	1506~1544	Jungjong	中宗	중종
(12)	1544~1545	Injong	仁宗	인종
(13)	1545~1567	Myeongjong	明宗	명종
(14)	1567~1608	Seonjo	宣祖	선조
(15)	1608~1623	Gwanghaegun	光海君	광해군
(16)	1623~1649	Injo	仁祖	인조
(17)	1649~1659	Hyojong	孝宗	효종
(18)	1659~1674	Hyeonjong	顯宗	현종
(19)	1674~1720	Sukjong	肅宗	숙종
(20)	1720~1724	Gyeongjong	景宗	경종
(21)	1724~1776	Yeongjo	英祖	영조
(22)	1776~1800	Jeongjo	正祖	정조
(23)	1800~1834	Sunjo	純祖	순조
(24)	1834~1849	Heonjong	憲宗	헌종
(25)	1849~1863	Cheoljong	哲宗	철종
(26)	1863~1907	Gojong	高宗	고종
(27)	1907~1910	Sunjong	純宗	순종

GLOSSARY

aegoe gyosaeng (액외교생, 額外敎生)	*gyosaeng* from the commoner status or the offspring of concubines
aengnae gyosaeng (액내교생, 額內敎生)	*gyosaeng* from the yangban class
Agency for the Arrest of Thieves (포도청, 捕盜廳)	the police bureau
amhaengeosa (암행어사, 暗行御史)	secret royal inspectors
Analects (논어, 論語)	Confucian classic containing sayings and ideas of Confucius
anchi (안치, 安置)	a form of banishment where royal family or high-ranking officials were sent to a specific location
Andong Gwon (안동 권씨, 安東 權氏)	the branch of the Gwon family whose ancestral seat is Andong
apseul (압슬, 壓膝)	a form of torture in which a person's knees were pressed down on with a heavy piece of wood
arakju (아락주)	the term for *soju* in Gaeseong
baegang (배강, 背講)	a type of class in which students recited texts from memory
Baegundong seowon (백운동서원, 白雲洞書院)	
Baekje (백제, 百濟)	one of the Three Kingdoms of Korea (18 BCE–660 CE)
baekjeong (백정, 白丁)	outcastes of commoner status who were in occupations associated with the low-born
Baekjung (백중, 百中)	the Ghost Festival
baekseong (백성, 百姓)	the people, the peasantry
Bak Jiwon (박지원, 朴趾源)	Silhak thinker and writer (1737–1805); author of *Jehol Diary*
banchan (반찬, 飯饌)	side dishes
bang (방)	store
bang (방, 坊)	a specially designated area where *baekjeong* lived
bangnap (방납, 防納)	a system in which low-level officials or merchants transported tribute goods submitted by commoners to the capital
beopgung (법궁, 法宮)	the main palace
beopjeon (법전, 法殿)	large hall within the palace grounds where official functions were held
Bibyeonsa (비변사, 備邊司)	Border Defense Command
bimo (비모, 婢某)	term for unfree people
Bincheong (빈청, 賓廳)	building where state ministers gathered before or after a meeting with the king
bo (보, 保)	the men who fulfilled their military service by providing the material necessities for the armed forces
bo (보)	reservoirs created by building dams across small rivers or streams
bobusang (보부상, 褓負商)	an organization of peddlers that received monopoly rights from local government offices

bom bori (봄보리)	spring barley
bon (본, 本)	main
bongwan (본관, 本貫)	ancestral seat
Book of Changes (주역, 周易)	*Yi Jing*
Book of the Later Han (후한서, 後漢書)	*Hou Han Shu*
borit gogae (보릿고개)	the barley hump
bu (부, 負)	unit for measuring land
bugok (부곡, 部曲)	district
Bugwon (북원, 北苑)	North Garden
buin bongjak (부인 봉작, 夫人封爵)	system in which *yangban* women received social positions based on the official rank of husbands
bukgamjeo (북감저, 北甘藷)	potato
Bukgwol dohyeong (북궐도형, 北闕圖形)	a large map with detailed information on the layout of Gyeongbok Palace
busa (부사, 府使)	a magistrate
byeolgam (별감, 別監)	officer in a *yuhyangso* who worked under the *jwasu*
byeoljang (별장, 別將)	merchants appointed in Seoul as officials by the government
byeolpo (별포, 別包)	the trade conducted by interpreters on tribute missions
byeoneo (변어, 邊語)	secret codes used by merchants
byeongjak (병작, 竝作)	the arrangement of tenants sharing the harvest equally with the landowner
byeonso (변소, 便所)	toilet
Byulsiwi (별시위, 別侍衛)	an army made up of yangban
cha (차, 茶)	tea
chaekgeori (책걸이)	a celebration held by parents for their children's teachers
Changdeok Palace (창덕궁, 昌德宮)	one of the main royal palaces in Seoul
Changgyeong Palace (창경궁, 昌慶宮)	one of the main royal palaces in Seoul
charye (차례, 茶禮)	ancestor memorial rites
cheajik (체아직, 遞兒職)	a system in which officials took turns handling duties
cheok(척, 尺)	the word given to call those of the *sillyangyeokcheon* class
cheonbang (천방, 川防)	another word for *bo*
cheongbang (청방, 靑房)	outhouse
cheongcheuk (청측, 靑厠)	outhouse
cheonghon (청혼, 靑渾)	outhouse
Cheongjanggwan jeonseo (청장관전서, 靑莊館全書)	the collected works by Yi Deokmu
cheongju (청주, 淸酒)	a type of clear liquor
cheonin (천인, 賤人)	low-born people
cheonmin (천민, 賤民)	low-born people
cheop (첩, 楪)	bowls with lids in which side dishes were served
cheukcheong (측청, 厠靑)	outhouse
cheukgan (측간, 厠間)	outhouse
cheuksil (측실, 厠室)	outhouse
chilbancheonyeok (칠반천역, 七般賤役)	the seven occupations that were regarded as the most lowly of the time

chilgeo jiak (칠거지악, 七去之惡)	the seven evil acts for which a husband could divorce his wife
chinyeongnye (친영례, 親迎禮)	wedding ceremony that welcomed the bride into the husband's family
Choe Inho (최인호)	South Korean novelist (1945–2013)
chon (촌, 村)	district
chongaekje (총액제, 總額制)	a system for the calculation of tax revenues
chonggak (총각)	another term for the head of a *dure*
chonggak daebang (총각대방)	another term for the head of a *dure*
chonggak daejang (총각대장)	the head of the *dure*
chonggak jwasang (총각좌상)	another term for the head of a *dure*
chonmin (촌민, 村民)	the peasantry
chubi (추비, 追肥)	the spreading of additional fertilizer while the rice plants are growing
chueotang (추어탕, 鰍魚湯)	loach stew
Chuncheon (춘천, 春川)	a city in Gangwon province
Chungchanwi (충찬위, 忠贊衛)	an army made up of *yangban*
Chungjangwi (충장위, 忠壯衛)	name of an army in the late Joseon period
Chungsunwi (충순위, 忠順衛)	an army made up of *yangban*
Chunguiwi (충의위, 忠義衛)	an army made up of *yangban*
Chunhyangjeon (춘향전, 春香傳)	*The Tale of Chunhyang*
chunju (춘주, 春酒)	another term for *samhaeju*, a type of *cheongju*
chupo (추포, 麤布)	roughly woven hemp cloth, also used as currency
Classic of History (서경, 書經)	*Shujing*
Classic of Poetry (시경, 詩經)	*Shijing*
dabang (다방, 茶房)	tea room
Daecheong (대청, 臺廳)	offices inside the palace for officials of the Office of the Inspector-General and the Office of the Censor-General
Daedongbeop (대동법, 大同法)	the Uniform Tax Law
daedongbo (대동보, 大同譜)	part of *sebo* that recorded the information of the entire extended family
daedonggye (대동계, 大同契)	another word for *donggye*
daegokjeonseok (대곡전석, 大斛全石)	term for twenty *mal*
daejanggi (대장기, 大將旗)	another term for *nonggi*
Daejeon hoetong (대전회통, 大典會通)	a code of law in the Joseon era
Daejol (대졸, 隊卒)	unit that young commoners could join by taking an examination
Daeryeong River (대령강)	a river in the northwest of the peninsula
Daewongun (대원군, 大院君)	the father of the king who was not a king himself; the father of King Gojong, who served as his regent
dambaecham (담배참)	tobacco break
dambaetong (담배통)	the part of the tobacco pipe that held the tobacco
dambago (담바고)	tobacco
Da Ming lu (대명률, 大明律)	*The Great Ming Code*
damo (다모, 茶母)	originally, the government slave whose job was to make tea; in the late Joseon period, undercover female detectives in the Police Bureau

danbo(단보, 段步)	unit of area equal to 300 *pyeong*
dang (당, 堂)	palace buildings that were a level lower in hierarchy to *jeon*
dangbaekjeon (당백전, 當百錢)	a currency equivalent to one *nyang*
Dangdaeseonwonnok (당대선원록, 當代璿源錄)	genealogy of the royal family
dangje (당제)	a shaman ritual
dangojeon (당오전, 當五錢)	a currency equivalent to five *pun*
Dangun (단군, 檀君)	the mythical founder of the first Korean kingdom
danmuji (단무지)	pickled daikon radish, called *takuan* in Japanese
dasik (다식, 茶食)	a kind of rice cake
ddungdol (뚱돌)	the name given to the stones used in the *deuldol* test in Jeju Island
deokdae (덕대, 德大)	a kind of mine operator
deokseokgi (덕석기)	another term for *nonggi*
Deoksu Palace (덕수궁, 德壽宮)	one of the royal palaces in Seoul
deongipan (덩이판)	a device used to break up soil into fine pieces
deuldok (들독)	the name given to the stones used in the *deuldol* test in Jeolla province
deuldol (들돌)	the test of lifting stones
dimchae (딤채, 淡菜)	pickled vegetables; later became the word kimchi
do (도, 徒)	penal servitude
Doctrine of the Mean (중용, 中庸)	*Zhong Yong*, one of the Four Books
doe (되, 升)	unit of volume
doenjang (된장)	fermented bean paste
doenjang soup (된장국)	fermented bean paste soup
dogyeol (도결, 都結)	an addition to the land tax that was calculated by assessing the value of all other taxes according to market prices
dohan (도한, 屠漢)	a term meaning *baekjeong*
doji (도지, 賭地)	a system in which land rent was fixed by a contract according to which tenants had to pay landlords a set amount every autumn
dokseodang (독서당, 讀書堂)	another word for *sasuk*
dong (동, 洞)	district
Dongdaemun (동대문, 東大門)	Great East Gate, one of the main gates of Seoul
Donggwol (동궐, 東闕)	Eastern Palace, residence of the crown prince
Donggwol dohyeong (동궐도형, 東闕圖形)	a large map with detailed information on the layout of Gyeongbok Palace (c. 1908)
donggye (동계, 洞契)	a communal organization that was a predecessor of the *dure*
donggye seodang (동계 서당, 洞契書堂)	a type of *seodang*, built to educate children of a specific clan
dongjae yusaeng (동재 유생, 東齋儒生)	another term for *aengnae gyosaeng*
Dongmong seonseub (동몽선습, 童蒙先習)	title of a textbook compiled in the sixteenth century
dongningye (동린계, 洞隣契)	another word for *donggye*
Doseongwi (도성위, 都城衛)	an army made up of yangban
doyusa (도유사, 都有司)	a member of the staff of a *hyanggyo*
du (두, 斗)	measurement of volume
dure (두레)	village organization of labor and mutual aid that coordinated farming work

Elementary Learning (소학, 小學)	*Xiaoxue*, a standard Confucian textbook
enuri (에누리)	the amount added to the original price of an item
eongwan (언관, 言官)	officials at the Office of the Censor-General
eungun (은군, 銀軍)	silver miners
eup (읍, 邑)	town
gabo (가보, 家譜)	a type of genealogy that focused on the family lineage of a specific individual
Gabo Peasants' War (갑오농민전쟁, 甲午農民戰爭)	a major peasant uprising in the year 1894
Gabo Reforms (갑오개혁, 甲午改革)	a reform program that started in the year 1894
gacheop (가첩, 家帖)	family book
gaekju (객주, 客主)	brokers
gaekto (객토, 客土)	a technique for improving the fertility of the land by adding new soil fertilizer to fields in early winter or spring
gaesi (개시, 開市)	international market
gaeul bori (가을보리)	autumn barley
gage (가게)	originally, a temporary store; today, a general term for store
gak (각, 閣)	palace buildings that were a level lower in hierarchy to *jeon* or *dang*
gamhongno (감홍로, 甘紅露)	a type of *soju* from Pyongyang
gamjeo (감저, 甘藷)	sweet potato
gan (간, 干)	the word term for people of the *sillyangyeokcheon* class
gan (간, 間)	a unit of area equal to the area between two columns
gang (강, 講)	class in a Confucian school
Gaoli tujing (고려도경, 高麗圖經)	*An Illustrated Account of Goryeo* by Xu Jing
Gapjin mannok (갑진만록)	a text by Yun Gukhyeong
Gapsa (갑사, 甲士)	an army made up of yangban
Gapsin Coup (갑신정변, 甲申政變)	a failed coup-d'état in December 1884
gasa (가사, 歌辭)	a type of poetry
gaseung (가승, 家乘)	a type of genealogy that focused on the family lineage of a specific individual
gat (갓)	a horsehair hat worn by yangban
gatbachi (갓바치)	*baekjeong* who worked as tanners, making shoes and other leather products
geogoljang (거골장, 去骨匠)	butchers
geomungo (거문고)	long-board zither
geum (금, 金)	gold
geumnanjeongwon (금난전권, 禁亂廛權)	the right of merchants to police commercial activity
Geumwon (금원, 禁苑)	name of a garden in the palace
Geumyang jamnok (금양잡록, 衿陽雜錄)	a fifteenth-century book on agriculture
geun (근, 斤)	unit of weight
geuru gari (그루갈이)	a practice of alternating barley and beans in the same field during a year
ggakdugi (깍두기)	kimchi made with daikon radish

gibi (기비, 基肥)	a method of coating seeds with fertilizer before they are sown
Gieon (기언, 記言)	title of a work by Heo Mok
gihopum (기호품, 嗜好品)	products such as alcohol and cigarettes that are consumed principally for pleasure
gil (길)	unit of height or length (one *gil* = several meters)
Gil Jae (길재, 吉再)	Neo-Confucian scholar, a progenitor of the *sarim* faction (1353–1419)
Gim Changjip (김창집, 金昌集)	official in the Noron faction who became Chief State Councillor (1648–1722)
Gim Deuksin (김득신, 金得臣)	royal court painter known for his genre paintings (1754–1822)
Gim Goengpil (김굉필)	Neo-Confucian scholar and official of the *sarim* faction
Gim Hongdo (김홍도)	artist known for his genre paintings (1745–c. 1806)
Gim Jongjik (김종직, 金宗直)	Neo-Confucian scholar; one of the founders of the *sarim* faction
Gim Okgyun (김옥균, 金玉均)	a leader of the Gapsin Coup (1851–1894)
Gimyorok boyu (기묘록보유)	a chronicle containing biographies of figures involved in the literati purge of 1519
gisaeng (기생, 妓生)	female entertainers
gisebae nori (기세배 놀이)	a custom in which a younger village used its banner to send new year's greetings to an older village
goguma (고구마)	sweet potato
gombangdae (곰방대)	a pipe with a short or no *seoldae*
gomtang (곰탕)	a dish made by boiling broth with meat
gongmin (공민, 公民)	taxpayers
gongwon (공원, 公員)	clerk
gongyong eun (공용은, 公用銀)	public-use silver
Goryeosa (고려사, 高麗史)	*History of Goryeo*
gosari (고사리)	fernbrake or buckwheat
Great Learning (대학, 大學)	*Daxue*, one of the Four Books
gu (구, 舊)	old
gukbap (국밥)	a dish served with rice already added to a soup
gun (군, 郡)	county
gung (궁, 宮)	palace
gungseong (궁성, 宮城)	a high wall surrounding a palace
gunjeok (군적, 軍籍)	military register
gunjeong (군정, 軍政)	military service tax
Gwanggaeto (광개토왕, 廣開土王)	the nineteenth king of Goguryeo (r. 391–413)
Gwangjang Market (광장시장, 廣場市場)	a market near Jongno-4-ga in Seoul
gwangjangnong (광작농, 廣作農)	a type of farmer that emerged in the late Joseon period
Gwangtong Bridge (광통교)	a bridge over Cheonggye Stream in Seoul
gwollaegaksa (궐내각사, 闕內各司)	an area inside the palace where government offices were located
gwoloegaksa (궐외각사, 闕外各司)	main government offices in front of the palace's main gate
gye (계, 契)	village organisation (a rotating credit association)
gyeol (결, 結)	unit for measuring land
Gyeongbok Palace (경복궁, 景福宮)	the original main palace of Joseon

gyeongdang(경당, 經堂)	name given to schools in Goguryeo
Gyeongdeok Palace (경덕궁, 慶德宮)	one of the royal palaces in Seoul
Gyeongdo japji (경도잡지, 京都雜志)	book about life in Seoul by Yu Deukgong
Gyeongguk daejeon (경국대전, 經國大典)	the code of laws of Joseon
Gyeonghui Palace (경희궁, 慶熙宮)	one of the royal palaces in Seoul
gyeongjaeso (경재소, 京在所)	the office that supervised the *yuhyangso*
Gyeongun Palace (경운궁, 慶運宮)	a royal palace that was later renamed Deoksu Palace
gyeonjongbeop (견종법, 耕種法)	method of planting seeds in the furrows
gyoim (교임, 校任)	the staff of a *hyanggyo*
gyorin (교린, 交隣)	neighborly friendship; term used to describe relations between Korea and Japan
gyosaeng (교생, 校生)	students over the age of sixteen at *hyanggyo*
Gyunyeokbeop (균역법, 均役法)	Equal-Service Law
Gyunyeokcheong (균역청, 軍役 廳)	Office of Equal Service
hab (합, 閤)	palace buildings that were a level lower in hierarchy to *jeon* or *dang* buildings
haengsang (행상, 行商)	travelling merchants
hagwa (하과, 夏課)	the summer study session
Hahoe (하회, 河回)	village in the North Gyeongsang province
halgeub hyuseo (할급휴서, 割給休書)	one of two methods of divorce used by commoners
Hangeul (한글)	the Korean script
Hanjungnok (한중록, 閑中錄)	the memoirs of Lady Hyegyeong, mother of King Jeongjo
Hanminmyeongjeonui (한민명전의, 限民名田議)	title of a work by Bak Jiwon
Heo Mok (허목, 許穆)	writer of *Gieon* (1595–1682)
heon (헌, 軒)	palace buildings that were used either as living areas for royal relatives or as work areas for government officials
heonminsu (헌민수, 獻民數)	ceremony in which the number of households was presented to the king
Heumhyul jeonchik (흠휼전칙, 欽恤典則)	a text on the standards and usage of instruments of punishment (1777)
hoechijang (회치장)	outhouse, toilet
Hoikwi (호익위, 虎翼衛)	an army made up of *yangban*
hojang (호장, 戶長)	the provincial ruling class of the Goryeo period
hojeok (호적, 戶籍)	household register
homi (호미)	weeding hoe
homi geori (호미걸이)	the festival held by the *dure* at the end of the year's faming
homi modeum (호미모듬)	the ritual held before the *dure* began work in the farming season
homi ssisi (호미씻이)	the name of *homi geori* in Jeolla province
honcheuk (혼측, 渾厠)	outhouse, toilet
Hong Gildong (홍길동, 洪吉童)	name of a legendary bandit
hongju (홍주, 紅酒)	a type of *soju* made on Jin Island

Hong Myeonghui (홍명희)	author of the novel *Im Ggeokjeong* (1888–1968)
honheon (혼헌, 渾軒)	outhouse
hop (홉, 合)	a unit of volume
huigwang (희광, 犧狂)	executioners who worked for prisons or the Ministry of Punishments
Hullyeon Dogam (훈련도감, 訓鍊都監)	an army established during the Imjin war
hungu (훈구, 勳舊)	a term referring to the political faction opposed to the *sarim* faction
hunjang (훈장, 訓長)	the headteacher
husi (후시, 後市)	large-scale private trade markets
Huwon (후원, 後苑)	Rear Garden
hwacheok (화척, 禾尺)	butchers or wicker makers
hwajangsil (화장실, 化粧室)	toilet
hwangdu (황두)	organisations similar to the *dure* in regions of dry-field cultivation
Hwang Hui (황희, 黃喜)	a state councillor (1363–1452)
hwangok (환곡, 還穀)	grain loan
Hwang Seogyeong (황석영)	South Korean novelist (b. 1943)
hwanjeong (환정, 還政)	the grain loan system
hyang (향, 鄕)	district
hyangan (향안, 鄕案)	the registry of local elites
hyangdo (향도, 香徒)	a communal organization that was a predecessor of the *dure*
hyangeum jurye (향음주례, 鄕飮酒禮)	wine-drinking rites
hyanggyo (향교, 鄕校)	secondary schools established by the government
hyanggyu (향규, 鄕規)	regulations for the operation of the *yuhyangso* and the maintenance of *hyangan*
hyangjeon (향전, 鄕戰)	incidents where *hyangan* were burned or destroyed
hyangni (향리, 鄕吏)	low or mid-level government functionaries
hyangsarye (향사례, 鄕射禮)	a ritual involving archery
hyangyak (향약, 鄕約)	community compact
hyeolju (혈주, 穴主)	mine operator
hyeon (현, 縣)	prefecture
Hyeongpyeong movement (형평운동, 衡平運動)	a movement in the 1920s whose goal was the liberation of the *baekjeong*
hyosu (효수, 梟首)	public displaying of heads after beheading
iganggo (이강고, 梨薑膏)	a type of *soju* made with pear and ginger extract
igung (이궁, 離宮)	the secondary royal palace
Im Ggeokjeong (임꺽정)	a legendary bandit who was active in the mid sixteenth century (?–1562)
Imwon gyeongjeji (임원경제지, 林園經濟志)	scholarly treatise on economic activities by Seo Yugu
induse (인두세, 人頭稅)	poll tax
Ingyeong Palace (인경궁, 仁慶宮)	a palace in Seoul built in the early seventeenth century
interpreter official (역관, 譯官)	*yeokgwan*
ipjeon (입전, 立廛)	merchant association with a monopoly over silk
jae (재, 齋)	palace buildings that were used either as living areas for royal relatives or as work areas for government officials
jaein (재인, 才人)	entertainers

jaerae sijang (재래 시장, 在來市場)	older types of market
jamchae (잠채, 潛採)	illegal mining without a government permit
jang (장, 杖)	heavy stick
jangajji (장아찌)	a type of pickled vegetable
jangdolbaengi (장돌뱅이)	itinerant peddler
jangdollim (장돌림)	itinerant peddler
Jang Gilsan (장길산)	a legendary bandit who was active in the mid sixteenth century; subject of a multi-volume historical novel by Hwang Seogyeong
jangin (장인, 匠人)	specialist
jangjuk (장죽, 長竹)	a pipe with a long *seoldae*
jangmun (장문, 場門)	town markets held twice a month
jangsi (장시, 場市)	rural markets
jangui (장의, 掌議)	a type of *gyoim* who took care of students and their living quarters
Japan House (왜관, 倭館)	Japanese settlement in Busan where trade was conducted
Japsaek Army (잡색군, 雜色軍)	an army made up of low-born
Jehol Diary (열하일기, 熱河日記)	title of work by Bak Jiwon about his trip to Qing China
jeohwa (저화, 楮貨)	a type of paper money
jeokjeon chingyeong (적전친경, 籍田親耕)	a ritual performed by the king in which he performed farming tasks and ancestor memorial rites
Jeollyul tongbo (전률통보, 典律洞補)	a guide to the criminal law sections of the country's legal code
jeolsu system (절수, 折受)	the right to reclaim a parcel of uncultivated land
jeomjang (점장, 店匠)	people in charge of mining
jeomsim (점심, 點心)	lunch
jeon (전, 殿)	palace residences for the king, queen, king's mother, or grandmother
jeon (전, 錢)	unit of currency (1 *jeon* = 10 *pun*)
jeonbang (전방, 廛房)	a store
jeong (정, 丁)	able-bodied man
jeong (정, 亭)	small leisure structures built in scenic settings inside the palace grounds
jeongbang (정방, 淨房)	outhouse, toilet
jeong buin (정부인, 貞夫人)	one of the titles given to women in the *buin bongjak* system
Jeongcheong (정청, 政廳)	building in a palace where officials from the Ministries of Personnel and Military Affairs handled personnel matters
Jeong Hagyu (정학유, 丁學遊)	author of "Nongga wollyeongga" (1786–1855)
jeongho (정호, 丁戶)	people required to perform specific types of physical labor and hereditary occupations during the Goryeo period
Jeong Mongju (정몽주, 鄭夢周)	Neo-Confucian scholar and official (1337–1392)
jeongpo (정포, 正布)	finely woven cloth officially recognized as currency
Jeong Yagjeon (정약전, 丁若銓)	brother of Jeong Yagyong
Jeong Yagyong (정약용, 丁若鏞)	Silhak scholar who wrote *Mongmin simseo* (1762–1836)
jeongyeong buin (정경부인, 貞敬夫人)	one of the titles given to women in the *buin bongjak* system
jeonjeong (전정, 田政)	the land tax system
jeotgal (젓갈)	a salted fermented food made with seafood

Jibong yuseol (지봉유설, 芝峯類說)	a kind of encyclopedic work compiled by Yi Sugwang
jigwol (직월, 直月)	official in a community compact
jigyeok (직역, 職役)	record of the military service and statute labor to be performed by each person
jijuje (지주제, 地主制)	the landlord system
jikjeonbeop (직전법, 職田法)	the Office Land Law
Jingbirok (징비록, 懲毖錄)	a text by Yu Seongryong about his experiences during the Imjin War
Jinhyulcheong (진휼청, 賑恤廳)	office that provided relief for starving farm families
jinsa (진사, 進士)	someone who has passed the *jinsa* part of the civil service examination
jinseteok (진세턱)	initation ceremony for new members of a *dure*
jjanji (짠지)	a type of pickled vegetable
jjigae (찌개)	stew
Jiphyeonjeon (집현전, 集賢殿)	Hall of Worthies established by King Sejong
jo (租)	land tax
jo (調)	household tax
joban (조반, 早飯)	a simple meal that was eaten before breakfast
jokbo (족보, 族譜)	family genealogy
jokdo (족도, 族圖)	lineage map
Jongbusi (종부시, 宗簿寺)	Office of the Royal Genealogy
Jongchinnok (종친록, 宗親錄)	genealogy of the royal family
Jongmyo (종묘, 宗廟)	the shrine for the former kings and queens of the dynasty
joseok (조석, 朝夕)	a meal
jo-yong-jo system (조용조, 租庸調)	the three main categories of taxes
jueup (주읍, 主邑)	a *gun* or *hyeon* with a magistrate sent from the central government
jugeum (주금, 酒禁)	a ban on the selling and drinking of liquor
juhyeonsi (주현시, 州縣市)	markets during the Goryeo period
jujangdangmyun (주장당문)	a form of torture where the body was pummeled with several red cudgels
juknyeokgo (죽력고, 竹瀝膏)	a type of *soju* made with bamboo sap
jumak (주막, 酒幕)	tavern
Jungguil (중구일)	the ninth day of the ninth lunar month
junggungjeon (중궁전, 中宮殿)	another term for the queen's quarters
junghwa (중화, 中火)	a midway meal eaten by travelers in taverns
jungin (중인, 中人)	a class whose status is lower than than of yangban but higher than that of commoners
jungjeon (중전, 中殿)	the innermost part of *naejeon* in a palace where the queen resided
Jungsamil (중삼일, 重三日)	the third day of the third lunar month
Jurchen people (여진족, 女眞族)	people originally from the Manchuria region
juri (주리)	a form of torture which involved placing two pieces of wood between legs at the shins of the suspect sitting in a chair and then pulling the wood downwards to twist the legs
Ju Sebung (주세붕, 周世鵬)	scholar who established the first *seowon*, Baegundong seowon (1495–1554)
jwasang (좌상, 左相)	the advisor of a *dure*
jwasu (좌수, 座首)	the head of a *yuhyangso*

Kaogongji (고공기, 考工記)	*Records of Trades*
kimchi (김치)	pickled vegetables usually flavored with chili pepper powder and garlic
Lady Hyegyeong (혜경궁홍씨, 惠慶宮洪氏)	the wife of Prince Sado and the mother of King Jeongjo (1735–1815)
Lu Dajun (呂大鈞)	(1031–1082)
Lushi xiangyue (呂氏鄉約)	Zhu Xi's emendation of the Lü Family Community Compact
maehwa (매화)	the king's feces
maeu (매우)	palace terminology for feces
maeuteul (매우틀)	the king's chamberpot
majigi (마지기)	area of a field necessary to plant one *mal* of seed
makgeolli (막걸리)	cloudy rice liquor
mal (말, 斗)	unit of volume
mangnani (망나니)	executioner
maryeongseo (마령서, 馬鈴薯)	potato
Memorabilia of the Three Kingdoms (삼국유사, 三國遺事)	*Samguk yusa*, a text compiled in the thirteenth century
Mencius (맹자, 孟子)	Chinese philosopher (372–289 BCE)
Micheon (미천왕, 美川王)	the fifteenth king of Goguryeo (r. 300–331)
minhoe (민회, 民會)	people's assemblies
Ministry of Punishments (형조, 刑曹)	Hyeongjo
Ministry of Taxation (호조, 戶曹)	Hojo
Mongmin simseo (목민심서, 牧民心書)	*A Book from the Heart on Governing the People* by Jeong Yagyong
mukpae (묵패, 墨牌)	documents issued by *seowon* to summon commoners
mulburi (물부리)	the part of the tobacco pipe which was placed in the mouth
mungwa (문과, 文科)	civil service examination
munseo jaebi (문서잽이)	a member of the staff of a *dure*
Muwonnok (무원록, 無冤錄)	a forensic text on examining corpses (1796)
myeon (면, 面)	district
myeongang (면강, 面講)	a type of class in which students used a book to recite
Naegeumwi (내금위, 內禁衛)	an army made up of yangban
naeoe (내외, 內外)	Korean term for husband and wife
nae sobak (내소박, 內疏薄)	the abandonment of the husband by the wife
Naeuiwon (내의원, 內醫院)	Office of the Palace Physicians
najang (나장, 羅將)	low ranking soldier
nak (낙, 烙)	a form of torture where a person's body was branded with a hot iron
namcho (남초, 南草)	tobacco
Namdaemun (남대문, 南大門)	Great South Gate
nammancho (남만초, 南蠻椒)	chili peppers
namryeongcho (남령초, 南靈草)	tobacco
nanjang (난장, 亂杖)	a form of torture which involved pulling out a person's toe

narae (나래)	soil leveler
natbap (낮밥)	a full midday meal
neungjicheocham (능지처참, 凌遲處斬)	a cruel form of execution where the head was cut off and the body into pieces
neungjicheosa (능지처사, 凌遲處死)	another word for *neungjicheocham*
nobi (노비, 奴婢)	unfree people
noju (노주, 露酒)	another term for *soju*
nomo (노모, 奴某)	term for unfree people
Nongga jipseong (농가집성, 農家集成)	book on advanced agricultural techniques compiled by Sin Sok
Nongga wollyeong (농가월령, 農家月令)	a book on agriculture written in the early seventeenth century
"Nongga wollyeongga" (농가월령가, 農家月令歌)	a work of *gasa* poetry by Jeong Hagyu
nonggi (농기, 農器)	farmers' banner
nongja cheonha ji daebon (농자천하지대본, 農者天下之大本)	"Farming is the Foundation of the World"
nongjang (농장, 農場)	agricultural estate
nongjongbeop (농종법, 壟種法)	method of planting seeds on the ridges created when fields were plowed
Nongsa jikseol (농사직설, 農事直說)	*Straight Talk on Farming* (1429)
nongsanggi (농상기)	another term for *nonggi*
nongyo (농요, 農謠)	farmers' songs
nu (누, 樓)	the second floor of two-story palace structures
nyang (냥, 兩)	unit of currency (1 *nyang* = 10 *jeon*)
oejeon (외전, 外殿)	the area of the palace where officials could meet the king
oe sobak (외소박, 外疏薄)	case of a husband abandoning his wife
Office of Special Advisors (홍문관, 弘文館)	Hongmungwan
Office of the Inspector General (사헌부, 司憲府)	Saheonbu
O Huimun (오희문)	Neo-Confucian scholar (1539–1613)
oiji (오이지)	cucumber kimchi
oisobagi (오이소박이)	stuffed pickled cucumbers
Oju yeonmun jangjeon sango (오주연문장전산고, 五洲衍文長箋散稿)	text written by Yi Gyugyeong in the mid-nineteenth century
Okjeo (옥저, 沃沮)	a state in the eastern coast of Korea before the Three Kingdoms Period
pabo (파보,派譜)	part of *sebo* that recorded specific branches of the clan
Paengbae (팽배, 彭排)	military unit that young commoners could join by taking an examination
paeraengi (패랭이)	a coarsely braided hat made of bamboo
paja (파자, 破字)	a system of separating Chinese characters into their constituent elements to produce words and phrases with different meanings
palpo (팔포, 八包)	eight bundles of ginseng
pichon (피촌, 皮村)	hide villages
pil (필, 疋)	roll of cloth (counting unit)
Pilwon japgi (필원잡기, 筆苑雜記)	a compilation of writings by Seo Geojeong

po (보, 包)	bundles (counting unit)
pojeon (포전, 布錢)	store with a monopoly over hemp cloth
pun (푼, 分)	unit of currency
pungheon (풍헌, 風憲)	an officer of the *yuhyangso*
putgut (풋굿)	*dure* in Gyeongsang province
pyeong (평, 坪)	unit of measuring area (one *pyeong* = 3.3 square meters)
pyeongmin (평민, 平民)	peasantry, the people
pyeonjeon (편전, 便殿)	the king's official office where the king and officials conducted meetings
Queen Inmok (인목왕후, 仁穆王后)	queen of King Seonjo (1584–1632)
Queen Regent Sinjeong (신정왕후, 神貞王后)	the mother of King Heonjong (1808–1890)
Records of the Grand Historian (사기, 史記)	*Shiji*
Red Turbans (홍건적, 紅巾賊)	*Honggeonjeok*
ri (리, 里)	unit of measuring distance (one *ri* = ~0.393 km)
ri (리, 里)	village
Rites of Zhou (주례, 周禮)	
Royal Library (규장각, 奎章閣)	Gyujanggak
ryu (류, 流)	banishment
sa (사, 死)	execution
sacheon (사천, 私賤)	private unfree people
sadae (사대, 事大)	literally, serving the great; term used to describe relations between Korea and China
sadaebu (사대부, 士大夫)	literati
saekjang (색장, 色掌)	a type of *gyoim* who took care of students and their living quarters
Sahak (사학, 四學)	the 'four schools' of Seoul
sajeong paui (사정파의, 事情罷意)	one of two methods of divorce used by commoners
Sajikdan (사직단, 社稷壇)	the altar for the ceremonies for the deities of land and grain
sajo (사조, 四祖)	a term referring to a person's father, grandfather, great-grandfather, and maternal grandfather
sajok (사족, 士族)	yangban families that produced high-ranking officials
sambeopsa (삼법사, 三法司)	a term referring to the Ministry of Punishments, the Office of the Inspector-General, and the Seoul city government
sambulgeo (삼불거, 三不去)	the three exceptions to divorce
samgeum (삼금, 三禁)	three kinds of prohibitions enacted by the government
samhaeju (삼해주, 三亥酒)	a kind of *cheongju*
Samhan (삼한, 三韓)	the confederacies of Byeonhan, Jinhan, and Mahan
samin (사민, 私民)	non-taxpayers
samjeong (삼정, 三政)	a term referring to the three main taxes paid by peasantry: the land tax, grain loans, and the military service tax
samjongjido (삼종지도, 三從之道)	the three obediences

sang (상, 上)	upper
sangchonin (상촌인, 上村人)	merchants who belonged to the *sijeon*
Sangdo (상도)	title of a novel by Choe Inho published in 2000
sangpyeong tongbo (상평통보, 常平通寶)	a copper-bronze coin
sangyeok (상역, 商譯)	merchant interpreters
Saongwon (사옹원, 司饔院)	the area where meals were prepared in the palace
sarim (사림, 士林)	a faction of Neo-Confucian scholars and officials
sasang dogo (사상도고, 私商都賈)	private merchants
sasuk (사숙, 私淑)	a type of *seodang* established by powerful families
Sayeogwon (사역원, 司譯院)	Training Center for Interpreters
sebo (세보, 世譜)	lineage records
sedo jeongchi (세도 정치, 勢道政治)	rule by in-law families
segyedo (세계도, 世系圖)	societal map
Seja Ikwisa (세자익위사, 世子翊衛司)	the personal guards of the crown prince
Seja Sigangwon (세자시강원, 世子侍講院)	area in the Eastern Palace where the crown prince received lessons
seodang (서당, 書堂)	village schools
seogak (서각, 西閣)	outhouse, toilet
Seo Geojong (서거정)	scholar-official who completed the compilation of the *Seonghwabo* (1420–1488)
seojae yusaeng (서재 유생, 西齋儒生)	another term for *aegoe gyosaeng*
seok (석)	a unit of measuring volume
seoldae (설대)	the part of the tobacco pipe which connected the *dambaetong* and the *mulburi*
seolleongtang (설렁탕)	a dish made by boiling broth, cooking meat, and then adding noodles
seom (섬)	a unit of volume
seonanggi (서낭기)	farmers' banner
Seonggyungwan (성균관, 成均館)	the highest educational institution in Joseon
Seonghwabo (성화보)	genealogy of the Andong Gwon family
Seong Hyeon (성현, 成俔)	scholar-official who wrote *Yongjae chonghwa* (1439–1548)
seonsang (선상, 船商)	a peddler that travelled over water routes
Seonwonnok (선원록, 璿源錄)	genealogy of Joseon's royal family
seotdeung (섯등)	the name given to salt wells in Jeolla province
seowon (서원, 書院)	private Confucian academies established by *sarim*
Seo Yugu (서유구, 徐有榘)	Silhak scholar who wrote *Imwon gyeongjeji* (1764–1845)
Seungjeongwon (승정원, 承政院)	Royal Secretariat
seungpo (승포)	a type of *chupo*
seupcheop (습첩, 拾妾)	custom in which the first man to find an abandoned woman on the road to a shrine early in the morning had the duty to take her in
Shanxi province (山西省)	
Sichuan province (西川省)	
sijeon(시전, 市廛)	merchant association
sikhwaju (식화주, 食火主)	the people who brought meals to farmers working in the fields

sillyangyeokcheon (신량역천, 身良役賤) — *yangin* who worked at low-born occupations
singgeonji (싱건지) — a type of kimchi
Sinhae Tonggong (신해 통공, 辛亥通共) — the new policy that abolished the monopolies of the *sijeon*
sinmungo (신문고, 申聞鼓) — a type of drum
Sinnong yueop (신농유업, 神農遺業) — "The Legacy of Shennong"
Sin Sok (신속) — (1600–1661)
Sin Sukju (신숙주, 申叔舟) — scholar-official who served as the Chief State Councillor (1417–1475)
Sin Yunbok (신윤복, 申潤福) — painter known for genre paintings (1758–?)
Six Licensed Guilds (육의전, 六矣廛) — Yuguijeon; the merchants houses granted monopolies from the government over six products: silk, cotton cloth, ramie cloth, thread, paper products, and fish products.
sobak (소박, 疏薄) — a method of separating from one's wife, in which husband and wife lived together but led separate lives
sobakdegi (소박데기) — an abandoned woman
sodongpae (소동패) — an organization of young people who had not yet joined the *dure*
Sogo Army (속오군, 束伍軍) — an army made up of people of lowborn status
sogokpyeongseok (소곡평석, 小斛平石) — term for fifteen *mal*
soim (소임, 所任) — the person responsible for morale and carrying out punishment in a *dure*
soin (소인, 小人) — a humble term of reference to oneself literally meaning 'small person'
soju (소주, 燒酒) — distilled rice liquor; literally, burnt liquor
sojutgori (소줏고리) — a distilling device used to make *soju*
Sokdaejeon (속대전, 續大典) — a revised legal code compiled in the mid-eighteenth century
sokhyeon (속현) — district
songgeum (송금, 松禁) — a ban on the cutting down of pine trees
Songpa sandae nori (송파산대 놀이) — Songpa Masked Drama
Spring and Autumn Annals (춘추, 春秋) — *Chunqiu*; one of the Five Classics
ssajeon (싸전, 差廛) — merchant association with a monopoly over the sale of rice
ssijok (씨족, 氏族) — family tree
Sugang Palace (수강궁, 壽康宮) — a palace built in 1419 that later was reconstructed as Changgyeong Palace
suk buin (숙부인, 淑夫人) — one of the titles given to women in the *buin bongjak* system
sulmak (술막) — tavern
sumeoseum (수머슴) — another term for the head of the *dure*
Sungnye Gate (숭례문, 崇禮門) — the official name of Namdaemun (Great South Gate)
sungnyung (숭늉) — scorched rice tea
sunureum (순우름) — the name of *dure* in Jeju Island
suryeom cheongjeong (수렴청정, 垂簾聽政) — system in which the queen mother served as regent and administered state affairs from behind a veil at court
susang (수상, 水商) — a type of peddler who travelled by water routes

sutmak (숫막)	another term for tavern
Swaemirok (쇄미록)	a diary written during the Imjin War by O Huimun
tae (태, 笞)	light stick
Taengniji (택리지, 擇里志)	A text on choosing settlements by Yi Junghwan written in 1751
takju (탁주, 濁酒)	cloudy rice liquors
Thousand-Character Classic (천자문, 千字文)	*Qian Zi Wen* (K. *Cheonjamun*)
tongjarak (통자락)	the name given to salt wells in Chungcheong province
tongyeong (통영, 統營)	the local military office
tsukemono (漬物)	Japanese pickled food
udae people (우대사람)	another word for *sangchonin*
*ugeum*ˆ(우금, 牛禁)	a ban on the killing of cows
Uigeumbu (의금부, 義禁府)	State Tribunal
ungdeongi (웅덩이)	salt well
Unhyeon Palace (운현궁, 雲峴宮)	the residence of the Daewongun, the father of Gojong
usang (우상, 右相)	the person who provided advice and assistance to the *jwasang*
Veritable Records of King Hyojong (효종실록, 孝宗實錄)	*Hyojong sillok*
Veritable Records of King Jungjong (중종실록, 中宗實錄)	*Jungjong sillok*
Veritable Records of King Myeongjong (명종실록, 明宗實錄)	*Myeongjong sillok*
Veritable Records of King Taejo (태조실록, 太祖實錄)	*Taejo sillok*
Waegwan (왜관, 倭館)	Japan House
waegyeoja (왜겨자, 倭芥子)	chili peppers
wiri anchi (위리안치, 圍籬安置)	a form of banishment where a thorny trifoliate orange tree was planted around the house of the exile
won (원, 元)	original
won (원)	places that provided food and lodgings to travelers
wonjang (원장)	large and round implements for use in beatings
Xu Jing (서긍, 徐兢)	scholar of Song-dynasty China
yakju (약주, 藥酒)	another term for *cheongju*
yangan (양안, 量案)	land register
yangban (양반, 兩班)	literally, the two orders; i.e., the civil and military officials
yangcheonje (양천제, 良賤制)	the social status system in which people were classified as either commoners or low-born
yangin (양인, 良人)	citizen, commoner in a broad sense
Yangju byeolsandae nori (양주별산대놀이)	Yangju Masked Drama
yangmin (양민, 良民)	commoners, peasantry
yangsucheok (양수척, 揚水尺)	another term for low-born people
yangyeok (양역, 良役)	military service tax

Yecheon Bak (예천 박씨, 醴泉朴氏)	the branch of the Bak family whose ancestral seat is Yecheon
Yemungwan (예문관, 藝文館)	Office of Royal Decrees
yeogaek (여객, 旅客)	an inn engaging in trade
yeogak (여각, 旅閣)	commission agents
yeogatarip (여가탈입, 閭家奪入)	the illegal act of a yangban seizing the house of a commoner
yeok (역, 驛)	places that provided food and lodgings to travelers
yeokbo (역보, 驛保)	messengers
yeokcham (역참, 驛站)	government offices that handled matters related to communication and transportation
yeokgwa (역과, 譯科)	civil service examination for translators
yeollyeo (열녀, 烈女)	a virtuous woman
yeom (염, 鹽)	the Chinese character for salt
yeomjeon (염전, 鹽廛)	merchant houses that had monopoly over the sale of salt
yeoncho (연초, 煙草)	tobacco
yeongeojiso (연거지소, 燕居之所)	buildings inside the palace where the king could meet with officials individually
yeongsang (영상, 領相)	the elderly supervisor of a *dure*
yeongun (연군, 鉛軍)	lead miners
yeori (여리, 餘利)	the amount of profit in excess of the amount taken by the storeowner
yeoriggun (여리꾼)	brokers who brought in customers to stores
Yi Deokmu (이덕무, 李德懋)	Silhak scholar and author of *Cheongjanggwan jeonseo* (1741–1793)
Yi Gwal (이괄)	military official who led a rebellion against the government in 1624 (1587–1624)
Yi Gyugyeong (이규경)	Silhak thinker (1788–1856)
Yi Hwang (퇴계 이황, 李滉)	also known as Toegye; a leading Neo-Confucian philosopher (1501–1570)
Yi Ik (이익, 李瀷)	Silhak thinker (1681–1763)
Yi Insang (이인상)	painter (1710–1760)
Yi Junghwan (이중환, 李重煥)	Silhak scholar, famous for writing *Taengniji* (1690–1756)
Yisan seowon (이산서원)	a *seowon* in North Gyeonsang province
Yi Seonggye (이성계, 李成桂)	a general who was the founder of Joseon and its first king
Yi Sugwang (이수광)	writer of *Jibung yuseol* (1563–1628)
Yi Sunsin (이순신, 李舜臣)	admiral who defeated the Japanese navy during the Imjin War (1545–1598)
Yi Yulgok (이율곡, 李栗谷)	Neo-Confucian philosopher and official (1536–1584)
yong (용, 庸)	statute labor; corvée labor
yongdanggi (용당기)	another term for a farmers' banner
yongdeokgi (용덕기)	another term for a farmers' banner
Yongjae chonghwa (용재총화, 慵齋叢話)	title of a book by Seong Hyeon
yongsulgi (용술기)	another term for *nonggi*
Yorowon yahwagi (요로원야화기, 要路院夜話記)	novel by Bak Duse (1678)
Yu Deukgong (유득공, 柳得恭)	Slhak scholar and writer of *Gyeongdo japji* (1749–1807)
Yuguijeon (육의전, 六矣廛)	Six Licensed Guilds
yuhyangso (유향소, 留鄉所)	self-governing organizations of the *sajok* in a village

Yukjo (육조, 六曹)	term for the six government ministries
yuksang (육상, 陸商)	a peddler who travelled by overland routes
Yun Gukhyeong (윤국형)	official who served in the Office of Special Advisors and the Royal Secretariat; writer of *Gapjin mannok* (1543–1611)
yusa (유사)	an official of the community compact
yuseoju (유서주, 柳絮酒)	another term for *samhaeju*
Yu Seongnyong (유성룡, 柳成龍)	official in the Southerner faction who served as Chief State Councillor (1542–1607)
Zhamen (책문, 柵門)	pronounced 'Chaengmun' in Korean
Zhu Xi (주자, 朱子)	pioneering Chinese Neo-Confucian philosopher (1130–1200)
Zhu Xi Jiali (주자가례, 朱子家禮)	"Family Rituals" by Zhu Xi

INDEX

Major terms are defined in the Glossary.